NEHRU

Utopian or a Statesman?

N.G. Rajurkar

Prof. Emeritus (Politicial Science),
Osmania University

Foreword by

Rajen Harshé

Former Vice-Chancellor, University of Allahabad,
Visiting Professor, Department of International Relations,
South Asian University, New Delhi

PENTAGON PRESS

Nehru: Utopian or a Statesman?

Prof. N.G. Rajurkar

First Published in 2014

ISBN 978-81-8274-799-9

Published by
PENTAGON PRESS
206, Peacock Lane, Shahpur Jat
New Delhi-110049
Phones: 011-64706243, 26491568
Telefax: 011-26490600
email: rajan@pentagonpress.in
website: www.pentagonpress.in

Branch:
Prime Arcade
Office #11
1154 Saifee Street
Opp. M.G.Road, Camp
Pune-411001
Email: pentagonpresspune@gmail.com

Printed at Aegean Offset Printers, Greater Noida, U.P.

Dedicated to
my wife - Anjali.
I only know what she means to me.

'What else is idealism, save the realism of tomorrow'.

—Jawaharlal Nehru

CONTENTS

Foreword *ix*
Preface *xv*
Acknowledgements *xvii*

1. The Man and His Charisma 1
2. Early Influences 8
3. '...And Then Came Gandhi' 15
4. Communism and the Communists 29
5. Towards Democratic Socialism 53
6. The Unity of India 72
7. Policies and Decisions in Perspective (I) 104
8. Policies and Decisions in Perspective (II) 130

Appendix I Jawaharlal Nehru's Role in Indian Politics: Before Independence 184

Appendix II Jawaharlal Nehru's Role in Indian Politics: After Independence 196

Bibliography 211

Index 216

FOREWORD

In this unusual study, Rajurkar has imaginatively captured a bird's eye view of Nehru's entire political career spanning over four decades, since the early Twenties till his death in 1964. In this process, a fairly wide range of ideas and events concerning Nehru, India and the world during the pre-independence as well as post-independence phases in India's contemporary history have been discussed with a sense of admiration for Nehru's visions. In my view, the unusual nature of this travail could be perceived in the following ways. To start with, it refrains from intervening in any recent or current scholarly debates on or about Nehru and his policies. Apparently, it has emerged in its present form because the author must have lived, intellectually as well as emotionally, with Nehru's writings as well as diverse events and questions that shaped Nehru's political career, during different times, for decades. He has mulled over what Nehru's critics had to argue and chosen to place Nehru's policies in a perspective to silence them. Being a sensitive scholar, the author has virtually stepped into Nehru's shoes to appreciate the circumstances in which he had to take decisions while dealing with difficult conditions.

Furthermore, Rajurkar's deeply sensitive mind also has made him receptive to Nehru's sensibilities, visions, and capacities to come to terms with social complexities of differing situations. There are also fairly appreciative remarks on Nehru's personal charisma and versatility of his personality. Thus, the author has alluded to Nehru's sacrificing spirit and the impact of Gandhi on him. Rajurkar's evocative narrative does highlight the nature of unparalleled mass appeal and popularity which Nehru enjoyed. Moreover, Nehru's progressive outlook that embraced secularism, his nationalism that was at once international and cosmopolitan, sense of history, statesman like qualities, feel for poetry and eminently readable writings seem to have literally charmed the author. Incontestably, the versatility of Nehru's charismatic personality has had a sense of romance and Rajurkar is deeply enmeshed in it. For, he certainly belongs to a generation of scholars who suffered the pangs of freedom and lived with optimism of Nehru era which believed in wiping out tears from every eye. Rajurkar also has been one of those rare contemporary historians who had the privilege of meeting and interviewing Nehru twice. Thus, his narrative on Nehru apart from capturing the essence of major milestones in India's history is also meant to inspire younger generation of scholars by concretely showing how that past still resides in India's present through institutions such as India's constitution, vibrant parliamentary democracy, planning commission, institutions of higher education and even the Non Aligned Movement (NAM).

If I were to locate this book, I would state without any hesitation that it resembles the pedagogy and sincerity of the late Sane Guruji (1899-1950). Sane Guruji was a well-known Gandhian, social reformer, author and an outstanding teacher who inspired generations of socialist leaders in Maharashtra. As a teacher, Rajurkar falls well within the tradition of pedagogy and sincerity that Sane Guruji has already established. Evidently, Rajurkar has made a sincere effort to communicate his protracted research and thinking on Nehru to students and scholars who are interested in Nehru as a phenomenon. Without losing sight of intricate complexities that surrounded any social reality in Nehru's times, he has taken a sympathetic view of Nehru and expressed himself in an eminently accessible style.

The impact of Nehru's ideas was quite profound on the Indian psyche. Indeed, if Gandhi was an undisputed leader of India during its freedom struggle, Nehru was the supreme architect of independent India. Nehru's ideas in different areas such as the nature of communist movement, foreign policy, socialism, secularism, nationalism, democracy and constitutionalism were evolving much before independence. This was well reflected in the resolutions of the Indian National Congress (INC) which often carried his stamp. Nehru's praxiological (uniting theory and practice) commitment to his ideas became real when as the first Prime Minister of India he had an opportunity to translate them into practice. Let me raise a few issues that have bearing on contemporary times, which Rajurkar has discussed with his characteristic feel for details and accuracy in stating them.

Rajurkar basically has built his arguments by consistently citing from Nehru's writings and speeches. His penchant for primary sources and persuasive way of placing them has shed light on the intellectual evolution of Nehru in different stages of his career. Being a historian, Nehru was attracted to Marxism as a method of thinking and given his passion for science he was quite favourably disposed to social scientific enquires. He also appreciated anti-imperialist streak among the communists. However, he was convinced that the communist movement in India was not rooted in India's past and it was looking for constant guidance from outside India. He went to the extent of dubbing the communists as reactionaries although they were supposed to be revolutionaries. Nehru was critical of minds that were shut and had blinkered vision. Has the communist movement in India changed fundamentally from the Thirties? One would still envy communist parties and their capacity to entertain fixed notions, speak in stereotypical manner on social problems that stem from dogmatic rigidities. However, like a true democrat Nehru had left a space for the communist to function. He enjoyed dissent even though in the initial days after India's independence the communists considered Nehru as running dog of Anglo-American imperialist.

Rajurkar has gone further while enumerating democratic socialism that Nehru had embraced which tried to balance equity and justice, on the one hand, and the rights of individuals with communities, on the other. Nehru conceived of several progressive measures like abolition of Zamanidari, Land Reforms and even Hindu code bill to take India forward. He also tried to establish parliamentary sovereignty by minimising the space for judicial activism in terms of deciding monetary compensation, once the land was taken over by the state. The very effort of synthesising liberty and equality through democratic socialism led to gradual progress which Nehru managed by playing accommodative politics involving umpteen numbers of divergent views that stemmed from different social groups within the Congress movement. Such act of balancing often placed Nehru in an unenviable position where critics on the left viewed Nehru as a good insurance against socialism while the critics on the right failed to appreciate his passion to expand the role of the state in developmental projects as well as state and nation building.

Reflecting on India's unity, Rajurkar has dealt with problems of Hindu–Muslim relations and resurgence of linguistic identities. By gently asserting that the phenomenon of the so called communalism cannot be entirely attributed to the designs of colonial power, Rajurkar has shown how gradually Muslims, who were the erstwhile rulers in India, in the course of history, began to nurture separatist sentiments by identifying themselves with Islam. Nehru was secular and saw no reason to partition India initially but had to reluctantly agree to the idea of partition as he could perceive that India would be dragged into a state of protracted civil war and strife with growing stridency of the attitudes of the Muslim League. Nehru was an unrepentant votary of persuasive means. Even while handling the language question, he pleaded with the enthusiasts of Hindi to go slow because of the obvious resistance of people belonging to Dravidian languages to accept Hindi as the only national language. As a democratic country India had to persuade people to develop consensus over the language issue. What is more, even the then authoritarian state of Yugoslavia was not able to impose any language on its people. Nehru's acceptance of the problems related to linguistic identities eventually led to the constitution of the state reorganisation commission in 1956. In a way, it did add towards the strength of quasi-federal India. The centralising as well as decentralising tendencies have been haunting India's polity till date and in spite of apparent chaos, India is working out creative solutions through constitutional and democratic methods to strike synthesis between these tendencies.

Rajurkar also has extensively underscored the evolution of heterogeneous organisation such the Congress by explaining differences between major leaders, Gandhi and Nehru over the notions of development. Similarly, controversy that erupted due to Subhash Chandra Bose's candidature for the Congress Presidency has also been analysed. The author is equally level headed in analysing the agreements and differences between Nehru and Patel within the Congress and later within the government. In fact, working through the consensus within the Congress as well as the government through discussions and persuasions was a hallmark of India's democratic polity. Nehru as a democrat and his faith in democratic attitudes seem to be a running thread that kept the Congress movement vibrant and growing during the Nehruvian phase which witnessed one party dominant system as Rajni Kothari has characterised it.

Nehru's faith in democracy also signified his love for peace. As a statesman Nehru while handling India's foreign policy chose to build bridges between the East and the West. Nehru's passion for peace and competence to be a peace activist was well demonstrated in Korean crisis (1950), Indo-China crisis (1954), Suez Canal crisis (1956) and the Congo crisis (1960). Apart from playing influential role in these crises India under Nehru consistently adhered to its anti-imperialist and anti-racist credentials. In fact during the fifties India played a disproportionately larger role compared to its actual power due to its policy of non-alignment and the way it was steered under Nehru's stewardship.

Irrespective of such stewardship, however, critics invariably blame Nehru for the intractable Kashmir problem and India's humiliation in Sino-Indian border dispute in 1962. Rajurkar has untangled the intricacies of the situation in Kashmir through several hard facts. He argues that it was not easy to humble the invaders, who were well armed, and get them evacuated during the winter season in the late Forties. Nehru was also committed to resolve the issue with reference to people and was committed to hold plebiscite in Kashmir under the auspices of the United Nations within the stipulated time of three months. However, Pakistan was dilly dallying and evasive because it was conscious of Sheikh Abdullah's disinclination to merge Kashmir within Pakistan.

Likewise, Rajurkar has provided ample evidence to show how Nehru was aware of the Chinese prowess. In his scheme of development Nehru preferred peace at the borders because the opposition parties were also critical of India's military expenditure. Rajurkar admits that India was militarily a weaker state than China and that humiliation in 1962 was due to failure in defence policy and not foreign policy. He also holds the view that Nehru had already realised that China was encroaching on India's territory and that he was never as naïve as to conclude that China was India's trustworthy friend. However, the author sincerely believes that Nehru failed to take the people of India into confidence and refrained from sharing his apprehensions about China with them. Evidently, the people remained in the dark and were even complacent when the Chinese aggression struck them all of a sudden!

Rajurkar has constantly emphasised Nehru's abilities to take cool and calculating decisions like a good realist without losing sight of his intrinsically idealist moorings. In effect, this interesting study almost captures *longue-durée* (long term) view of the eventful years of the last century in almost Braudelian sense and provides a useful backdrop to understand the on-going events in this century in India's domestic polity as also foreign policy. For instance, events like the formation of new states in the Indian Union, including the on-going and persistent demand for the formation of Telangana, or unresolved Kashmir dispute between India and Pakistan and sustained Sino-India differences over existing border between the two countries can never be understood without taking a careful look at Rajurkar's meticulously constructed and ably presented analysis. I would like to thank as well as congratulate him for this work. Incontestably, it is an indispensable reading for students and scholars of contemporary Indian history, Indian political process and foreign policy of India !

New Delhi **Rajen Harshé**

PREFACE

Critics of Jawaharlal Nehru have referred to him far too often as an idealist, implying thereby that his ideas and policies were devoid of realism. As a keen student of Nehru's policies and approach to problems for the last five decades or more, I feel that this description is indicative of a somewhat inadequate understanding of the rationale behind his policies, based as they were on a proper understanding of ground realities and the capacity to look at things in the perspective of today and tomorrow. If Nehru was an idealist, he was so only in the sense in which Nehru himself had on one occasion described idealism. 'What else is idealism,' Nehru had stated, 'save the realism of tomorrow'. The question mark at the end of the title of the book is indicative of the riddle in the minds of the people about Nehru's policies and approach to problems, which appear to them idealistic rather than pragmatic. Through an analysis of the relevant facts, I have attempted to show as to how his idealism was not divorced from realism.

I have discussed in this book some of the controversial decisions of Nehru before and after India's freedom, such as Nehru's refusal to form a ministry in U.P. in 1937 with the help of the Muslim League, his role in the Subhash Bose controversy of 1939, his press conference of July 10, 1946 vis-a-vis the Cabinet Mission Plan, his support to the June 3, 1947 plan of Lord Mountbatten and his Kashmir and China policy. While discussing Nehru's controversial decisions, I have made an honest effort to examine all relevant facts, known and hitherto unknown, that governed those decisions. I have often wondered as to whether, on balance, decisions other than those that he took were either possible or desirable. More often than not we tend to lose sight of the fact that the choice before a leader at any given point of time is not always between good and better, sometimes it is between bad and worse and considerations such as these are a pre-requisite for the proper evaluation of the decisions made or policies pursued.

Chapters two to five of this book are largely based on my doctoral thesis, entitled 'Nehru's ideas on nationalism, democracy and socialism', whereas parts of chapters six and seven have the thesis material for their basis. Matters germane to the topic of research, provide the theoretical framework which I hope will contribute to a better understanding of Nehru's approach to problems, his policies and the crucial decisions that he took at different stages of his political life, whether on the national or international plane.

The references provided at the end of every chapter will enable the readers to appreciate the fact that this is a research-oriented book. I have taken every care to check facts and figures on which my conclusions are based.

The two speeches that I had delivered at The Center of Nehru Studies, Department of Political Science, Shivaji University Kolhapur (incorporated in the appendix part of the book), represent in brief, my understanding of Nehru's role in Indian politics, before and after India's freedom.

N.G. Rajurkar

ACKNOWLEDGEMENTS

My grateful thanks to Prof. Rajen Harshe for his Foreword to the book, which bears testimony to his erudition and insight, as also for the valuable help that he rendered in the publication of this book.

My daughter-in-law Jyoti, cheerfully took upon herself the ardous task of meticulously checking the references, going carefully through the proofs of the printed matter and preparing the final script. She was ably assisted by my granddaughter Ankita and my grandson Aditya. It was because of their help that my task became much easier.

Finally, I thank Shri Rajan Arya, CEO, Pentagon Press, New Delhi and his entire team, for bringing out the book in a very attractive and presentable form.

N.G. Rajurkar

With Jawaharlal Nehru, 27th October, 1960, New Delhi

With Indira Gandhi at Raj Bhavan Hyderabad on the 23rd of June, 1966

1

THE MAN AND HIS CHARISMA

No one in the recent history of India has meant so much to so many, in so many different ways, as Jawaharlal Nehru. The rich had in their minds a soft corner for him, as socially Nehru belonged to their class, though he championed the cause of the poor and the down-trodden. For the middle and the poor class people, Nehru was of course a hero, because it was for their betterment that he strove ceaselessly. The intellectuals respected Nehru because of his education at Harrow and Cambridge, and his intellectual attainments. And what fascinated one and all was his strikingly handsome face and grand figure. To see Nehru standing erect in a motor car with folded hands, acknowledging the greetings of an admiring crowd, was always an aesthetically satisfying and emotionally thrilling experience. No wonder that people waited for hours and hours together, just to catch a glimpse of him. Those who were too young when Nehru passed away or, were born later, could be told about almost everything that Nehru possessed, except his handsome looks almost verging on beauty, and his extremely magnetic personality, as they could never be adequately described. One feeble way of describing his personality to those who never saw him, is to say that Nehru would have attracted the attention of a person, even when he (Nehru) was in a crowd of thousands and when that person had not the faintest idea as to who he was.

Many are the stories of Nehru's hypnotic effect on people, especially on a crowd. A friend of mine was an eye witness to one such scene in New Delhi. A group representing some political party was staging a demonstration in front of the Parliament. The demonstrators were intermittently raising anti Nehru slogans also. Nehru arrived at the Parliament House a little later. When he was told about the demonstration, he briskly moved to the place where the group was raising the slogans. In spotless white sherwani and the Gandhi cap, with a red rose bud tucked in one of the buttons of the sherwani, with folded hands and a charming smile on his face, Nehru stood before the demonstrators. And all of a sudden the scene changed. The demonstrators were captivated by Nehru's personality; they forgot their wrath against him and shouted, 'Jawaharlal Nehru ki jai'.

A large number of people, who never agreed with Nehru's politics, admired him tremendously for his qualities of head and heart. Here was a man, who on his own, gave up a life of luxury and comfort and spent the best years of his life behind prison bars, because the call of the nation was too strong for him. And while in prison, he didn't idle away his time but made the best possible use of his enforced idleness and came out almost after every long imprisonment with a great book written in superlative English.

Nehru's literary style was captivating. It was graceful and artistic. In fact, the artist in him never left him, not even in the midst of very heavy work. In his message to the All-India Teachers' Conference (which he must have dictated during the course of a tremendously busy day, as all days were for him) in a certain year, there was a very artistic expression. Nehru stated: 'These days, while wealth shouts, knowledge whispers.' In fact, there was this artistic touch in everything that he wrote, be it a book, an article, a letter or a message.

Sometimes, Nehru caught his readers completely unawares by introducing a witty remark in the midst of serious writing. While describing his life in the Naini prison, Nehru wrote: 'My barrack and enclosure were popularly known throughout the jail as the Kuttaghar—the Dog House. This was an old name which had nothing to do with me'.[1]

Nehru wrote English with absolute ease and mastery. His choice of words was always appropriate and the presentation of facts forthright and vigorous. In short, going through his writings is a rare artistic experience. It was not without reason that John Gunther referred to Nehru in his Inside Asia as one of the best contemporary writers of English.

The intensely human side of Nehru's mental make-up is revealed by one of the incidents described by him in his Autobiography. When Nehru was in the Dehra Dun Jail, he used to feed three puppies, left there by a bitch. 'One of the puppies fell ill with a violent distemper and gave me a great deal of trouble. I nursed her with care, and sometimes I would get up a dozen times in the course of the night to look after her. She survived, and I was happy that my nursing had pulled her round.'[2]

The anecdote about Nehru, narrated by Tensing Norgay—the Everest hero, is equally interesting. Tensing called on Nehru at his house, a little before the former's departure for England. Nehru asked him whether he had enough warm clothes with him for his journey abroad. Tensing hesitated a little before telling Nehru that he did not have enough warm clothes with him, but for Nehru's point blank question, he wouldn't have told Nehru about it. Nehru thereupon took Tensing to another room, opened his wardrobe and asked Tensing to try different clothes on him and take all those that fitted him. Very hesitatingly, Tensing chose a few of Nehru's clothes. Nehru then took out a sherwani from his wardrobe for which he had great sentimental attachment, as it was his father's, and asked Tensing to wear it. On finding that it was just his size, Nehru parted with that sherwani also. It is worth remembering that Nehru thought of Tensing's needs amidst a day of interviews, meetings, official work and other preoccupations.

Nehru was a man of rare courage and in no period of his life did his courageous nature manifest itself to the extent to which it did, immediately after India became free. Being secular to the very core and acutely aware of his responsibilities as the prime Minister, he made every attempt to crush the fierce communal riots that broke out in different parts of the country during that period. Moreover, he personally took the lead in helping the minority community. On one occasion, he saved two Muslim children who were about to be murdered by a mob. On yet another occasion, he rushed unarmed into a furious mob which was looting Muslim shops in Connaught Circus, New Delhi, and tried to bring the situation under control.

Another true story of this period is worth narrating. News reached the ears of the then Vice-Chancellor of Jamia Milia Dr. Zakir Hussain that the University would be attacked on a certain night. That day, from the evening itself, Dr. Zakir Hussain, the teachers of the University staff and the students kept a vigil in order to save the university from being ransacked. Nothing happened during the: evening and then came the night. Those on the campus could see flames leaping up in the adjoining villages, and could hear the shrieks and shouts of rioters and their victims, as the communal frenzy was in full swing. And then, almost at the midnight hour, a taxi-cab arrived at the campus and there stepped out of it, Jawaharlal Nehru, in order to stand by the side of Zakir Hussain, during that hour of danger. He had left the capital without informing any one (except perhaps the person who fetched the taxi for him), and come to Jamia Milia through the danger belt! What else could offer a better proof of reckless courage and unwavering faith in secularism!

A certain anecdote narrated by H.V.R. Iyengar throws light not only on Nehru's capacity to put in extremely hard work (which was a well known fact), but also on his ability to concentrate on any subject, even under the most unfavourable and trying circumstances and during a period of great stress and strain.

Iyengar, who was the principal private secretary to Nehru, accompanied him in August 1947, on a tour to East and West Punjab, which were in flames. Nehru had jointly undertaken the tour with Liaquat Ali Khan, the Prime Minister of Pakistan. The tour started at 6 a.m. and by the time the day's work was over, it was midnight. When Iyengar went to bed at that hour, completely exhausted in body and spirit, he was not too happy to remember that another programme 'equally heavy and tragic' was to begin at six in the morning the next day.

During the tour on that day, Nehru had covered long distances by car and jeep through dusty roads, had seen a caravan of hundred thousand people rendered homeless, had visited places where the dead were still lying about. He must have felt his dreams and his faith in human nature crashing down to pieces on that saddening day. Iyengar naturally imagined that Nehru too, after that long and tiring day – a day of shocking sights, must have gone to bed at midnight, as others in the party had done. But he was wrong! When Iyengar got up with some difficulty early in the morning the next day, in order to go to the airport, the P.A. showed him a pile of letters, telegrams and memoranda, which Nehru had dictated after everybody had dispersed. Nehru himself did not go to bed till 2 a.m., but was ready to start another day at 5.30 a.m. Though the schedule of the day was somewhat unusual, it is worth remembering that Nehru for years together, worked for about 17 hours a day.

On that particular morning, the plane took off at 6 a.m. from Lahore. When everybody on the plane was looking weary and miserable, Iyengar found Nehru quietly reading a thin book. When he asked Nehru about that book Nehru told him that it was a translation of Shudrak's Mricchakatika, which his brother-in-law, Ranjit Pandit had asked him to read when the latter was in the Ahmadnagar prison.[3] This was an example of phenomenal detachment. A person who could concentrate on the translation of a Sanskrit play at 6 in the morning, during a period of shocking experiences and that too after having worked for more than twenty hours on the previous day, must certainly have been a very extra-ordinary person.

Nehru was known for his promptness in replying to letters and his punctuality. I had personal experience of both these qualities of Nehru. When I wrote a letter to him sometime in the first week of October, 1960, seeking an interview with him, Nehru was in New York. He returned to India from the States on the 12th or 13th of October. I did not expect a reply to my letter for at least two weeks after his return as I thought that he would be very busy with other matters and a reply to my letter would obviously be delayed. To my pleasant surprise, I received Nehru's reply on the 19th morning, asking me to come over to Delhi for the interview. It was a Diwali day and it could not have brought happier news.

The two lengthy interviews that I had with Nehru, started exactly at the very minute they were scheduled to start. Just a minute before the second interview, Nehru came to the visitors' room, put his arm across my shoulders and said in a most affectionate way, 'come on Rajurkar' and led me to his room.[4]

Nehru's immense desire to see everything being done well, big or small drove him to do things which a Prime Minister would hardly care to do. On the occasion of the proclamation of the Republic of India (January 26, 1950), before the arrival of the members of the Cabinet, diplomatic corps and the guests, Nehru was seen darting about the room, rearranging chairs, verifying the place cards for the ambassadors and so on. Similarly, in the preceding year, at the Second Asian Conference, Nehru was seen going from desk to desk of the foreign delegates (before the delegates had arrived), just in order to make sure that there were pens, pencils paper etc. for the delegates. In fact, he looked into every inkwell, just in order to satisfy himself that there was ink in each of it.[5]

Nehru nursed the infant democracy in India with the tenderness and devotion of a mother, so that it may grow to its fullest and become strong and sturdy. He taught the Parliament to conduct its affairs with dignity and decorum. Like a school teacher, he reprimanded the Members of the

Parliament, whenever he felt that their behaviour was inconsistent with the dignity of the Parliament. In fact, Nehru himself functioned as an ideal Parliamentarian. In spite of his mercurial temperament, he used to sit in both the Houses of Parliament for long periods listening to speeches, good and bad, so that he may know every point of view. His speeches in the Parliament were always balanced, restrained and dignified.

Nehru took good care to safeguard the rights and privileges of the members, but was always very keen to make them conscious of their duties and responsibilities as members of an August Assembly. He felt greatly upset whenever the members did something that was not in keeping with the best traditions of democracy. When a vote of no-confidence was moved by the Opposition Members of the Lok Sabha against its first Speaker-Mavalankar, Nehru felt irritated, not because of the no-confidence motion as such, but because of the vague charges and flimsy grounds on which it was based. His speech in reply to the motion of no-confidence was intended not so much to defend Mavalankar as to create in the members as awareness in regard to the absolute need of responsible, dignified and mature parliamentary behaviour. In fact, Nehru's constant anxiety was to lay down ideal parliamentary traditions, so that they may be followed in the years to come.

A person who spends almost his entire adult life in the domain of politics will necessarily become crude and vulgar and his behaviour would lack polish. Nehru was a rare exception. Even in the midst of the crude political atmosphere, Nehru continued to remain a man of charm, grace, refinement and polish. His love of poetry and music never left him, and he found time for them in spite of his bewildering pre-occupations. On a certain occasion, he stayed long at a Music Party, just because he had not heard sitar since long and that item was lower down the programme.

Nehru was a lover of Nature-of-snow-capped mountains, running brooks and waterfalls. He loved flowers, and the rose bud on his sherwani was symbolic of his aesthetic sense and love of beauty. He felt very happy in the company of children and simple village folks, as they represented purity and innocence. And yet, he always resisted the temptation of spending much time in the company of Nature or of children, because he had 'promises to keep'.

As a man, Nehru was 'greater than his deeds and truer than his surroundings.'[6] The people of India loved him, as they rarely loved anyone else, not only because of his sacrifices and sufferings, nor merely because of his political wisdom or multi-sided personality, but above all for his being 'the most civilized among us all, when many of us are not even civilized'.[7]

NOTES

1. An Autobiography, Jawaharlal Nehru, The Bodley Head, London, 1953, p. 218.
2. Ibid., p. 358.
3. A Study of Nehru, edited by Rafiq Zakaria, A Times of India Publication, Second revised edition, January 1960, pp. 177-178.
4. Author's interview with Nehru, October 1960.
5. Nehru: The Years of Power, Vincent Sheean, London, Victor, Gollanez Ltd, 1960, pp. 280-281.
6. Tagore's words about Nehru (A Bunch of Old Letters, written mostly to Jawaharlal Nehru and some written by him, Asia Publishing House, Bombay, 1958,p. 187).
7. C. Rajagopalachari quoted in the periodical 'Andhra Pradesh', July 1964 (Nehru Number), p. 24.

2

EARLY INFLUENCES

The attitude of a person towards different problems, his ideas on various issues and his likes and dislikes, are primarily a result of the impact on his mind of events, ideas and personalities, during the earlier part of his life. A careful examination of all such factors becomes all the more necessary, when an attempt is being made to understand a complex personality like Jawaharlal Nehru and the motivating considerations behind his political actions, for a period of more than forty years. In Nehru's case, however, it becomes essential to take into account the influences on him not merely during his childhood and adolescence, but even beyond the fortieth year of his life, in order to interpret correctly, the policies that he pursued during the later part of his life, more specially so, after he became the Prime Minister of the country in August 1947.

Much of the difficulty in understanding the politics of Nehru arises from our failure to comprehend the fact that Nehru was first and foremost a nationalist-one who had the country's interests uppermost in his mind, and that his role as an internationalist and a humanist did not prevent him from pursuing policies which were in the first instance advantageous to his country, without of course being injurious to the larger cause of international peace and co-operation.

Since nationalism was the principal force behind Nehru's actions, it becomes necessary to trace those events which were responsible for turning Nehru into a nationalist. As a child, Nehru very often listened to the talk of his cousins (who were much older than him)—talk which was invariably related to the overbearing character and insulting manners of the English people and the Eurasians towards Indians. He came to know from such talks as to how the people of India suffered at the hands of their alien rulers. An Englishman, who killed *an Indian,* was almost always acquitted by a jury of his countryman. Compartments were reserved for Europeans in railway trains, which the Indians were not permitted to occupy even when they were empty and when the train otherwise was terribly crowded. There was also reservation of benches and chairs for Europeans in parks and other places. This policy of discrimination and one that resulted in the humiliation of the Indian people at the hands of their British rulers, filled Nehru's mind with anger and resentment against the British authority in India. This coupled with the stories that he heard from his father's munshi-Munshi Mubarak Ali, about the excesses committed by English troops during the revolt of 1857, made Nehru anti-British authority in India even at that young age, though he did not entertain feelings of anger against individual Englishman.[1]

In May 1905, Nehru sailed for England in order to join the Harrow Public School. It was at Harrow that he got as a prize one of G.M. Trevelyan's Garibaldi books. The story of Italian movement captured his imagination and he obtained the other volumes and read with great interest the whole Garibaldi story. The exploits of Joseph Mazzini, Count Cavour and Garibaldi stirred his imagination and very often he imagined doing similar things for the emancipation of his country.[2]

India was pulsating with life when Nehru was studying at Harrow. There were terroristic activities and also a boycott of British goods, which was accompanied by a drive to support Swadeshi, or home-made products. The idea of partitioning Bengal, which was wholly unacceptable to the people of India, resulted in the Indian nationalism taking a more assertive form since 1904. The emergence of Bal Gangadhar Tilak on the political scene led to the Moderates losing some of their influence in the Indian National Congress.

Tilak was a great believer in incessant agitation, direct and indirect, to be reinforced by violence if necessary. He along with the great orator Bipin Chandra Pal and the Cambridge educated Aurobindo Ghose, led the anti-partition (Bengal) movement. And as for Punjab, there was unrest there also. The agrarian grievances manifested themselves in political demonstrations and the agitation there was led by Lala Lajpat Rai and Sardar Ajit Singh, both of who were deported by the British Government.

Young Nehru was greatly agitated by the news from India right through the years 1906-1907. Though the accounts he got from British papers were meagre enough, he could easily make out that big events were taking place in India. The news of the happenings in India stirred Nehru tremendously.

Nehru joined Trinity College, Cambridge in October 1907, when his age was about eighteen years. The events that were taking place in India influenced Nehru and other Indians in England greatly and almost all of them became strong supporters of the aggressive policy pursued by Tilak and his followers. India at that time was seething with unrest and for the first time since the Revolt of 1857, it was trying to defy foreign rule instead of submitting to it meekly. Nehru points out in his Autobiography, as to how Tilak's activities and his conviction stirred all of them in England and how almost without an exception they were Tilakites or Extremists, as the new Party was called in India.[3]

Even after he left Cambridge, Nehru continued to be a Tilakite and therefore did not like the politics of his father, who had cast his lot with the Moderates. It irritated Motilal Nehru to find most of the Extremists, who were young (apart from a few leaders in Bengal and Poona), going their own way and criticizing the Moderates. He hit at these young Extremists whenever he could. A little after he had left Cambridge, Nehru read an article of his father, which annoyed him greatly. He wrote a rather impertinent letter to his father, in which he suggested that it was not surprising that the British Government was greatly pleased with his activities.[4] Nehru's reaction to his father's activities as a Moderate, shows that his antipathy to the Moderates in the Congress and subsequently to the Liberals,[5] who followed a similar policy, dates back to his years in England as a student.

During those years, whenever a speaker talked about horrors in Africa or in India or something similar, Nehru the young nationalist, instinctively thought of such person as an ally. Moreover, books written by Indians or Englishmen, which brought out the harm done to India by British rule appealed to him almost immediately.[6]

However, almost up to early 'twenties, nationalism for Nehru was little more than a feeling of antagonism towards the alien rule over India-a rule which was responsible for the humiliation of the Indian people. In a statement made at his second trial on May 17, 1922, Nehru laid stress on the fact that he was forced to rebel against the Government in India, in spite of the fact that he was in his mental make-up and attitude towards life, more English thanIndian (due of his lengthy stay in England), because the Indians were subjected by that Government to miseries and insults.

In the concluding part of the statement Nehru emphasized the fact that the people of India were fighting for their freedom only and that they neither desired to injure any nation or people, nor did they wish to have dominion over others.[7] This part of Nehru's statement reveals the fact that even as early as 1922, Nehru represented a constructive and healthy type of nationalism.

An important event, which had profoundly affected Nehru during his boyhood, was the Russo-Japanese war of 1904-1905. Japanese victories made him very enthusiastic and he waited eagerly for the papers for fresh news daily. He invested in a large number of books on Japan and tried to read some of them. Years later, in a letter to his daughter, he described the Japanese victories as 'a great pick-me-up for Asia.'[8]

A little earlier, Nehru had got interested in the Boer War (1899-1902) and had sympathised with the Boers (possibly because of his antipathy to the British—the rulers of India), but as compared to the Boer War, the Russo-Japanese war excited Nehru more and stirred his sentiments to a greater degree because Japan symbolized an Asian country in conflict with an European power. This war injected in him an awareness of Asia and its lot under foreign domination. Probably the Russo-Japanese war marked the beginning of Asia-consciousness in Nehru, which became so pronounced in later years.

As stated a little earlier, almost upto early 'twenties, Nehru's antipathy to the British rule in India was based not so much on an awareness in regard to the manifold evil consequences that flowed out of such a rule, but rather had for its basis the ill-treatment of the Indian people at the hands of their foreign masters. As such, he stood for the liberation of his country from foreign domination, so as to save the people of India from shame and humiliation. However, gradually from 1920 onwards, his nationalism became more and more broad-based because of the impact on his mind of Mahatma Gandhi's ideas and the Marxist-Leninist literature. At this stage, however, it would be appropriate to assess the influence of environment (apart from the factors that turned him into a nationalist, as these have been already discussed), ideas and persons on Nehru's mind, from the period of his childhood to the year 1912—the year in which Nehru returned from England, after a sojourn of seven years in that country. Nehru was twenty three years old at that time.

Nehru grew up in North India, where there was a mixture of what was sometimes called Muslim culture in language, in ways of living, in food etc. and since childhood Nehru got used to this composite kind of cultural life.[9] This influence of the composite culture on his life could be considered as one of the important reasons for Nehru becoming a great secularist in later years, as a person living in such atmosphere would naturally develop breadth of mind and tolerance.

The influence of his father on young Nehru was very great. If Nehru became a rebel in later days, determined to oust out the British from India that in no small measure could be attributed to the impact on his mind of the forceful personality of his father, who rebelled against many social customs. In a letter written to John Gunther in 1938, Nehru stated that his father and Gandhi were the chief personal influences on his life.[10] Years later, Nehru stated that Motilal created a very great impression on him, not only because Motilal was his father but because of what he was, and according to Nehru, Motilal was a great fighter and specially a fighter when the odds were against him.[11]

Motilal Nehru's visits to Europe had created a storm in the Kashmiri Brahmin community and pressure had been brought on him to perform, '*prayaschit*' or purification ceremony. Motilal Nehru, who revolted against all superstitious customs and beliefs, not only refused to perform the purification ceremony but took a lead in doing away with all such out-moded practices.[12] Jawaharlal Nehru thus had in his veins the blood of a rebel and it is no wonder that he became in later years a rebel himself, challenging British authority in India as well as all such social customs and traditions amongst Indians which were out-moded and out-dated.

During this formative period of Nehru's life, a very real influence was that of his young Irish Tutor, Ferdinand T. Brooks,[13] who was a theosophist and a disciple of Annie Besant. Brooks not only got Nehru interested in sciences but also brought a new influence to bear on Nehru—the one of Theosophy, but this influence did not last long. It was because of Brooks that Nehru got interested in the great books of the Hindu religion like the Upanishads and the Bhagwad Gita. The influence of these great books, coupled with that of the stories from Ramayana and Mahabharata, which he used to hear from his mother and aunt during his childhood, perhaps account for his attraction to the moral side of Gandhi's movement for India's freedom. In late 'thirties, he once again took to the study of India's ancient literature, which impressed him powerfully and made him proud of India's past.[14]

Nehru, as has already been stated, returned to India in 1912 after a stay of about seven years in England. His faith in a democratic way of life and secularism in later years could primarily be attributed to his education in England and the consequent impact of 19th century Liberalism on his mind. The seeds of socialism, which Nehru was to consider as the panacea for India's social, economic and political evils in later years, were sown in his mind when he was at Cambridge. It was during this period that he was vaguely attracted to Fabian and other socialistic ideas.[15] The policy of gradualism that Nehru adopted during the post—Independence period in regard to the introduction of changes on socialistic lines could partly be attributed to the influence of Fabianism on him. Moreover, because of his study of sciences, firstly in his childhood at the hands of F.T. Brooks and subsequently at England, he developed a scientific attitude towards various problems and ideas. One of the reasons for Nehru's attraction to Marxism in later years was its scientific approach to political and economic problems.

The first four years after Nehru's return from England were hardly of any importance from the political point of view. But the period from 1916 onwards was very important in Nehru's life and it could be broadly stated that the period from that year to 1939 represents one particular phase in his life, the two major influences on Nehru's political ideas and politics during this period being those of (1) Mahatma Gandhi's personality, ideas and approach to political problems, and (2) the Marxist-Leninist literature and the policies and achievements of Soviet Russia in the post-Revolution period.

It must be borne in mind that Nehru came to socialism almost via communism, his college day ideas about socialism having receded into the background of his mind after his return to India.

The socialistic and Gandhian ideas continued to influence Nehru almost till the very end of his life-the influence of communism on his thoughts being relatively short-lived, though profound.

NOTES

1. *An Autobiography*, Jawaharlal Nehru, The Bodley Head, London, 1953. pp.6-8.
2. Ibid., p.19.
3. Ibid., loc. cit.
4. Ibid., p. 24
5. Ibid., pp. 410 & 413.
6. Conversations with Mr. Nehru, Tibor Mende, Secker and Warburg London 1956, pp. 14-15.
7. Important Speeches of Jawaharlal Nehru (from 1922-1925), edited by J.S. Bright, The Indian Printing Works, Kacheri Road, Lahore 1945, pp. 39 and 44.
8. *Glimpses of World History*, Jawaharlal Nehru, Lindsay Drummond Ltd., 2 Gilford Place, London, W.C.1., Fourth Edition, January 1949 p. 401.
9. Conversations with Mr. Nehru, Tibor Mende, Secker and Warburg London, 1956, p. 10.
10. *Inside Asia*, John Gunther, Harper and Brothers, New York and London, 1942, p. 441.
11. Jawaharlal Nehru's Speeches (1949-1953) Vol. III, The Publication Division, Ministry of Information and Broadcasting, Calcutta, Delhi, 1959, p. 480.
12. *An Autobiography*, Jawaharlal Nehru, The Bodley Head, London, 1953, p.13.
13. Ibid., pp. 14-15.
14. *The Discovery of India*, Jawaharlal Nehru, Signet Press, Calcutta-20, Fourth Printing, September 1948 p. 31.
15. *An Autobiography*, Jawaharlal Nehru, The Bodley Head, London, 1953, p. 25.

3

'... AND THEN CAME GANDHI'

Between the years 1920 and 1947, Gandhi and Nehru were the two persons who influenced the minds of the Indian people most. These two worked in close co-operation in the Indian movement for freedom, in spite of the fact that temperamentally they were not very similar. Moreover, on many issues, mainly economic, they held different views. And yet, so close they were to each other that Gandhi had no hesitation in declaring Nehru as his political heir and Nehru on his part considered Gandhi as his master.

A careful analysis of what drew Nehru to Gandhi and made him the latter's disciple, as also of the matters on which Gandhi and Nehru agreed with each other and those on which they didn't, would considerably facilitate the understanding of Nehru the man and Nehru the political leader. The Gandhi-Nehru relationship warrants an elaborate discussion because Gandhi's was perhaps the single greatest influence on Nehru, even greater than that of his father.

It was in the beginning of 1915 that Gandhi returned to India from South Africa. On the advice of Gokhale, his political master, as Gandhi called him later, he stayed away from active politics for a year and devoted that time for touring the country, so that he might get acquainted with the conditions therein. It was about two years after Gandhi's return from South Africa that Nehru met him for the first time. The impact of Gandhi's personality on young Nehru's sensitive and impressionable mind was tremendous. And yet, as far as approach to political problems was concerned, Gandhi seemed to Nehru 'very distant and different and un-political', though he had admired Gandhi's heroic fight in South Africa.

Gandhi, the man, impressed Nehru profoundly. In him, he found someone after his heart's desire; one who symbolised action and one who was devoid of all fear. Being himself a rebel, he admired the rebel in Gandhi. To Gandhi courage had been the one sure foundation of character and without it there was no morality, no religion and no love. Cowardice was a contagious crime. In the masses of India he inculcated fearlessness and a sense of pride and created a rebel out of every ordinary man and woman. While most others merely talked and talked loudly, Gandhi put into practice all that he preached.

Gandhi's insistence on fearlessness had an immense effect onNehru. Gandhi desired not only bodily courage but the absence of fear from the mind. 'The dominant impulse under the British rule was that of fear, pervasive, oppressing, strangling fear; fear of the official class; fear of the laws meant to suppress, and of prison ... it was against this all pervading fear that Gandhiji's quiet and determined voice was raised: Be not afraid.'[1]

Gandhi made the Congress a dynamic organization and discouraged all empty and fruitless talk. Before Gandhi's advent the Congress had indulged in merely talking and passing resolutions. Whereas most of the other leaders of the day excelled only in platform platitudes and tall talk, Gandhi was quiet and yet a man of action. Though he was always peaceful and courteous, he never submitted to anything that he considered evil. To the earnest Nehru, full of patriotic zeal, Gandhi's insistence on action appealed all the more as he was tired of the empty talk, pious platitudes, long speeches and noisy politics of the day. Gandhi's approach was entirely different from the Congress approach upto that period of passing futile and ineffective resolutions, which were not taken very seriously by anybody. Nehru was greatly drawn towards Gandhi because the latter's politics was of action and not of talk.[2]

Nehru first came under Gandhi's spell when the latter started the Satyagraha Sabha as a sequel to the rejection of his appeal to the Viceroy not to give his consent to the Rowlatt Bills. Its members were to disobey the Rowlatt Act as well as any other objectionable laws to be specified from time to time that might be applied to them. When Nehru read about the formation of the Satyagraha Sabha, his first reaction was one of tremendous relief. The action proposed by Gandhi appealed to Nehru as it seemed effective and was one of open defiance.

Though Gandhi seemed somewhat different and un-political to Nehru when he first met him, his opinion underwent a complete change soon afterwards. Nehru worked as some kind of a secretary to Gandhi, when the latter visited Punjab soon after the Jallianwala Bagh tragedy. It was during this period that Nehru's faith grew in the wisdom and political insight of Gandhi. Time and again, Nehru was surprised at the appraisal of the situation by Gandhi and the directions that he gave in regard to what was to be done. The first reaction of Nehru and others was invariably unfavourable to Gandhi's proposed action, but subsequently they found out that Gandhi's was the right policy. It was because of such experiences that Nehru gradually started relying on Gandhi's judgment, apart from basic principles.[3]

Gandhi's insistence on the adoption of good means for the achievement of good ends also met with Nehru's approval. Gandhi thought that the Machiavellian dictum, 'ends justify means' was wrong ethically and harmful even from a practical point of view. To him means and ends were convertible terms and as such should be equally pure. Gandhi likened the means to a seed and the end to a tree and thought that there was the same inviolable connection between the means and the end as there was between the seed and the tree.[4] Thus, according to Gandhi, if one took care of the means the end would take care of itself.[5] Nehru spoke almost Gandhi's language, when he addressed the Columbia University in October 1949. He said that there was always a close and intimate relationship between the end that was aimed at and the means that were adopted with a view to attain it. Even if the end was good, its goodness would necessarily be vitiated, if bad means were adopted for its attainment. It was just not possible to separate the means from the ends as they were connected very intimately and inextricably.[6]

Nehru had read Gita occasionally in his earlier days and had admired it, but under Gandhi's influence he read it again and again. Numerous parts of it had a powerful effect on him and he was particularly influenced by those parts of Gita which put forward the view that if a person did the right thing, right results would flow from it. And yet, his scientific training made it difficult for him to accept any viewpoint unless he could find a scientific explanation for it. Thus, gradually he began to develop the thought to apply his scientific mind to that matter and came to the conclusion that since every action had a result, every right action would necessarily have, to that extent, a right result, and similarly every wrong action, a wrong result.[7]

Though Nehru's faith grew progressively in Gandhi's leadership, it did not affect adversely his socialistic leanings. Again, it was almost during this period that he was greatly attracted by the events that were taking place in Russia-Bolshevik revolution and Lenin's regime subsequent to it. And yet, his faith in Gandhian ideas on one hand and socialistic and communistic ideas on the other did not produce any intellectual crisis in his life. 'I believed more and more in socialism. More and more even in some parts of communism, not the action part but the theory part of it, a communist society somewhere in the future. But I always conditioned it that the methods should be peaceful, broadly speaking peaceful and not wrong'.[8] This showed the extent of the impact on Nehru's mind of the Gandhian view that the ends and means should be equally good.

Nehru accepted Gandhi's programme of non-violent struggle for the achievement of India's freedom on ethical as well as pragmatic considerations—more so because of the latter. He, of course, admired and approved the moral and ethical side of non-cooperation movement and satyagraha, though he did not give absolute allegiance to non-violence or accept it forever. He was attracted towards it more and more because the belief grew on him that in the context of India's background and traditions and also that of the existing conditions that was a right policy for them to pursue. As already stated, the spiritualisation of politics at Gandhi's hands appealed to Nehru as he thought that Gandhi's insistence on the purity of means was not only ethically right but was also beneficial from a practical and pragmatic point of view, as bad means often defeated the end in view and created fresh problems.[9]

Nehru was convinced of the futility of violent methods for the achievement of freedom and thought that acts of terrorism and the killing of individual officers by bomb or pistol was a bankrupt's creed. It was simply absurd and ridiculous, thought Nehru, to imagine that such acts could shake a powerfully organized Government, however much they might terrify and frighten individuals. Years later, in his Presidential address at the Lucknow Congress (April 12, 1936), Nehru described terrorism as a sign of 'political immaturity in people'.[10] It was therefore very understandable that he should have welcomed Gandhi's programme of non-cooperation which promised good results. Gandhi had placed it before the country not only because it was a right method but also because it was very effective.[11] To Nehru however non-violent method of resistance was not an unchangable creed or dogma. It was for him essentially a policy and a method which promised certain results and in the ultimate analysis it was to be judged by those results only.[12]

It should not however be imagined that Nehru's faith in the efficacy of non-violent methods for the achievement of independence, never wavered. He had his moments of doubts about its effectiveness and one such moment of grave doubt came when Gandhi suspended the non-cooperation movement early in February 1922, because of the Chauri Chaura incident.

Near the village of Chauri Chaura, an angry mob of villagers had defied Police authorities in a violent way and had set fire to the Police Station, as a result of which half-a-dozen policemen were killed. Nehru realized the inevitability of such occurrence, for it was not possible to train three hundred and odd millions of Indians in the theory and practice of non-violent action before they could move forward. If that was the sole condition of the function, then the non-violent method would always fail. However, Nehru's confidence in Gandhi's leadership did not diminish as he came to the conclusion after deep thought that the suspension of the civil resistance could not have been the result of Chauri Chaura alone and that Gandhi must have realized almost instinctively that the movement was gradually losing its strength, though apparently it looked quite powerful.

To Nehru's satisfaction, Gandhi explained a little before the Civil Disobedience Movement of 1930 that the movement would not be abandoned because of the occurrence of sporadic acts of violence. This lent support to Nehru's view that the suspension of the non-cooperation movement, could not have been due to Chauri Chaura alone. In a sceptic mood he wrote: 'whether this interpretation which widened the scope of non-violent action represented an evolution in his mind or not I do not know'.[13]

Nehru's Autobiography and his other writings as well as his speeches make it fairly clear that but for his faith in the effectiveness of the non-violent movement, he would not have supported it. The pragmatist Nehru realized more quickly than others that Gandhi's method was the only feasible and effective method in those circumstances. It was highly probable that he would have lent his support even to violent methods, if he had been convinced of their utility. In his Presidential speech at the Lahore Congress (1929), Nehru pointed out that very often violence brought with it reaction and demoralisation and might even lead to disruption in a country like India. The Indian people had neither the material nor training for organized violence and in the absence of those pre-requisites, it was a folly to attempt violent methods. Individual or sporadic violence was of little use and was merely indicative of a state of desperation amongst people. The majority of the people of India, thought Nehru, looked at the question of the advisability or otherwise of violence, not from a moral point of view but from a practical one. They rejected the way of violence because they felt that it did not guarantee the desired results. Any effective movement for the liberation of a country should necessarily be one which had mass support and such mass movements had to be peaceful except when there was an organized revolt.[14] In the *Glimpses of World History* Nehru gave expression to similar views. He pointed out as to how for the disarmed people of India, a great majority of which was not acquainted even with the use of arms, armed rebellion was out of the question. Even if the people of India did make such an attempt, it could be very easily put down by the British authority in India.[15]

How did Nehru reconcile his faith in the adoption of good means for the achievement of good ends with his readiness to take recourse to violent means, if they could be effective. His answer could perhaps be obtained from his statement that while violence was bad, slavery was worse and that even Gandhi, the great apostle of non-violence had preferred violence to keeping quiet out of cowardice.[16] This leads us to the conclusion that though Nehru was all in favour of adopting good means for good ends, he found it necessary to compromise a little over the means if good means could not be adopted, as the alternative would be inaction and submission to a greater evil. '...the right means may well be beyond the capacity of infirm and selfish human nature. What then was one to do? Not to act was a complete confession of failure and a submission to evil; to act meant often enough a compromise with some forms of that evil, with all the untoward consequences that such compromises result in.'[17]

That Nehru never accepted non-violence as a creed was proved by a statement he made years later, in a vastly different set of circumstances. When he spoke on the creed of non-violence that time, he was no longer an agitator for his country's independence but independent India's first Prime Minister and the occasion was a debate on Goa in Lok Sabha, the Lower House of the Indian Parliament. Nehru in his reply to the debate spoke about the Government's anxiety to bring about the union of Goa with India and turned to the question of the methods that were to be employed for that purpose. Nehru stated that Acharya Kripalani had asked him a straight question as to whether the Government was pledged to non-violence, and his reply was that it was not. He could not conceive any Government pledged to non-violence in the circumstances that existed. If a Government was pledged to non-violence, it would neither maintain army, navy or air force nor perhaps even a police force. One might have an ideal and yet one might not find the circumstances conducive enough to give a concrete shape to that ideal. He reminded the members of the Parliament that a person like Gandhi, the very symbol of non-violence, gave his blessings to the idea of Indian army going to Kashmir, so that Kashmir could be saved from the raiders. The right of the State to resort to violence in defence was conceded even by Gandhi and the Government could not give up that right in the context of contemporary conditions.[18]

How would one account for Nehru's attraction to the ethical side of Gandhi's movement for freedom? As already stated in Chapter 2, it was perhaps because of the impact on his mind (during his childhood) of the great Hindu books like the Bhagwad Gita and the Upanishads, as also the stories from Ramayana and Mahabharata.

Though Nehru admired the moral side of Gandhi's movement, he got worried over the inroad of religion into politics under Gandhi's leadership, as that was encouraging the movement of revivalism and was indirectly helping the reactionary forces in the country. Gandhi always laid stress on the religious and spiritual side of the movement and in spite of the fact that there was no element of dogmatism in his religion, it did amount to religious outlook on life,[19] and this in turn had a great impact on the movement and for the masses it assumed a revivalist character. Nehru got worried over the entry of the religious element in Indian politics, on the Hindu as well as the Muslim side. Many things that were said by the Moulvies and Maulanas on the Muslim side and Swamis and the like on the Hindu side appeared wrong to Nehru and he particularly disliked the religious twist that they gave to everything, thus rendering clear thinking on any matter almost impossible. Some of Gandhi's favourite phrases jarred upon Nehru and he didn't quite like Gandhi's constant reference to Ram Raj as a golden age which was to return. However, as for Gandhi's use of those words, Nehru consoled himself with the thought that Gandhi used them because they were understood by the masses.[20]

Nehru did not however worry himself much over the religious element in Indian politics because he considered that matter as trivial and also because of his faith in Gandhi's greatness and his leadership, in spite of the fact that sometimes it was difficult to understand the working of Gandhi's mind and his language on occasions was incomprehensible.[21] Though Nehru and others accepted Gandhian ideas and the Gandhian lead without much murmur and though they tried (Nehru in particular), to rationalise some of Gandhi's apparently out-dated ideas, they did not wholly agree with many of Gandhi's ideas. They discussed Gandhi's fads and peculiarities amongst themselves' quite often and said half-humourously that in free India those fads should not receive any encouragement or support.[22]

Though Nehru did not quite like the religious over-tones of the Gandhian movement, he was greatly drawn towards the economic aspect of Gandhi's programme. 'Mahatma Gandhi taught us to view our national struggle always in terms of the under-privileged and those to whom opportunity had been denied. Therefore, there was always an economic facet to our political struggle for freedom. We realized that there was no real freedom for those who suffered continually from want and because there were millions who lacked the barest necessities of existence in India, we thought of freedom in terms of raising and bettering the lot of these people.'[23]

Nehru's attraction towards the economic facet of Gandhi's movement became far greater in 1920, due to an unforgettable personal experience, which widened his vision and changed his mental outlook. Till then Nehru was totally ignorant of labour conditions in factories and his outlook on life was entirely 'bourgeoisie'. Gandhi's agrarian movement in Champaran (Bihar) and Kaira (Gujarat) had induced him to take some interest in the problems of the peasantry. He was of course aware of the colossal poverty of the Indian people and had always thought that the first problem a free India should tackle must be that of poverty. However, his first contact with the peasantry left a deep mark on his mind. In May 1920, about two hundred peasants from the Pratapgarh district of Allahabad marched fifty miles and came over to Allahabad and spoke to the important politicians of their miserable condition. Nehru along with some colleagues went to the villages of the Pratapgarh district where they were all very enthusiastically received by the villagers. When Nehru saw their misery and their appalling poverty, he was overwhelmed with a feeling of shame and sorrow at the very comfortable life he led and the petty politics of the urban areas, which did not take into account the sad plight of the poverty-stricken millions of India. 'A new picture of India seemed to rise before me, naked, starving, crushed, and utterly miserable. And their faith in us casual visitors from the distant city, embarrassed me and filled me with a new responsibility that frightened me.'[24]

The people living in the cities then were totally ignorant of the problems of the peasantry and even the nationalist movement had remained till then, totally divorced from rural people and their problems. Thus, Nehru's outlook which had naturally remained bourgeoisie till then due to his comfortable urban life underwent a radical change after that incident.

That incident greatly strengthened Nehru's consciousness of peasant India, which had taken roots in his mind due to Gandhi's influence. Nehru sometimes wondered as to what would have happened, if he had not gone to the villages of Pratapgarh. He however thought that sooner or later, he would have been drawn towards the Indian peasantry, though the manner and effect of such a contact with the rural world of India, would have been different.[25]

Gandhi symbolised rural India and its manifold problems and his ambition was 'to wipe every tear from every eye'.[26] To him the salvation of India lay in villages. The Gandhian programme of rural uplift was in complete harmony with Nehru's recently awakened consciousness of rural India. Inevitably, he drifted more and more towards Gandhi's broad-based politics. Even before the Pratapgarh episode Nehru had occasions to pass through villages and talk to the peasantry. But somehow, he had not fully realized the gravity of the rural misery and its complete realisation came to him only during, his Pratapgarh visit and 'since then his mental picture of India was one which contained that starving naked mass'.[27]

Gandhi asked Congressmen to go to the villages and get themselves acquainted with the economic conditions of the poor people living there. Thus Nehru and others went to the villages where they saw the villager being pursued by the dark shadow of hunger. They learnt their lessons in Indian Economics not so much from books and scholarly lectures but from their visits to villages, where they came face to face with the realities of Indian economic conditions.[28]

Nehru not only appreciated Gandhi's stress on the economic betterment of the people belonging to rural India but he also approved the method suggested and advocated by Gandhi to achieve this end in view, viz., the method of spinning wheel and village industry. Gandhi's knowledge of the Indian villages and the problems with which the villagers were faced was unrivalled and the programme of spinning wheel and village industry that he evolved was a result or his experiences in regard to the conditions prevailing in Indian villages. Nehru thought that there was no other way than the one suggested by Gandhi, if the very large number of unemployed or partially employed persons were to be given immediate relief; if the standards of the villagers were to improve and if they were to become self-reliant, especially in view of the fact that all those things had to be accomplished without much of capital.[29]

Though Nehru approved Gandhi's emphasis on village industry he did not agree with the latter's views on the use of big machines. Gandhi was shocked at the vast gulf that stretched between the rich and the poor, in their ways of living and their opportunities of growth and one of the two principal causes for this vast difference between the rich and the poor seemed to him the capitalist industrial civilisation of the West as embodied in the big machine.[30] So Nehru, whose views were contrary to those of Gandhi stated that few of them agreed with Gandhi on the question of machinery and modern civilisation and yet the Gandhian ideology influenced many people and they in their turn became critical of machinery and its consequences.[31] On his part, stated Nehru, he was all in favour of tractors and big machinery as he felt convinced that the only way of solving many of India's urgent problems such as those of poverty of the people, relieving the pressure on land, improving the standards of living etc., was through the rapid industrialization of the country.[32] However, as Nehru pointed out, Gandhi's attitude to the use of machinery gradually underwent a change as he expressed his opposition not so much to the machinery as to the craze for it. Gandhi stated that he would not object to the villagers plying their implements and tools with electricity, if it was possible to have electricity in the house of every villager. Gandhi however opposed the big machine on the ground that its inevitable consequence was the concentration of power and wealth in the hands of the few. He even stated that he was prepared to lend his support to heavy industries, public utilities etc. provided they were owned by the State and did not affect adversely certain kinds of cottage industries, which were essential in his view.[33]

Nehru always held the view that the economic progress and prosperity of India primarily depended on the growth of large scale industries in it. Industrialization had become necessary for every poor and backward country, not only for the purpose of eradicating poverty but also from the point of view of perpetuating political independence and preventing the country from falling a prey to economic imperialism (which rendered the country's independence nominal), a very probable consequence of economic insufficiency. 'It can hardly be challenged', wrote Nehru, 'that in the context of the modern world, no country can be politically and economically independent, even within the frame-work of international interdependence, unless it is highly industrialized and has developed its power resources to the utmost. ... An Industrially backward country will continually upset the world equilibrium and encourage the aggressive tendencies of more developed countries. Even if it retains its political independence, this will be nominal only, and economic control will tend to pass to others. This control will inevitably upset its own small scale economy which it has sought to preserve in pursuit of its own view of life. Thus, an attempt to build up a country's economy largely on the basis of small-scale industries is doomed to failure. It will not solve the basic problems of the country or maintain freedom, nor will it fit in with the world framework, except as a colonial appendage.'[34]

The passage quoted above shows very clearly as to how Nehru's understanding of the problem of the industrialization of the country was deeper than that of Gandhi. Gandhi while dealing with that problem took into account its economic implications and not the political ones. Nehru on the other hand, not only considered carefully the economic implications of industrialization on the national level, but also took into account the possible political consequences of a policy of depending on small scale industries only and opposing large scale industrialization. Thus Nehru brought out very clearly the essential relationship between industrialization and the survival of a nation as an independent entity politically, with real freedom to pursue its own policies without outside interference or influence.

Nehru's bold lead in matters of the rapid industrialization of the country in the post-Independence period, could thus be attributed, not only to his intense desire to raise the standards of the people and make them economically better off but also to his desire to prevent India from falling a victim to economic imperialism.

As on big machines, Nehru also did not agree with Gandhi on the latter's concept of trusteeship. The idea of trusteeship appeared to Nehru, wholly impracticable and unrealistic. To give unchecked power and wealth to an individual and expect him to use it entirely for the public good was, according to Nehru, entirely unreasonable, as even the best of us could not be trusted that way. Perhaps it would have been difficult even for Plato's philosopher king to function as Gandhi expected a rich man to do. Unfortunately what the world had were frail human beings and not supermen, whose actions were governed by motives of self-aggrandisement and not with those of public good.[35]

When Nehru opposed Gandhi's concept of trusteeship, it was the socialist in him that was staging the revolt. Nehru believed that good men who were prepared to consider their wealth as a 'trust' of the poor, to be used exclusively for the poor, were rare exceptions and the behaviour of such people should not form the basis for the formulation of political concepts or policies. History, according to Nehru, had always showed that political outlook of groups and classes were moulded by economic interests. Neither reason nor moral considerations override these interests. Individuals may be converted, they may surrender their special privileges, but classes and groups do not do so: 'The attempt to convert a privileged class into forsaking power has therefore always failed and there seems to be no reason whatsoever to hold that it will succeed in the future.'[36]

From what has been discussed above in regard to Gandhi-Nehru relationship and their views on different matters it can be safely concluded that though Nehru was tremendously impressed by Gandhi's personality and had faith in his political wisdom, he (Nehru) did not accept many ideas of Gandhi. Nehru had the, ability to arrive at his own conclusions on different issues—political and economic, conclusions which at times were not only at variance from those of Gandhi but even diametrically opposite. Moreover, he had the mental courage to place before the Indian people his point of view through his writings.

The main problem in the pre-Independence period was the one of carrying on a very effective movement against the British rule in India so as to end it. Nehru almost entirely approved of the programme that Gandhi placed before the country for that purpose and the strategy that he advocated and as such Nehru became Gandhi's lieutenant.

The differences between Gandhi and Nehru were mainly on issues which were of no immediate relevance. Moreover, Nehru knew as to how important Gandhi's leadership was in the context of the freedom movement and Gandhi on his part knew the worth of the younger man.

Thus, the roles played by these two men in the national movement were complementary to each other, resulting in the movement gaining greater strength and added effectiveness.

NOTES

1. *The Discovery of India,* Jawaharlal Nehru, Signet Press Calcutta-20 Fourth Printing, September 1948, p. 299.
2. *Glimpses of World History,* Jawaharlal Nehru, Lindsay Drummond Ltd, London, Fourth Edition, January 1949, p. 713.
3. Conversations with Mr. Nehru, Tibor Mende, Secker and Warburg, London, 1956, p. 23.
4. *Hind Swaraj,* M.K. Gandhi, Navjivan Publishing House, 1909, p. 60.
5. *Harijan,* February 11, 1939, p. 8.
6. Jawaharlal Nehru's Speeches (1949-1953), The Publication Division, Ministry of Information and Broadcasting, Govt Of India, Calcutta, 1954, p. 396.
7. Conversations with Mr. Nehru, Tibor Mende, Secker and Warburg,, 1956, p. London 31.
8. Ibid., pp. 31-32.
9. An Autobiography, Jawaharlal Nehru, The Bodley Head, London, 1953, p. 73.
10. Important Speeches of Jawaharlal Nehru (1922-1945), edited by J.S. Bright, The Indian Printing Works, Kacheri Road, Lahore 1945, p. 9.
11. An Autobiography, Jawaharlal Nehru, The Bodley Head, London, p. 82.
12. Ibid., p. 84.
13. Ibid., loc. cit.
14. Important Speeches of Jawaharlal Nehru (1922-1945), edited by Jagat S. Bright, The Indian Printing Works, Kacheri Road Lahore, p. 138.
15. *Glimpses of World History,* Jawaharlal Nehru, Lindsay Drummond Ltd, London, Fourth Edition, January, 1949, p. 116.
16. Important Speeches of Jawaharlal Nehru (1922-1945), Edited by Jagat S. Bright, The Indian Printing Works, Kacheri Road, Lahore, 1945, p. 138.
17. *The Discovery of India,* Jawaharlal Nehru, Signet Press Calcutta-20 Fourth Printing, September 1948, p. 10.
18. Jawaharlal Nehru's Speeches, Volume III, March 1953-August 1957, The Publication Division, The Ministry of Information and Broadcasting Govt. of India, Calcutta, Delhi, 1959, p.382.
19. In September 1932, Gandhi decided to fast unto death in disapproval of the separate electorates given by Mr. Ramsay Macdonald's Communal Award to the Depressed Classes. While making a mention of that fast. Nehru wrote: 'I felt angry with him at his religious and sentimental approach to a political question, and his frequent references to God in connection with it. He even seemed to suggest that God had indicated the very date of the fast. What a terrible example to set.' (An Autobiography, Jawaharlal Nehru, The Bodley Head, London, 1953, p. 370).
20. Ibid., p. 72.
21. Ibid., pp. 72-73.
22. Ibid., p. 73.
23. Independence and After: A Collection of the more Important speeches of Jawaharlal Nehru from September 1946 to May 1949, The Publication Division, Ministry of Information and Broadcasting, Govt. of India, Calcutta, p. 160
24. An Autobiography, Jawaharlal Nehru, The Bodley Head, London, 1953 p. 52.
25. Ibid., p. 51.

26. *The Discovery of India*, Jawaharlal Nehru, Signet Press, Calcutta 20 Fourth Printing, September, 1948, p. 304.
?27. An Autobiography, Jawaharlal Nehru, The Bodley Head, London 1953, p. 57.
28. *The Discovery of India*, Jawaharlal Nehru, Signet Press, Calcutta, 20 Fourth Printing, September, 1948, p. 302.
29. Ibid., p. 339.
30. Ibid., loc. cit.
31. An Autobiography, Jawaharlal Nehru, The Bodley Head, London, 1953, pp. 76-77.
32. *The Discovery of India*, Jawaharlal Nehru, Signet Press, Calcutta-20, Fourth Printing, September,1948, p. 340.
33. Ibid., p. 342.
34. Ibid., loc. cit.
35. An Autobiography, Jawaharlal Nehru, The Bodley Head, London, 1953, p. 528.
36. Ibid., p. 544.

4

COMMUNISM AND THE COMMUNISTS

Nehru was profoundly influenced by the happenings in Russia in the post-revolution period as also by the Marxist-Leninist literature almost for a period of two decades. During this period, Nehru interpreted political happenings all over the world in terms of the ideas of Marx and Lenin. Moreover, because of the impact of the philosophy of Communism on his mind, Nehru's ideas in regard to nationalism became more broad-based and made him feel that India's movement for freedom had a global significance.

Those who read Nehru's speeches and writings during that period rather superficially almost felt that Nehru had become a Communist. Again, in the post-Independence period Nehru's attitude towards Soviet Russia was softer as compared to that towards the U.S.A. and, this coupled with Nehru's reliance on Krishna Menon's (who many considered the Communist Trojan Horse in the Congress government headed by Nehru) advice on matters of international importance, brought back to the minds of the people the memories of those days when Nehru was greatly enamoured of Communism, and made at least some of them feel that Nehru was a 'fellow-traveller'.

In order to understand the Nehru of the period between the First and the Second World Wars and in order to ascertain his exact attitude towards Communism, it becomes highly necessary to subject his writings and speeches during that period as also later to a close and careful scrutiny.

Nehru got greatly interested in Russia when the Kerensky and Bolshevik Revolutions took place there, and Lenin came to power subsequent to those events. The happenings in Russia excited Nehru, as he had read about the tyrannous rule of the Tsar's and naturally he was drawn to Lenin, who led the revolutionary movement. Of course, he did not know much about the Marxist philosophy at that time and the reactions of Nehru were those of a nationalist in revolt against an oppressive power, being drawn to similar events elsewhere.

For a nationalist struggling for the liberation of his country, no other country could have a greater appeal than the one that was opposed to imperialism[1] in every shape and form. Nehru was greatly drawn towards Russia in the post-revolution period because of Lenin's policy towards other countries. His policy towards China was very considerate as he gave up immediately extra-territoriality and the special privileges of the Russians there.[2] Nehru considered Russia the greatest opponent of imperialism and was of the view that her record with the nations of the East had been just and generous. In countries like China, Turkey and Persia, Russia gave up her valuable rights and concessions, while the British were acting in an entirely different way. They bombarded the thickly populated cities of China, causing thereby deaths on a large scale, as the Chinese were guilty of protesting against British imperialism.

When the Russian Ambassador went to the city of Tabriz in Persia for the first time, he spoke before the people of that city and tendered formal apology on behalf of Russia for the evil deeds of the Tsars. Russia was welcomed in the East as it went there not with the pride of a superior race but as equal. Moreover, unlike England and other countries of the West, Russia was wholly free from feelings of racial prejudice.

Thus, in the early twenties, Nehru was enamoured of Russia, because her policies symbolized: (a) anti-imperialism; (b) racial equality and what was more important; (c) a very considerate attitude towards Asian countries.

Another factor which drew Nehru towards Communist Russia was his faith in her peaceful intentions. He thought that Russia was the most peace loving country in the world and her policies were free from all aggressive designs.[3]

Nehru's visit to Europe in 1926 was very significant from the point of view of the impact of socialistic ideas on his nationalism. This visit profoundly influenced Nehru's mind and since then socialistic ideas became an integral part of his nationalism. The Nehru that reappeared on the political scene of India, after a sojourn of a year and nine months in Europe, was a Nehru with a broader vision. That visit to Europe could rightly be considered as a turning point in his life as it changed and modified many of his political ideas.

During his visit to Europe, Nehru attended the Congress of oppressed Nationalities held in Brussels in 1927. At that Congress Nehru met various socialist and communist leaders and was rather irritated by the attitude of the British socialists to the question of India's freedom. The communists, he thought, were at least not 'hypocritical and imperialistic', whatever might be their other faults. Nehru particularly approved the attitude of Russia towards other countries, though he was irritated by the communist methods, which he considered vulgar.

His visit to Russia in 1927 was particularly important from the point of view of the change that came over him. By and large, he was favourably impressed by the changes that were taking place in Russia. The articles that he contributed to Indian newspapers and which were later published in the form of a book, revealed a balanced assessment of the conditions and happenings in Russia.

During the early 'thirties, Nehru studied several books on Marxism and was greatly drawn towards it. In his *The Discovery of India*, Nehru stated as to how he was profoundly influenced by the Marxist-Leninist ideas during that period. 'A study of Marx and Lenin produced a powerful effect on my mind and helped me to see history and current affairs in a new light. The long chain of history and of social development appeared to have some meaning, some sequence, and the future lost some of its obscurity.'[4]

Nehru's early education in Science at home and subsequently at Cambridge impelled him to reject everything that was based on superstition and dogma and drew him instinctively to all those concepts and ideologies which had for their basis the scientific approach. In a letter that he wrote to his daughter on February 16, 1933, Nehru pointed out as to how Marxism attempted to reduce human history, past, present as well as the future to a system that was rigidly logical. Though Nehru expressed his doubts in regard to the correctness of the view that life was that logical, he approved of the Marxian method of surveying history as a scientist and drawing some conclusions from it.[5] Thus, it could be said that Nehru's attraction to Marxism was also due to its more or less scientific approach to social, economic and political problems. And yet ironically enough, Nehru drifted away from Marxism in later years because of the tendency amongst the Marxists to treat that philosophy as a dogma which could not be varied and modified.

Though Nehru was not prepared to accept Marxism as a gospel truth, there was no doubt about the fact that the Marxist-Leninist ideas as a whole had an immense impact on his mind. He gained a new perspective on history and thence forward considered India's struggle for freedom as one of the world problems, in which people elsewhere ought to be equally interested. It was a typical example of imperialist domination and the success of Britain in retaining its hold over India had tempted other countries to undertake imperialist adventures.[6]

India's fight against the British was described by Nehru as one against imperialism. In his Presidential address to the U.P. Conference on October 27, 1928, Nehru stated that it was not England that was their enemy, but it was imperialism and wherever imperialism, existed, there they could not willingly remain.[7]

Again, the emergence of Fascism on the ideological scene of Europe was also interpreted by Nehru in terms of the Leninist interpretation of imperialism. Nehru pointed out as to how capitalism in its difficulties manifested itself in the form of Fascism and was instrumental for the brutal suppression of all those things which the Western civilisation was said to symbolise. It could not but function in a few of its home-lands in a manner in which its imperialist counter-part had been functioning in the subject countries. Thus, Imperialism and Fascism became the two manifestations of decaying capitalism and though the national characteristics as well as economic and political conditions influenced the form they took in different countries, basically they represented the same force of reaction. Moreover, they lent support to each other as they could not do otherwise, since in their very nature such a conflict was inherent.[8]

Apparently, there was little that was common between Britain, which stood for democracy and the Fascist Italy or the Nazi Germany. The decadent capitalism in Italy gave rise to the usual manifestations, characteristics of that stage of economy, those of authoritarianism at home and imperialism abroad. Individual liberty was completely crushed and there was the glorification of the State. As opposed to this, Britain stood for complete individual freedom and yet that apostle of democracy, did little to arrest the spread of the Nazi and the Fascist influence, as Britain on one hand and the Nazis and the Fascists on the other represented the same forces of reaction and they had as stated already, conflict inherent in them.[9]

Years later, in a statement at his trial held in Gorakhpur prison (November 3, 1940), Nehru stated as to how for years past he had consistently raised his voice of protest against Nazism as well as Fascism, as everything in him revolted against those ideologies, and how he had been extremely critical of the policy of the British Government which was pro-Fascist and one of appeasement. He had been an unhappy observer of the developments that had taken place in the recent past and his mind had been filled with anguish at the betrayal of Manchuria, Abyssinia, Spain, China etc. in the name of this appeasement. And yet it did not take long for him to realize that the only way for imperialism to function without weakening its ideological foundations, was one of appeasing its rival imperialism. In case it did not do so, it would be left with no other alternative save that of liquidating itself in order to make way for democratic freedom, which it obviously would not be inclined to do.[10]

Nehru's ideas in regard to democracy underwent a very noticeable change during the 'thirties as a result of the study of the Marxist-Leninist literature. Democracy, felt Nehru, was incompatible with capitalism; as such, any super-structure of democracy built on the foundations of capitalism was bound to come down sooner or later. Inspite of the mutual incompatibility between democracy and capitalism, they grew together in Europe in the 19th century. The incompatibility arose out of the basic contradiction between the two, democracy symbolising the power of the many and capitalism giving power only to the few. It was however possible for this pair with mutually antagonistic interests to carry on, as the democracy of the political parliamentary type was a democracy in a very restricted way and it did not adversely affect either the growth of the monopoly or power concentration. But such an ill-assorted pair as the one of democracy and capitalism could not but break up sooner or later and the time had come for such a separation. Parliamentary democracy, which in itself was beyond reproach, had come into disrepute and was being severely criticised because of its many acts of omission and commission.[11]

The famous definition of democracy as being a Government of the people, by the people and for the people could not materialise in practice, because the Government under a capitalist set up could only be that of the possessing classes for the advancement of their interests. It would be possible to have a Government by the people and for the people only when the power went into the hands of the masses and, that happened only under socialism.[12]

As stated in the preceding paragraph, Nehru believed in the 'thirties that the acceptance of a democratic form of Government by a country with a capitalist economy did not render it democratic in spirit. The capitalistic system was full of fundamental economic inconsistencies that resulted in the inequalities of wealth and the ultimate pursuit of imperialistic policies. Great Britain was democratic at home and autocratic abroad because it had based its democracy on a capitalistic order and the inherent incompatibility between the two (democracy and capitalism), hindered its growth and prevented it from achieving its desired ends. Hence, Britain inspite of its loud professions about democracy followed an imperialistic policy in the 19th century and was making a desperate effort to cling to the acquired territories in our own century. Capitalism inevitably led to imperialism and to the conflicts of imperialist powers that were seeking colonial areas where they could obtain raw produce and also markets for the goods manufactured in their respective countries. The actions of imperialist powers could not but lead to greater conflicts with the rising nationalism of colonial countries as well as to social conflicts with working class movements. It's inevitable consequence had been the occurrence of crisis after crisis in the political and economic domain, they in turn leading to tariff wars as also to the wars of a political nature.[13] Thus capitalism according to Nehru was the negation of democracy as it nullified all those basic principles and values for which democracy had always stood. Countries like Britain and France, inspite of their democratic political set up at home were compelled to follow a policy of imperialism abroad and thus come into conflict with democratic urges as represented by nationalist movements in colonial countries as a result of their adherence to capitalism which stood for interests wholly opposed to those of democracy. A capitalistic democracy functioned in an undemocratic way not only on the international plane but also on the national level. On the national level it led to maldistribution of wealth and privileges, leading to acute poverty and unemployment in the midst of prosperity and plenty. Thus, those democratic countries, which clung to capitalism, had perforce to live up with Fascist forces on the international level (as British policies during the 'thirties' so clearly revealed), and represented reaction at home as they had governments neither of the people but those of the possessing classes for the advancement of their own interests.[14]

During the 'thirties, the influence of Marxian and Leninist ideas on Nehru's mind led him to the conclusion that throughout the world there was a conflict between two forces, one represented by Fascism and imperialism and the other by freedom and democracy.[15] About Fascism he wrote: 'I dislike Fascism intensely and indeed I do not think it anything more than a crude and brutal effort of the present capitalist order to preserve itself at any cost,[16] The test of the faith of those countries (Britain and others) in democracy was the Spanish struggle for democracy and freedom. Britain was actually guilty of indirectly aiding the Fascist rebels in Spain.[17]

Nehru looked at the Spanish struggle in the context of a world conflict between Fascism and imperialism on the one side and democracy and freedom on the other. He wanted the Indians who stood for Spain to clearly understand that by implication they stood for putting an end to Fascism and empire and all that they symbolised.[18] Nehru's reaction to the Spanish War showed very clearly as to how he considered India's struggle for independence as an integral part of a much wider movement against colonialism and imperialism. More and more he began to think of the political or economic problems of the different parts of the world, either those of China, Abyssinia, Spain, Central Europe, India or any other part, not in isolation or separately, but rather as the different facets of a world problem.[19]

To Nehru, India's freedom was not an end in itself but a means towards an end—the end being the betterment of the Indian people, socially and economically. Apart from national considerations, Nehru also felt that only an independent India could offer an effective resistance to the spread of Fascism. He passionately believed in countering Fascism at the national as well as the international level and came to the conclusion that it could be done only by relying on democracy and by encouraging it everywhere. India under foreign yoke was an undesirable phenomenon even from the international point of view as it weakened the democratic front and rendered resistance to Fascism less effective.[20]

It was clear to Nehru that there was nothing common between the nationalism of the East and the narrow nationalism of the Fascist countries. The former represented the historical urge for freedom, whereas the latter was the last refuge of reaction. Thus, it was the desire of Nehru that India should strengthen the forces of democratic socialism on the international plane so that Fascism's spread might be arrested, but even for that the pre-requisite was an independent India, and Nehru was acutely conscious of that. A free India, stated Nehru, would willingly throw her entire weight on the side of democracy and freedom. Only free and democratic countries can help freedom and democracy elsewhere. If Britain is on the side of democracy, then its first task is to eliminate empire from India. That is the sequence of events in India's eyes, and to that sequence, the people of India will adhere.[21]

It was but natural that Nehru, who was convinced of the inefficacy of a democracy based on the foundations of a capitalist system, should advocate a complete break with the existing order. He was convinced that the only remedy for the mal-distribution of wealth and other concomitant evils was the acceptance of socialism. He ruled out the possibility of any via media and thought that the world should either accept capitalism or socialism. Advocating a break with the past, Nehru pointed out that it was not possible to have two processes that were contradictory as well as conflicting to continue side by side. It was necessary that a choice should be made and for those who aimed at socialism there could not but be one choice.[22] For Nehru, Reformism was an impossible solution for any vital problem at a critical moment when the basic structure had to be changed and however slow the progress might be later on, the initial step must be a complete break with the existing order, which had fulfilled its purpose and was now only a drag on future progress.[23]

With all his love for democracy, Nehru in this period was highly doubtful about the possibility of introducing socialism in a country by democratic means. The Marxian concept of class war influenced his thinking greatly and he felt convinced that the interest of the two classes in the society were so opposed to each other that no democratic method would resolve that class conflict. In theory, thought Nehru, it seemed possible to bring into existence a socialistic society through democratic means subject to the condition that full democratic process was available. However, one realized that in practice it presented great difficulties as those who were opposed to socialism could not but reject that method as that would strike at the very roots of their power. Inspite of its many victories, the democratic method had not succeeded in ending the conflict in regard to the state's or society's basic structure. It was obvious that the group or class that controlled the governmental machinery would not give up their power voluntarily because the majority demanded it.[24]

It could be said that roughly from 1917 to the out-break of the Second World War (1939), Nehru was greatly under the influence of Soviet Russia. The Russian Revolution attracted him as also the subsequent approach of the Bolshevik Government to national and international problems. His visit to Soviet Russia in 1927 drew him nearer still to that country. His study of the literature on Communism, specially the works of Marx and Lenin in the early 'thirties, resulted in his gaining new perspective on history and also enabled him to look at the Indian struggle for independence in the larger context of a world struggle between the forces of imperialism and Fascism on the one hand and those of democracy and freedom on the other. By 1935, his intellectual adherence to communism had become so complete that he came to the conclusion that the world had to choose between socialism and capitalism and that there was no middle way. Thus, we find that during that period Nehru was very considerably influenced by the theory of communism as well as by what Russia was doing and the changes that were taking place there. 'I am strongly attracted towards communism and I feel that the only reasonable and scientific explanation of history is the communist one. I do not approve of many things that have taken place in Russia nor I am a communist in the accepted sense of the word. But taking everything together, I have been greatly influenced by the Russian experiment.'[25]

The influence of the Marxist-Leninist literature on Nehru's nationalism revealed itself from Nehru's writings and speeches of the 'thirties'. In his presidential address to the Lucknow Congress (April 1936), in which Nehru analysed different problems, national and international, from the Marxist-Leninist point of view, we find the impact of the Leninist ideas on the analysis that he made of the nature of the Indian nationalist movement and the change that he sought in it. He pointed out as to how the direct action struggles in the past, in India, had for their basis the masses and more particularly so the peasantry, though the leadership inevitably came from the middle classes. The middle classes, according to Nehru, were a vague group or groups. At the top there were a handful of persons who were closely allied to British imperialism, whereas at the bottom were the dispossessed and the other groups who were increasingly being crushed by economic circumstances and from whose ranks came the advanced political workers and revolutionaries. In between were the centre groups, which usually threw their lot with the advanced elements, but which also entered into alliances with the upper groups and entertained the hope of joining their superior ranks. Thus, the middle class provided a leadership which was often distracted as it looked into two directions at the same time.[26] 'And yet, paradoxically, it is only from the middle class intellectuals that revolutionary leadership comes, and we in India know that our bravest leaders and our stoutest comrades have come from the ranks of the middle classes.'[27] Though this would inevitably happen, they must look, 'more and more towards the masses and draw strength and inspiration from them.'[28]

The *Glimpses of World History*, written by Nehru in the early thirties, showed a marked influence of the Marxist-Leninist ideas on Nehru's ideas about nationalism. In this book, he pointed out as to how the inevitable result of capitalism was imperialism as capitalism necessarily required raw materials and new markets. The wealth that was accumulated by the imperialist nations of Europe and the betterment in the standard of living of their people was at the expense of the Asian and African people and also of the people belonging to other non-industrial areas. The wealth amassed by these capitalistic countries through the exploitation of the people of Asia and Africa, did conceal for a while the inherent contradictions of capitalism and yet the difference between the rich and the poor went on growing and the distance between them became all the greater.[29]

Britain, a typical capitalist country, inspite of itself, became the agent of a great historical process—the one which transformed the feudal India into the modern type of Industrialized Capitalist state.[30]

What the British did not understand was that capitalism as well as imperialism (the latter being the progeny of the former) carried with them their own seeds of destruction—the Indian nationalist movement itself being a part of that inexorable historical process. That process, thought Nehru, would ultimately throw the great British Empire into dustbin and individuals would not be able to do much against the mighty forces at work, which would determine the speed and direction of the world's relentless onward march.[31]

Nehru knew that nationalism was bound to be the strongest force in Asia as countries under alien domination inevitably thought in terms of nationalism. But he was also aware of the fact that powerful economic forces,[32] bringing about changes in the world, were increasingly influencing nationalism in Asia, with the result that almost everywhere, nationalism was appearing in 'socialistic garb'.[33] Gradually, the nationalist struggle for political freedom was also assuming the character of a social struggle aimed at economic freedom.

The internationalism inherent in socialism was also taken into account by Nehru. He stressed the fact that from an economic point of view the world was essentially international, though 'political structure' still lagged behind and continued to be 'narrowly national'. The difficulty with today's world was that the rivalries between nations were rendering very difficult the solution of the economic problem, which was essentially an international problem. The intensification of nationalism by the Fascists could never succeed as it went against the modern world economy which as stated earlier was essentially international in character. As such, for one who professed to believe in socialism, nationalism could not have any meaning.[34]

The influence of the Marxist-Leninist ideas on Nehru's nationalism also became evident when Nehru opposed the idea of Dominion status for the country on the ground that it would deprive India of its capacity to work for the independence of other countries under foreign domination and would actually become a party to Britain's exploitation of other countries.

The Second World War brought dis-illusionment to Nehru, not only because of the betrayal of the democratic cause by the democratic countries of the world but also because of the rather dubious and opportunistic role played by Soviet Russia during the war period. 'As the war progressed, new problems arose or the old problems took new shape, and the old alignments seemed to change, the old standards to fade away. There were many shocks and adjustment was difficult. The Russo-Japanese Pact, the Soviet's invasion of Finland, the friendly approach of Russia towards Japan; were there any principles, or any standards of conduct in the world, or was it all sheer opportunism.'[35] At yet another place Nehru gave expression to his great disappointment at Russia's policy of opportunism and expediency, so different from the policy pursued by her during the previous twenty years or more. Russia was guilty of bartering away her moral prestige and friendship of her numerous friends for what she considered to be advantageous to her politically. Russia the symbol of hope and fulfillment for her admirers and champions degraded herself by sacrificing moral principles at the altar of political expediency.[36]

Though there was no necessary connection between Soviet Government's policies and the philosophy of communism, the attitude of Russia during the period of Second World War shook Nehru's faith in communism as he had always looked at Russia as a country symbolising communism in practice. Hence Russia's role during the war period might be considered as the starting point of Nehru's dis-illusionment in regard to the communist approach to various problems.

Though Marxist-Leninist ideas influenced Nehru's thinking profoundly for more than a decade, and though he was enamoured of post-Revolution

Russia, it would be incorrect to infer that he was a communist at any stage of his life. In fact, a close study of his utterances and actions since 1939 and more particularly so after India attained freedom, would convince us that Nehru was opposed to the communist way of life. An attempt has been made in the remaining pages of this chapter to trace the various factors which contributed to Nehru's allergy for communism and the communist party of India.

A close study of Nehru's life and the influences thereon would convince us that Nehru could not but be a democrat. As he was a great believer in a democratic way of life, he disliked communism which stood for the regimentation of speech and action and reduced an Individual in the State to a position of nothingness. 'I am too much of an individualist and believer in personal freedom', stated Nehru, 'to like over much regimentation'.[37] Moreover, his democratic mental make-up disliked intensely the communist habit of denouncing everybody who did not agree with them.[38] Almost twenty five years earlier Nehru had stated that civil liberty was for him neither an airy doctrine nor a pious wish but was something which was highly necessary for the proper development of a nation as well as for its all round progress and advancement. To make an effort to crush an opinion or, to prevent a person from expressing it as it was not to one's liking, was analogous to cracking the skull of a person whom one disliked. When one cracked the skull of one's opponent, he might die, but in the case of suppressed opinions such an end was improbable, whatever might be the extent of force that was applied for its extinction.[39] In a letter written to John Gunther in 1938, Nehru stated that he was not a communist chiefly because he was too much of an individualist. Nehru further stated that he did not like being told as to what he should think and do.[40] Thus one of the principal reasons for Nehru's opposition to communism was his love for a democratic way of life and allergy to the regimentation of thought and action, which were characteristic of communism and the communist way of life.

Nehru disliked the very dogmatic and rigid approach of the communists to various problems. He did not like the tendency amongst the Marxists to treat Marxism as a dogma which could not be varied. He believed implicitly in the scientific approach to life and its problems, as opposed to the dogmatic approach. To Nehru the scientific approach was the only correct approach to a question. As science was advancing, the less dogmatic it was becoming and also more hesitant in its answers to the questions that were put to it. However, science was greatly helping us in the understanding of life and was enabling us to lead a better life and one which was more purposeful. Science had always succeeded in illumining the dark corners of life and had always facilitated the process of facing reality, thus enabling us to see our path clearly, instead of groping in the darkness of vague confusion of unreason.[41]

To Nehru, who had an open mind and who was essentially a believer in the scientific approach to problems, the very dogmatic attitude of the communists to various problems appeared very wrong and even detrimental from the point of view of the progress of the people in the right direction. The Indian communists according to Nehru showed a complete lack of awareness in regard to the problems with which India was faced and the manner in which they were to be solved. They advocated exclusive adherence to Marxian principles and for them any deviation from those principles or even a variation in them was a blasphemy. This dogmatism irritated Nehru as he believed that the Marxian thinking was conditioned by the political and economic conditions prevailing in the nineteenth century and that it did not have much relevance to the problems of the twentieth century, particularly those of the under-developed areas.

Nehru cautioned the communists against the tendency amongst them to rely on Marx whose ideas had become completely out-of-date and on the writings of other communist thinkers either belonging to the nineteenth century or to the early twentieth century. The conditions in which they lived were entirely different from the conditions of today, and what was more important was that, they were written in the context of the problems of Europe and America and not in the context of under-developed areas like India.[42]

Since the times of Marx, new factors had intervened and new conditions had developed, rendering thereby the Marxian approach to problems, out-of-date. The approach of Marx was certainly very appropriate so far as the problems of Industrial Revolution period in England were concerned, but it had little applicability to the problems of the under-developed areas of the world today. Marxism was essentially the outcome of the beginnings of the Industrial Revolution in England when the conditions were abnormal and abominable.[43]

For the problems with which Indians were faced, solutions could be found out only by thinking of them in the context of the contemporary conditions in India as well as those prevailing in the other parts of the world. The Marxian solutions might have been proper for the conditions prevailing in the nineteenth century, but they could not be applied to our problems, and that was one of the reasons for Nehru's opposition to the dogmatic insistence on the solutions suggested by Marx.[44]

Moreover, the analysis made by Marx of historical forces and the like was a correct analysis so long as other forces coming into the picture were not taken into account. Marx unfortunately did not take into consideration the other forces that might start operating at a future date. It could not have been otherwise as Marx used the conditions of his times as the premises for his conclusions. It was after Marx that other forces came into play the most important of them being political democracy that rendered peaceful change possible. In the absence of political democracy during Marx's time, it was not possible to bring about changes in the constitutional or democratic manner, and therefore they had to be made through violent means. The doctrine of 'revolutionary violence' was thus a result of the political conditions that were prevailing during Marx's time. The right of franchise given on a large scale to the people in different countries after Marx's time made vital differences. It was an effective Instrument for the purposes of exercising effective pressures towards social change and that was something that Marx did not visualise as the picture was not before his mind's eye.[45]

Later still, other democratic factors entered into the picture, such as, those of trade union organizations, workers organizations, peasant organizations etc. and they exercised effective pressures upon the rich ruling classes and that was how the beginnings of economic democracy were made. The Marxist apprehension in the context of the Industrial Revolution, about the concentration of wealth in the hands of very few and the increasing poverty of the great majority in consequence, did not really take place. The pressures such as those exercised through democratic methods and also those that were exercised through the trade unions etc. succeeded considerably in limiting both. The economic tendency that Marx had apprehended, did manifest itself but it was always 'limited and inhibited' by those objective conditions.[46]

The urge for social justice and the desire for social change were accelerated by the political conditions which were constantly undergoing radical changes. While that was happening new types of organizations were developing in the political background and at the same time great technological developments were revolutionising the world, things which were not foreseen either by Marx or anyone else during the nineteenth century.[47]

The period in which Marx lived was one in which the principal problem was one of distributing something that was not adequate and that was responsible for conflicts of all sorts. In those conditions, as was to be expected, the stronger and the wealthier got hold of most of what there was and the poor inevitably suffered in consequence. The intensity of the conflicts would obviously be in proportion to the shortages and since the scientific and technological developments were bringing (in the modern period) the goal of material prosperity within reach of people, those conflicts were lessening in many parts of the world.[48]

The United States of America had in modern days the biggest apparatus of production and though the difference between the American billionaire and others was great, the conditions of living as also the standards of life were very high. In fact in America, there was no proletariat of the Marxian conception. Whatever had happened in the U.S.A. in the economic domain did not synchronise with the Marxian prophecy about what would happen. 'Capitalism itself has changed, is changing all the time, though it sticks to its basic grab-instinct and tends towards monopolies and aggregation of economic power. But the urge for social justice is there even in the capitalist system.'[49]

The intervention of new factors and more particularly so the two features of political democracy and technological progress had rendered the review of Marxism essential. The problems of the contemporary period were such that Marx could not have applied his mind to them.[50]

Thus, according to Nehru, dogmatic adherence to the Marxian approach to various problems was meaningless and unwise, as the whole set of circumstances had undergone a radical change since Marx lived. It was therefore but natural for Nehru to be allergic to the tendency amongst the Communists to ignore the peculiar present day conditions and to advocate blindly the Marxian solutions that had little bearing on the present day problems.

It was Justice Mahadev Govind Ranade, who had declared at the beginning of the twentieth century that India had its own economics. He had strongly deprecated the tendency amongst Indian Economists to follow blindly, Adam Smith, Ricardo and others and to advocate methods suggested by them. Like Ranade, Nehru also believed that the economic problems of India were very different from the economic problems of those countries which did not fall in the category of under-developed countries and as such a blind adherence to the methods followed by other countries was not only undesirable but positively detrimental. The dogmatic attitude of the Communists who refused to take into account the peculiarities of the Indian problems and who suggested that India should totally follow the methods employed by Russia for its prosperity, impelled Nehru to refer to them not as revolutionaries but as 'great reactionaries'. 'Let us come to the communists' stated Nehru, 'these brave revolutionaries whose revolution consists not in an application of intelligence but in trying to find out what is happening 5,000 miles away, and trying to copy it, whether it fits in or not with the present state of India. Their mind is a kind of inverted mirror which reflects something that happened not today but sometime ago in some other country.... Unfortunately our friends of the Communist Party of India have so shut their minds and have so spent all their time and energy in learning a few slogans of the past that they are quite unable to appreciate what is happening in India. In fact, these great revolutionaries of the Communist Party of India have become great reactionaries.'[51] In yet another speech, Nehru stated that the approach of the Communists to various matters was comparable in rigidity to that of old religious bigots and added that he on his part had always refused to bow to the bigotry of any religion and that his attitude would be the same to the bigotry of this new religion of communism.[52]

Nothing could meet with greater disapproval of a nationalist than the tendency in any group in the country to look to other countries for inspiration and guidance. The attitude of the communists left a deep mark on Nehru's mind. When the whole country was making a last bid for the overthrow of British rule in India, the communists betrayed the country and co-operated with the British authority in India. For the communists, Russia's participation in the war rendered it a peoples' war from one that was being fought by imperialists, and thus necessitated co-operation with the British Government of India.

Since the sudden somersault of the communists in India during the Second World War period, Nehru had become very critical of them. In late 1945, a special committee of the Congress of which Nehru was a member, recommended the expulsion of the communists from the Congress as a sequel to their anti-national role during the Second World War period.[53] About seven years after India became free, Nehru condemned the communists in India in a very categorical way for their policies which were dictated to them from outside. The communists in India had always condemned India's foreign policy but it became praiseworthy to them the moment Soviet leaders approved of it. With utmost frankness and courage, he declared: 'They (the communists) have no moorings in the land of their birth, but always look to outside countries for inspiration and guidance.'[54]

One of the reasons for Nehru's adherence to the policy of non-alignment was his intense desire to enable India to function independent of foreign pressures. In February 1952, he stated in the Parliament that the people of India decided for themselves and that they pursued a policy which they considered right without outside interference.[55] Thus, for a nationalist like Nehru who was proud of India's past and who held the belief that India was capable of looking after itself and moreover who reacted very strongly against any foreign interferences, the habit of the communists to get dictates from other countries had become a source of constant irritation. In a speech that he delivered in December 1955, Nehru referred to the visit of the Soviet Union leaders to India and the friendly and cordial welcome that was given to them. He pointed out as to how the Soviet Union was friendly with India and how India wished her leaders well. 'But wishing them well doesn't mean that we should lock up our own minds and intelligence and forget our own experiences and our own country. India is some definite entity in the world. And I cannot understand how anyone can simply imagine that India's mind and heart can be locked up and made to follow a dictated policy from somewhere else. Is that the kind of independence and freedom that we have achieved?'[56]

Nehru's opposition to the communists would have been lesser if they had functioned as a national group like any other political group or party in the country. But on the contrary the communists not only looked for inspiration and took guidance from other countries but sometimes functioned in a way that was highly detrimental to the national interests. The powers to whom the Communist Party was tied up could utilise the party to gain their own ends. Thus, the Governments in various newly independent countries of Asia were afraid of what the bigger powers would do through the political groups that were loyal to them in their respective countries and not of what they would do officially. In the past one country, was against another whereas in recent times there were international groups in each country which opposed the national group. If the Communist Party in any country was like other parties with a definite political and economic programme, nobody would have objected to it. But the trouble arose because that party was tied up intellectually and mentally with outside nations.[57] As stated earlier, it was always possible for certain countries to advance their own interests by utilising the communist groups in other countries.[58]

The communists, according to Nehru, had no roots in the country's past. National memories and traditions did not inspire them nor did famous figures in national history have any appeal to them. The present inherited from the past vast stores of wisdom and knowledge and it was the height of folly for the people not to profit by that rich legacy. A country's past had much to offer to its present and more particularly so, when the country was an ancient country like India with a great and glorious past. Apart from other things, the past of a country enabled the people belonging to its present, to look at things in perspective and in their proper context. During his last term of imprisonment (1942-1945), Nehru discussed India's past with his scholarly colleagues and read a lot about it and was very powerfully impressed by India's achievements in various fields, more particularly so in the realm of thought.[59] It was but understandable that Nehru should disapprove of the communist attitude of ignoring the past completely and clinging only to what had happened in Russia in 1917 and subsequently. Writing about this peculiar and abnormal attitude of the communists to the country's past Nehru observed: 'I cannot speak with much knowledge of what happened elsewhere, but I know that in India the Communist Party is completely divorced from, and is ignorant of the national traditions that fill the minds of the people. It believes that communism necessarily implies contempt for the past. So, far as it is concerned, the history of the world began in November 1917 and everything that preceded this was preparatory and leading up to it. The Communist Party ... has cut itself off from the springs of national sentiment and speaks in a language which finds no echo in the hearts of the people. It remains an energetic and small group with no real roots.'[60]

Though Nehru was conscious of class struggle, he disliked the Communist methods of resolving it through violence. He believed in the Gandhian approach of solving problems peacefully and in a friendly way and felt that the Marxian approach to the problem of class struggle was out-of-date. Gandhi, thought Nehru, was perhaps not conscious of the class struggle aspect in the way many others of his times were and yet the solutions suggested by him had greater applicability to modern conditions and particularly to India. Gandhi's advocacy of the peaceful solutions of problems was in harmony with India's history and traditions. Nehru also thought that class struggle need not be ended by intensifying it first and then resolving it through violence and conflict. He considered the Gandhian method far more desirable-one of lessening the conflict by winning over people, rather than taking recourse to violent means.[61]

The peaceful approach to the problem of class war had become imperative because of the atom bomb which threatened the extermination of human race. This very destructive weapon had made it impossible to think in terms of solving class conflict through violent means. 'Hence, from any point of view, the concept of class struggles or wars has been out-dated as too dangerous at a time when not only nations but groups of individuals can be put in possession of weapons of enormous destructive potentiality. So we have to appreciate and follow the Gandhian solution of synthesis, co-operation, co-existence and progressive equalisation.'[62]

Nehru was opposed to the Communists as excessive violence was associated with their methods. Being greatly influenced by Gandhi's creed of non-violence and his emphasis on the adoption of good means, Nehru could not but dislike the violent communist methods.

While expressing his disapproval of the adoption of violent methods for the achievement of any goal, Nehru stated in the Parliament that though he admired the achievements of great countries like Russia and China, he wondered whether the leaders and people of Russia would not try other means of reaching their ideals, in case they had another chance, rather than pay the colossal price which they had to pay during the period of Revolution in their country.[63] Inspite of Soviet Union's many achievements, Nehru was not drawn towards communism as its association with violence had become too close. 'Even if it does not indulge normally in physical violence, its language is of violence, its thought is violent and it does not seek to change by persuasion or peaceful democratic pressures, but by coercion and indeed by destruction and extermination. This is completely opposed to the peaceful approach which Gandhiji taught us.'[64]

Nehru was also opposed to the communists because the way of life that they advocated and which they would eventually force the country to follow in case they got into power, was one which did not meet with his approval. *The Discovery of India*, written by Nehru during the year 1944, revealed a very considerable modification in his views in regard to Marxism. He had always been enamoured of the scientific approach to life and it was primarily because of this, that he was greatly drawn towards Marxism in the earlier days. And yet a deep study of India's ancient literature during the 'forties drew him further away from Marxism, as he realized that an 'integral vision of life could not be developed merely by relying on the scientific approach to life. What was required was a somewhat, different approach to life, one which would combine the approach of science with philosophy and which would have for its basis reverence for all that lay beyond. It was necessary for the people to develop the integral vision of life, which embraced in its scope the past and the present and which could look towards the future with serenity.'[65]

The philosophical teachings of Vedanta and the moral example of Gandhi, also increased Nehru's dissatisfaction with the Marxist philosophy. Marxism lacked much on the metaphysical and ethical side something which Nehru did not appreciate or approve. Marxism failed to satisfy Nehru completely as it could not provide answers to the questions that he had in his mind and almost unconsciously he was drawn towards the Vedanta approach to life.[66] Years later, in his foreword (September 1955) to a book by Ramdhari Singh 'Dinkar', Nehru stated that Marxism failed to find a remedy for the crisis of the spirit and though it had some virtue as an economic approach, it could not provide answers to many questions and could not resolve the basic doubts of the people. Though economic growth was important, life was something more than that.[67]

Some spiritual standards had become absolutely essential as one of the biggest problems which America and other economically advanced countries would have to face in the next decade would be that of the proper utilisation of leisure. One read about cases of youth delinquency, which were becoming more and more common in prosperous countries and perhaps the incidence of such cases in America was the greatest. How were the people belonging to the countries which were going for the automation in a big way, to solve the problem of the proper utilisation of leisure? 'I wonder if a problem like this could be tackled scientifically to the exclusion of other values. What appears to be wanting is...an ethical aspect...some spiritual solution ... I believe that the human mind is hungry for something deeper in terms of moral and spiritual development without which all the material advance may not be worthwhile.... I do not happen to be a religious man, but I do believe in something, call it religion or anything you like, which raises man above his normal level and gives the human personality a new dimension or spiritual quality and moral depth.'[68]

The real problem of today was one of creating a fully integrated human being, and even those countries which had made great material progress had failed to create an atmosphere which would be conducive to the growth of a fully integrated life. When the problem of employment was solved, a bigger problem propped up and that was one of employing leisure itself. Obviously when a person got the material comfort that he desired, his mind would hunger for something spiritual and ethical.[69]

The trouble with the problem of leisure was that the human being would utilise it very wrongly, unless he was sufficiently developed. Of course this problem was always there but it did not come to the surface in countries like India, specially, where a person had to work constantly in order to make both ends meet, and where the struggle for life was very fierce. But in countries where the social and economic problems were solved, as had happened in the more developed countries, and where automation relieved a person of his work also, new problems propped up in a big way, such as those of juvenile delinquency, sexual outrages and crimes, alcoholism, destructiveness, anarchy and a hundred other viruses of spiritual sickness and moral collapse.[70] The problem in developed countries thus was one of what a person was to do when he had enough money and other essentials. The moment his physical wants were satisfied he got engulfed in a spiritual vacuum and in consequence we had the 'angry man' so characteristic of this generation. This aspect of the problem was not taken into consideration by Marx as it had not revealed itself during his times. It was very clear however that in the context of modern problems, the aspect which was assuming more and more importance was the ethical one. Whether it was leisure or the nuclear energy or space rockets—the problem before our generation was the one of using them properly. 'All these new discoveries take you outside the normal economic domain. You cannot argue about them in terms of Marxist economy or any other set pattern. There must be a new approach, a modern approach, a moral or ethical approach.'[71]

Thus, Nehru was opposed to the communists who believed that Marxism was the panacea for all human evils and as such, should be adhered to totally. Nehru considered the Marxian philosophy as inadequate for the purposes of solving one of the biggest problems of the day, viz., the one of the growth and development of an integrated personality and of integral vision amongst the members of the society. Marxism could not prove equal to the task as it had contempt for the moral and spiritual side of life and as it deprived human behaviour of certain standards and values.[72]

It is hardly necessary to state by way of conclusion that inspite of the impact on his mind of Marxist-Leninist ideas, as also of the policies of Soviet Russia during the post-revolution period and the progress that it made, Nehru could (for reasons given above) never become a communist during any part of his life. On the contrary he made every effort to prevent communism from taking roots in India, during the post-freedom period. However, it must be pointed out that his accurate analysis of different political phenomena on the national as well as the international plane (during the pre-independence period), was primarily a result of his study of the writings of Marx and Lenin.

NOTES

1. After the First World War, Winston Churchill had envisaged the idea of a great middle-Eastern Empire, stretching from India to Constantinople, the countries which were practically in possession of the British at that time. 'I liked the developments in Russia (in the post Revolution period) as a counterpoise to all this. I have no doubt that it made a great difference to Iran and Turkey and all those countries in those days.' (Conversations with Mr. Nehru, Tibor Mende, Secker and Warburg, London, 1956, p. 17).
2. Ibid, loc. cit.
3. Important Speeches of Jawaharlal Nehru (1922-1945), Edited by J.S. Bright, The Indian Printing Works, Kacheri Road, Lahore, 1945, pp. 101-102.
4. *The Discovery of India*, Jawaharlal Nehru, Signet Press, Calcutta 20, Fourth Printing, September 1948, p. 12.
5. Ibid., p. 544.
6. *India and the World*, Jawaharlal Nehru, George Allen and Unwin Ltd., London, 1936, p. 16.
7. Important Speeches of Jawaharlal Nehru (1922-1945) Edited by J.S. Bright, The Indian Printing Works, Kacheri Road, Lahore, p. 111.
8. Ibid. p. 5.
9. Ibid., loc. cit.
10. Ibid., pp. 188-189.
11. *An Autobiography*, Jawaharlal Nehru, The Bodley Head, London, 1953, p. 529.
12. *China Spain and the War*, Kitabistan, Allahabad and London, 1940, p. 31.
13. *Recent Essays and Writings*, Jawaharlal Nehru, Kitabistan, Allahabad. 1934, p. 15.
14. Ibid., p. 31.
15. *The Unity of India*, Jawaharlal Nehru, Lindsay Drummond, London, W.C. 1, 1948, pp. 294-29.5.
16. *Recent Essays and Writings*, Jawaharlal Nehru, Kitabistan, Allahabad, 1934, p. 126.
17. *The Unity of India*, Jawaharlal Nehru. Lindsay Drummond, London, W.C., 1948, p. 295.
18. *Eighteen Months in India*, Jawaharlal Nehru, Kitabistan, Allahabad and London, 1938, p. 113.
19. *An Autobiography*, Jawaharlal Nehru, TheBodley Head, London, 1953, p. 601.

20. *China, Spain and the War*, Jawaharlal Nehru, Kitabistan, Allahabad and London, 1940, p. 116.
21. Ibid. p.187.
22. *India and the World*, Jawaharlal Nehru, George Allen and Unwin Ltd, London, 1936, pp. 181-182.
23. *An Autobiography*, Jawaharlal Nehru, The Bodley Head, London, 1953, p. 362.
24. *India and the World*, Jawaharlal Nehru, George Allen and Unwin Ltd, London, 1940, p. 182.
25 *Recent Essays and Writings*, Jawaharlal Nehru, Kitabistan, Allahabad, 1934, p. 123.
26. Important Speeches of Jawaharlal Nehru: Being a Collection of the most significant speeches delivered by Jawaharlal Nehru from 1922 to 1945, Edited by J.S. Bright, The Indian Printing Works, Kacheri Road, Lahore, pp.9-10.
27. Ibid., p. 10.
28. Ibid., loc. cit.
29. *Glimpses of World History*, Jawaharlal Nehru, Lindsay Drummond Ltd, London, W.C. 1. p. 403.
30. Ibid., p. 413.
31. Ibid., loc. cit.
32. *Recent Essays and Writings*, Jawaharlal Nehru, Kitabistan, Allahabad, 1934, p. 18.
33. Ibid., loc. cit.
34. *Glimpses of World History*, Jawaharlal Nehru, Lindsay Drummond Ltd, London. 403.
35. *An Autobiography*, Jawaharlal Nehru, The Bodley Head, London, 1953, p. 609.
36. *China, Spain and the War*, Jawaharlal Nehru, Kitabistan, Allahabad and London, 1940, p. 250.
37. *The Discovery of India*, Jawaharlal Nehru, Signet Press Calcutta-20, Fourth Printing, September 1948, p. 13.
38. *An Autobiography*, Jawaharlal Nehru, The Bodley Head, London, 1953, p. 163.
39. *The Unity of India*, Jawaharlal Nehru, Lindsay Drummond Ltd, London, W.C. 1, 1948, pp. 67-68.
40. *Inside Asia*, John Gunther, Harper and Brothers, New York and London, 1942, p. 441.
41. *Glimpses of World History*, Jawaharlal Nehru, Lindsay Drummond Ltd, London, W.C. 1, Fourth Edition, January 1949, p. 870.
42. Jawaharlal Nehru's Speeches (1953-1957), The Publication Division, Ministry of Information and Broadcasting, Govt, Of India, Calcutta, Delhi, 1959, p. 84.
43. *The Mind of Mr. Nehru*, R.K. Karanjia, George Allen and Unwin Ltd., 1960, p. 28.
44. Ibid., loc. cit.
45. Ibid., p. 29.
46. Ibid., pp. 29-30.
47. Ibid. p. 30.
48. Ibid., p. 31.
49. Ibid., loc. cit.
50. Ibid., loc. cit.
51. Jawaharlal Nehru's Speeches (1953-1957), The Publication Division, Ministry of Information and Broadcasting, Govt. of India, Calcutta, Delhi, 1959, pp .136-137.
52. Jawaharlal Nehru's Speeches (1949-1953), The Publication Division, Ministry of Information and Broadcasting, Govt. of India, Calcutta, 1954, p.32.

53. Text of the Committee's Report in Congress Bulletin, No.2, Delhi, 24th January 1946, pp. 24-37.
54. To a public meeting in New Delhi, 28th November 1954, (The Times of India, Bombay, November 29, 1954).
55. Jawaharlal Nehru's Speeches (1953-1957), The Publication Division, Ministry of Information and Broadcasting, Govt. of India, Calcutta, Delhi, 1959, p. 136.
56. Ibid., loc. cit.
57. The Central Secretariat of the Communist Party of India at its meeting in New Delhi (November 1, 1962), passed a resolution in which the Chinese aggression over Indian territory was condemned and support to the Indian Government was assured. It was however significant that several communist leaders and workers were taken into custody under the Preventive Detention Act, even after the resolution was passed. The Times of India, Bombay (dated 22nd November 1962), stated, 'In a countrywide operation, the police on Wednesday took into custody over 350 members of the Communist Party of India, including some of the Party's leading workers in various States. Among the arrested are a member of the Lok Sabha, 30 members of the State Legislative Assemblies and Councils, five Ministers of the first Communist Government in Kerala.'
58. Jawaharlal Nehru's Speeches (1953-1957) The Publication Division, Ministry of Information and Broadcasting, Govt. of India, Calcutta, Delhi, 1959, pp. 272-273.
59. *The Discovery of India.* Jawaharlal Nehru, Signet Press, Calcutta, 20, Fourth Printing, September, 1948, p. 31.
60. Ibid., p. 437. .
61. *The Mind of Mr. Nehru*, An Interview by R.K. Karanjia, Allen and Unwin Ltd, London, 1961, pp.76-78.
62. Ibid., p. 77.
63. Jawaharlal Nehru's Speeches (1949-1953), The Publication Division, Ministry of Information and Broadcasting, Govt. of India, Calcutta, 1954, p, 33.
64. *The Tragic Paradox of our Age*, Jawaharlal Nehru, New York, Times Magazine, 7th September 1958, p. 13.
65. *The Discovery of India*, Jawaharlal Nehru, Signet Press, Calcutta, 20, Fourth Printing, September, 1948, p. 435.
66. Ibid., p. 13.
67. Jawaharlal Nehru's Speeches (1953-1957), The Publication Division, Ministry of Information and Broadcasting, Govt. of India, Calcutta, Delhi, 1959, p, 414.
68. *The Mind of Mr. Nehru*, An interview by R.K. Karanjia, Allen and Unwin Ltd, London,1961, pp. 32-33.
69. Ibid., p. 34.
70. Ibid., pp. 34-35.
71. Ibid., pp. 35-36.
72. 'The Tragic Paradox of Our Age', Jawaharlal Nehru, New York, *Times Magazine*, 7th September 1958, p. 13.

5

TOWARDS DEMOCRATIC SOCIALISM

Almost since the date of his arrival on the political scene of India, Nehru started advocating the acceptance of the socialistic ideal and, stressing the fact that only through socialism could India solve its basic problems. His first major pronouncement in favour of socialism came through his presidential address to the Lahore Congress of 1929. In this address, Nehru stated that he was a socialist and a republican and that he did not believe either in kingship or in the capitalist order, which produced kings of industry. Further, he added that there could almost be no two opinions in regard to the advisability of accepting the goal of socialism and almost the only disputed point was in regard to the pace and the methods of advancing towards that goal. India too, would have to go the socialistic way if she sought to end her poverty and inequality, though she might evolve her own methods and might adapt the ideal of socialism in such a way as to suit the 'genius of her race.'[1]

Nehru's presidential address revealed that even in 1929, his approach to socialism was not doctrinaire and rigid, and that his pragmatic mind was engaged in evolving a method for the achievement of the socialistic ideal which would suit India, and was anxious to adapt the ideal of socialism to its conditions and its people.

Though Nehru's adherence to socialism became a matter of all India knowledge only after the Lahore Congress, he had gone a long way in the socialist direction by that time. His interest in socialism, as stated in Chapter 2, dated back to his days at Cambridge and even that academic interest receded into the background of his mind when he took a plunge into the political movement after his return to India.

Again, as stated in Chapter 2, Nehru came to socialism via communism. Though he read a few books on socialism while at Cambridge and subsequently during the First World War period, the socialistic ideal did not take deep roots in his mind till his visit to Soviet Russia in 1927. It was roughly during the late 'twenties that he did considerable reading of the Marxist-Leninist literature and this coupled with his visit to Russia, resulted in his becoming a confirmed believer in the socialistic goal, though he did not approve the communist method of reaching it. Since 1927, Nehru had consistently put forward the view that socialism alone offered a solution to India's problems and more particularly to India's problem of acute poverty, of which he had the first, painful but revealing experience when he visited some vi llages of Pratapgarh in 1920.

Why did Nehru accept socialism? He accepted it because he believed that socialism alone could root out the evils which had taken deep roots in the soil of India in particular and in that of the world in general. For him, socialism was not merely an economic doctrine promising better economic standards and the removal of poverty; it was for him in the final analysis, a way of life which called for a profound transformation in the habits and instincts of men and which would establish a new civilization wholly different from the modern capitalist order.[2]

After his return from Europe, Nehru became the General Secretary of the Congress—the year being 1928. As the General Secretary, he directed the attention of the people to social and economic changes. He was particularly desirous of spreading socialistic ideas amongst the Congress workers and the intelligentsia, as they were the backbone of the national movement. He spoke at different places on the need of achieving political independence in the shortest possible time and emphasized the fact that it was the pre-requisite for social freedom.[3]

There were many socialists in India before Nehru became one, but his importance lay in his being a prominent Congressman. Some leading Congressmen shared Nehru's views on socialism, but their number was very small and amongst them it was Nehru who took the initiative in giving a socialistic bias to the national movement.

In 1928, Nehru presided over four provincial conferences and had the opportunity of visiting rural areas in the U.P. and also of addressing industrial workers. Wherever he spoke, he tried to interpret nationalism as a means towards the achievement of a socialistic society. How Congress was taking to his ideas in regard to socialism could be gauged by the fact that as early as 1926, the U.P. Provincial Congress Committee tried 'to draw up a mild socialist programme'.[4] In 1929, the Nehru inspired U.P. Provincial Congress Committee passed a resolution, which was wholly on socialistic lines. The All India Congress Committee (A.I.C.C.) meeting in Bombay that summer adopted the preamble of the U.P. resolution and thus accepted the principle of socialism underlying the whole resolution. However, the resolution was passed by the A.I.C.C. without giving serious consideration to it and probably the members did not quite realize its implications.[5]

Nehru also tried to quicken the pace of the spread of socialistic ideas by including the U.P. branch of the Independence for India League (which consisted entirely of principal Congress workers in the Province)to function wholly on socialistic lines. The League, which ultimately merged into the Congress in 1930, had in fact social freedom as one of its objects.

In 1929, a little before the Lahore Congress, Nehru presided over the All-India Trade Union Congress, held at Nagpur. It was quite unusual for the same person to preside over the Indian National Congress as well as the Trade Union Congress, one after the other, within a range of few weeks. By associating himself with the Trade Union Congress, Nehru hoped to be 'a link between the two and bring them closer to each other—the National Congress to become more socialistic more proletarian, and organized labour to join the national struggle.'[6]

Nehru's associates however were not very keen about socialism, the governing passion with them being the removal of foreign authority from the country. Nehru, though equally keen on eliminating British rule from India was also passionately eager to discuss socialism in the context of India's problems—economic, social and political, so that the people of India might know about the real content of 'Swaraj' to come. Thus, Nehru got irritated, whenever his colleagues in the Working Committee showed indifference to socialistic ideas and treated them as a fad of Nehru. In a lengthy letter to Gandhi (dated August 13, 1934), Nehru accused the Congress Working Committee of deliberately encouraging 'vagueness in the definition of our ideals and objectives'.[7] In this connection, he particularly drew Gandhi's attention towards the political objectives. He thought that it was high time for the Congress to do some clear thinking on social and economic issues, though he conceded that education on those issues took time and that the Congress as a whole might not be able to go as far then as he would like it to go. The Working Committee, thought Nehru, made no attempt to understand the views held by him and a few others on socialism and was too willing to denounce them for their views. 'A strange way of dealing with the subject of socialism is to use the word, which has a clearly defined meaning in the English language, in a totally different sense. For individuals to use words peculiar to themselves is not helpful to the commerce of ideas. A person who declares himself to be an engine-driver and then adds that his engine is of wood and is drawn by bullocks is misusing the word engine driver.'[8]

This accusing and sarcastic letter of Nehru showed the extent to which he was pained not only by the frequent criticism of his ideas by the members of the Working Committee but also by a 'loosely worded' resolution passed by the Congress Working Committee. It was stated that the resolution became necessary in view of the rather loose talk about the confiscation of private property and necessity of class war. The resolution also asserted that the Karachi Resolution neither contemplated the confiscation of private property without just cause nor had it advocated class war. Nehru was exasperated by that clumsy resolution, 'as apart from being loosely worded, it exhibited a certain amount of ignorance on the part of the framer as to what class war was.'[9]

During those years, Nehru was preaching socialism tenaciously. Inspite of the lukewarm attitude of his colleagues in the Working Committee towards the ideology of socialism, he realized that it was very necessary not only to consider the question of applying socialism to Indian conditions, but to speak of socialism to the people of India, 'in the language of India', if it was to become popular. It was probable that Gandhi, who always reached the hearts of the people by speaking a language which the people of India understood, must have served as an example to Nehru. While emphasizing the importance of speaking to the people in a language they understood, Nehru stated, 'I am referring to the language which grows from a complex of associations of past history and culture and present environment. So long as we do not speak in some language which has that Indian mentality for background, we lose a great measure of our effectiveness. Merely to use words and phrases, which may have meaning for us but which are not current coin among the masses of India, is often wasted effort. It is this problem of the approach to socialism that occupies my mind, how to interpret it in terms of India, how to reach the hearts of the people, with its hope giving and inspiring message.'[10]

Throughout his political career, Nehru lent his support, to the ideology of socialism with a surprising degree of consistency and constantly stressed the fact that it was most essential to bear in mind the needs of the country while accepting it. He had all along held the view that it was very detrimental to the interests of the country to ignore the peculiar conditions prevailing in it and accepts blindly a certain form of socialism as it had paid rich dividends in some other country. It must however be said that one did not find much evidence in Nehru's speeches, of words and phrases which were current coin among the masses of India. In that respect, Gandhi was more successful than Nehru, as he used phrases familiar to the people of India such as Ram Rajya, Daridri Narayan etc.

Nehru reiterated his belief in socialism and in a non-doctrinaire approach to it, when he stated in 1960, that he had believed in socialism for the previous five decades and that he would continue to believe in it and work for it unless someone convinced him that he was wrong in doing so. Modern thinking observed Nehru, was increasingly becoming socialistic and those who thought otherwise could be deemed as being totally out of touch with contemporary trends. Inspite of his faith in socialism, Nehru did not like the idea of accepting any particular dogma of socialism and thought that it was wrong to be rigid either about the form of socialism or about the approach to it. What he broadly desired was that every individual should be given equal opportunity and that there should not be inequalities, at least in respect of the opportunities that were given. Moreover he desired that the gulf between the rich and the poor should be narrowed down as far as possible.[11]

While emphasizing the need of accepting that form of socialism which was in accordance with a country's genius, Nehru gave the example of Buddhism and pointed out that though Buddhism took its birth in India it put on the garb of the country to which it went. In China, it took on a Chinese orientation and so on, in Burma, Japan etc. In other words it meant that Buddhism got itself engrafted in nation's soul, wherever it went. Thus, while accepting the ideology of socialism for one's own country, it was necessary to choose a form which was compatible with the country's genius and which could be an answer to the country's peculiar needs and requirements.[12]

At this stage it would be very relevant to discuss Nehru's socialism vis-à-vis democracy. Nehru's public utterances for more than three decades, made it abundantly clear that he had always desired to raise the super-structure of socialism in India, on the firm foundations of democratic principles. Nehru's faith in a democratic way of life primarily resulted from the influence of the Indian way of life and that of the 19th century liberalism on his mind. Probably, it was also the result of the impact on Nehru's mind, of the evils of the suppression of individual liberty and the denial of basic rights, a normal feature of the British rule in India.

Nehru stressed the fact that the people of India had always been known for their democratic way of life. The Indian tradition was a democratic tradition, in matters of conducting the affairs of political, social, commercial and religious institutions. The democratic way was not only well-known but was a common method of functioning in social life, in local government, trade guilds, religious assemblies etc. Caste, with all its evils, kept up the democratic habit in each group. There used to be elaborate rules of procedure, election and debate.[13]

Nehru's support to and attraction for a democratic way of life, could primarily be attributed to his faith in the value of individual freedom. In the Unity of India, Nehru stated: 'Civil liberty is not merely for us an airy doctrine or a pious wish, but something which we consider essential for the orderly development and progress of a nation. It is the civilized approach to a problem on which people differ, the non-violent way of dealing with it.'[14]

How enamoured Nehru had always been of individual liberty, could be gauged by the resolution on Fundamental Rights and Economic Programme (drafted by Nehru), adopted by the Karachi Congress of 1931, which would be quoted and discussed at some length in the next chapter.

It must be pointed out at this stage that the Karachi Congress indicated unmistakably the socialist trend in the Congress, due primarily to Nehru. Though the leading members of the Congress were not much interested in resolutions on economic programme, the acceptance of the resolution on Fundamental Rights and Economic Programme did constitute a definite advance on the socialistic path, as that resolution was clearly on socialistic lines. The impact of Nehru's socialistic views on Indian nationalism, which was discernible since 1929, became more pronounced from the Karachi Congress of 1931 onwards.

Being a great believer in individual freedom, it was but natural that Nehru should find the British rule over India intolerable, as it resulted in the denial of the rights of free expression of opinion and free association.

Through his Presidential address to the Lucknow Congress (April 12, 1936) Nehru gave expression to his righteous indignation at the tremendous deprivation of civil liberties in India through various laws that suppressed press and literature, that banned innumerable organizations and were responsible for many such unjust and undemocratic acts.[15]

The impact of 19th century liberalism on Nehru's mind was indeed very great and it contributed largely to his faith in a democratic way of life. In his Autobiography he pointed out as to how his roots were partly in the nineteenth century and how greatly he was influenced by the humanist liberal tradition.[16]

Since his return from Soviet Russia, Nehru the democratic socialist was trying to popularize the idea of planning in India and this finally resulted in the setting up of the National Planning Committee under the auspices of the Congress in 1938, of which Nehru became the chairman. Since different groups were represented on it, ranging from representatives of provincial governments (Congress as well as non-Congress), native States, Business community as well as Socialists and near-Communists, it was not very easy to carry on the work. The Big Business in particular was 'definitely apprehensive and critical and probably joined up because it felt that it could look after its interests better from inside the Committee than from outside.'[17] The Committee also faced a few other difficulties. The data and statistics at its disposal were inadequate and the attitude of the Government of India towards the Committee's work was one of indifference, thereby rendering its work more difficult. What was still worse was the attitude of some important elements in the Congress itself, who looked upon the Committee 'as an unwanted child, not knowing how it would grow up and rather suspicious of its future activities.'[18] Moreover, there was a certain element of unreality about the work which the Committee had taken up, as the Planning was for an unascertained future. Thus, it became all the more clear to Nehru that comprehensive planning was possible only under a free national Government, strong enough and popular enough to be in a position to introduce fundamental changes in the social and economic structure. The attainment of national freedom and the elimination of foreign control, therefore, became an essential pre-requisite for planning.[19]

Though the Committee was faced with numerous difficulties and its members sometimes pulled in different directions, the work done by it was quite satisfactory and its conclusions on the whole were on socialistic lines. The plan aimed at a socialist structure which would limit the acquisitive factor in society and would pave the way to a rapidly expanding social structure by removing the hindrances in the way. The plan had for its primary aim the raising of the standards of the common man and providing him with opportunities of growth so that the best in him might come out.[20]

Nehru was well aware of the fact that planning normally brought about control and co-ordination to a very considerable extent and that inevitably resulted in interference with individual freedom in some measure. Yet he had absolutely no doubt in his mind that in the context of India it would lead to a great deal of increase in freedom. Moreover, if India adhered to the democratic state structure and followed the policy of encouraging co-operative enterprises, the dangers of regimentation and concentration of power could be avoided to a very great extent.[21] These views of Nehru revealed very clearly that even in 1938, Nehru was constantly applying his mind to the problem of introducing planning in India in such a way as not to jeopardize individual liberty and allow for regimentation.

During late twenties and almost throughout the thirties Nehru was constantly applying his mind to a very vital problem with which India was faced viz., the problem of landlordism. During this period, he referred to this problem quite frequently through his speeches and writings and the views of Nehru found an echo in some of the Congress resolutions of that period. Thus, it would not be incorrect to say that the Congress policy on land reforms was primarily a result of Nehru's efforts in that direction. Even in the post-Independence period, it was Nehru who took initiative in this matter and also in that of bringing amendments to the Constitution so as to facilitate land reforms. The speeches made by Nehru on these occasions make extremely interesting reading as they represent a mind that was dynamic, progressive and democratic.

It did not take long for Nehru the socialist to realize that the acute poverty from which the people of India suffered, could not be wiped out from the country unless radical land reforms were introduced and the old system of Zamindari introduced in India by the British, was abolished.

The first time Nehru spoke his mind on the question of landlordism in India was in 1928. In his presidential address to the U.P. Conference (Jhansi, October 27, 1928), Nehru referred to the Zamindari system in his province and pointed out as to how it had affected very adversely the economic condition of the vast masses of people. The only solution to the problem of landlordism, opined Nehru, was its abolition. There could not be any 'half-way house. It is a feudal relic of the past utterly out of keeping with modern conditions. The abolition of landlordism must therefore occupy a prominent place in our programme.'[22]

Though Nehru had referred to the Zamindars in U.P. he obviously had the question of Zamindari in mind in the larger context of India. Nehru opposed the idea of giving any compensation to Zamindars in return for their lands on the ground that it would require a large amount of money and that it would go against the attempt at equalisation. At any rate, he was wholly opposed to the idea of giving full compensation as apart from the monetary implications of such a proposition, such a course of action had failed to bring any relief or solution of the problem, in other countries. Confiscation, though perfectly justifiable from the point of view of equity might lead to hardships in many cases; as such in cases of that sort some compensation might be given, though never to the extent of making those people rich again.[23] Nehru's views on land reforms in India became Congress views when a resolution on Agrarian programme, drafted by Nehru, was adopted in 1936 at the Lucknow Congress. The adoption of this resolution by the Congress indicates as to how Nehru was making it increasingly conscious of the social and economic problems with which India was faced. The resolution emphasized at the very outset that the most important and urgent problem before India was 'the appalling poverty, unemployment and indebtedness of the peasantry, fundamentally due to antiquated and repressive land tenure and revenue systems.'[24] It further stated, 'the final solution of this problem involves the removal of British imperialistic exploitation, and a thorough change of the land tenure and revenue system.'[25]

A little before the Lucknow Congress, Nehru reiterated his view that the idea of giving full compensation to the landowners after the confiscation of their lands was impracticable and would not serve the purpose intended. He stated that it was desirable to give some compensation so that conflicts which would be wasteful and costlier than the compensation itself could be avoided. Giving full compensation in the shape of bonds, thought Nehru, amounted to mortgaging the future of the land as the burden on the peasantry would continue in yet another form. He thought that a method of giving compensation should be devised which would unburden the peasantry and would also minimise the distress of the landlords during the period of transition. Broadly speaking, he was of the view that the compensation for the bigger landlords should be proportionately less and for the middle landlords proportionately more.[26]

The socialist Nehru looked at the question of giving compensation to the landlords, whose lands were to be confiscated, from different angles. Firstly, he was anxious that the remedy of confiscating lands in order to lessen the burden on the peasantry, should not prove almost as bad as the disease of the misery of the peasants. That Nehru thought, could be avoided by not paying full compensation to the landlords. Secondly, human as well as pragmatic considerations prompted Nehru to suggest that some compensation might be given to the landlords, not only in order to lessen their distress during the period of change over but also to avoid conflicts and legal squabbles over such questions.

Since Nehru was very anxious to carry out land reforms and fulfill thereby his off-repeated pledge to the nation in that respect, he proposed an article of the Draft Constitution (September 10, 1949), pertaining to the question of compensation for compulsory acquisition of property. That draft article was in the nature of an amendment to Article 24 of the Draft Constitution. While proposing the draft article, Nehru made it clear that there would not be any expropriation without compensation, so far as that Constitution was concerned. If property was required for public use, there was a well established law which laid down that even by compulsion the State should acquire it and pay the compensation, if necessary. That law had also laid down the methods by which such compensation was to be determined. In normal course of things, such acquisitions were made with a view to improve a town or for purposes of that sort, and in such cases the acquisition usually was of small properties, and the law on all such matters was very clear. But the problem with which India was faced was of a different nature. The community had to grapple with very large schemes of social reform, social engineering etc. and they presented a problem of a different order. Such schemes could materialise through legislation, but the time factor was important. The piece of legislation was considered highly essential by the community from the point of view of the overall progress of the country. It was very obvious therefore that it could not be subjected to frequent and time consuming litigation in the courts of law. If that happened, it would very adversely affect the future of India's millions and it could shake the very foundations of the state. Of course, when the state desired to expropriate property, it would have to pay a compensation that was 'fair and equitable' and yet it had to be remembered that equity was as applicable to the community as it was to the individual. 'No individual can ultimately override the rights of the community at large. No community should injure and invade the rights of the individual, unless it be for the most urgent and important of reasons.'[27] Thus, what was required was a balancing of the two, partly by legal means of course, but in the ultimate analysis it could be done by the Sovereign Legislature of the country, as that alone was capable of taking an overall view of any problem by considering its public, political and other implications. Article 24, thought Nehru, made an attempt to deal with this problem in a manner that was consistent with equity and justice.[28]

The observations made by Nehru while dealing with the question of compensation for compulsory acquisition of property were very important, as they revealed Nehru's intense desire to strike a balance between individual and social rights. Here, we saw Nehru the democratic socialist making a great effort to harmonise the democratic and the socialistic urges within him. Of course, those observations revealed a slight shift in his stand from the one that he took in the 'thirties. He no longer stood for some compensation but had become agreeable to fair and equitable compensation. It must however be remembered that though Nehru spoke about fair and equitable compensation, he favoured the idea of judging the fairness and equity of compensation not merely in the context of those who received it but also in that of the community as a whole.

Three important points emerged from the observations made by Nehru while speaking on Article 24 of the Draft Constitution: (1) Property would not be expropriated without fair and equitable compensation. (2) The individual should not be allowed to transgress the domain of community rights nor should the community be permitted to violate the sacred domain of individual rights, except in very extra-ordinary circumstances. (3) The Legislature and not the courts would have the final authority of determining as to what constituted fair and equitable compensation.

About the draft Article itself, Nehru explained as to how the first clause in that Article laid down the basic principle that no person should be deprived of his property save by the authority of law. The next clause said that the law should provide for compensation for the property acquired and should either fix the amount of the compensation or specify the principles according to which or the way in which the compensation was to be determined. It was clear, therefore, that it was a matter for the law or for Parliament and not for the judiciary, as there was no reference to any judiciary. A great deal of thought, explained Nehru, had been given to the question as to where the judiciary should enter into the picture, and eminent lawyers had told the Government that in normal course of things it did not come into the picture at all. The Parliament either fixed the compensation itself or laid down the principles which should govern compensation and they were not to be challenged except when it was thought that the law had been grossly abused or where there had been a fraud on the Constitution. Obviously, it was presumed that the Parliament which represented the entire nation would be the last institution to commit fraud on its own Constitution and it would always be its endeavour to do justice to the individual as well as the community.[29]

While defending the right of the Parliament to fix compensation amount or lay down principles for determining compensation, Nehru reminded the Parliament that no concept was static and that of property in particular, was subject to constant change. It would be well for the defenders of property to remember that the concept of property was a very dynamic one and had been changing throughout the ages. Not only the meaning of property was undergoing a change today but also its ownership, as new elemental forces were at work throughout the world and that should be borne in mind by those who talked about the sanctity of the right to property in a manner as if the meaning of the term was very static. In fact, the conception of property had undergone great changes and was undergoing very quick changes. There was a time in the history of the world when even human beings were considered as property. Then there was a time when property was measured in terms of cows, bullocks, etc. At a later stage property in land assumed importance. The idea of property underwent gradual changes not so much due to legislation but rather due to the development of human society. In the context of today, land was an important kind of property, though it should also be borne in mind that in many industrially advanced countries, other things also were coming in the category of property. In fact, a stage had been reached when property consisted of 'chiefly...a bundle of papers in the millionaires hands and these papers represent millions in securities, promissory notes and so on. That is the conception of property today.'[30] The idea of property was thus a changing one and the changes in that idea were a result of rapid changes in society.[31]

Another change that had taken place was the one in regard to the ownership of the property, which was becoming progressively general. The individual was sharing large properties with others rather than owing exclusively a small property. Co-operative undertakings and also to a certain extent joint stock system had come into existence. Recent days had revealed the tendency, for monopoly of wealth as well as property in industrially advanced countries, which had resulted in the domination of the scene by those monopolists; with all the wealth at their command those monopolists, could very easily squeeze out the smaller businessmen and the latter would vanish from the scene without getting the slightest compensation. Thus, in context of those developments it had become imperative for the state to protect the individual's right to property.

Article 31, of the Constitution needed modification soon as the judgement of the Bihar High Court hindered land legislation. The Bihar High Court brought in Article 14 of the Constitution to apply to a question of land reforms. Article 14 states: 'The State shall not deny to any person equality before the law or the equal protection of the laws within the territory of India.' Nehru stated in the Parliament that the entire object of Article 31, 'was to take away the question of Zamindari and land reform from the purview of the courts.'Since the decision of the Bihar High Court created difficulties for the law makers two sub-articles were added to Article 31, giving thereby complete power to the legislatures to decide upon the quantum of compensation. Articles 31 and 31A, necessitated further amendment in order to facilitate land reforms. Through these amendments, the right of deciding the amount of compensation in all cases pertaining to the compulsory acquisition of agricultural and industrial property was taken away from the courts. While speaking on these amendments, Nehru reiterated his view that a Legislature alone should have the right to decide upon the amount of compensation. Speaking on the Bill to amend Article 31(2) in the Lok Sabha in April 1955, Nehru said; 'the quantum of compensation will be determined by the Legislature. I cannot say off hand what in a particular case the Legislature might do. But, by and large, if you have to govern this country democratically, you have to trust the Legislature not only in this but in a hundred other matters of far greater moment....It seems to me a basically wrong approach to single out this question of compensation and to take it out of the purview, of the Legislature in the sense of somebody else revising the Legislature's decision. Such a course can be thought of only if you think that property is something semi divine and that the protection of private property is to the largest good of the nation, which hardly anyone will say today, obviously.'[32]

The debate, in the Parliament over land reforms, revealed unmistakably not only the views of Nehru on land reforms but also threw much light on his intense desire to function in a democratic way; democracy, according to Nehru, demanded that not Judiciary but the Legislature should have the final authority of deciding the amount of compensation in cases where compulsory acquisition of land took place.

How far was Nehru correct in demanding the right for the Legislature of deciding the compensation amount instead of leaving it to the Judiciary? That was obviously a controversial issue and unanimity of opinion over it was hardly possible. It should however be borne in mind that whatever might be the value of the judiciary from the point of view of protecting the rights of the individuals in the long run, it could slow down considerably the process of urgent changes in the social structure as evidenced by the decisions of the courts in regard to the Zamindari abolition legislation. The Legislature could play a more effective role in bringing about social changes of importance and could do so more quickly, if it were given the necessary powers for that purpose.

In the period of transition at least, the Legislature should be unfettered to bring about the change that it had envisaged. Otherwise there would be the very real danger of social change not keeping pace with social requirements, thus creating fresh social, economic and political problems.

Moreover, it would be difficult to find fault with Nehru's argument that the country trusted the Legislature in hundred ways and there was no reason as to why trust should not be reposed in it, in matters of deciding upon fair and equitable compensation for the property compulsorily acquired.[33]

What a subsequent party in power would do and the extent, to which its policies would affect the individual's property in the absence of judicial safeguards, was a hypothetical question. Wasn't it likely that a party in power subsequently might as well scrap up the provision in regard to the compulsory acquisition of property itself? When Nehru made the suggestion in regard to the Legislature being given the right of determining the compensation for compulsory acquisitions he was not putting forward the proposition that it should be so for all times to come. As Nehru stated: 'for us to think what may happen at a distant future is not a very useful or profitable occupation at any time much less at a time when the world itself is in a transitional stage.'[34]

To put it very briefly, one could not but feel that in a newly independent country, at least in the first few years the Legislature should be armed with sufficient powers to bring about far reaching changes in the society, in the shortest possible time. Though Nehru laid emphasis on the point that the Legislature represented the sovereign will of the people, there was hardly any reason to believe that his stand on the compensation issue was based on mere technicalities. On the contrary, Nehru seemed convinced about the fact that the onward march of the country would be hindered, if the matter was not entrusted to the Legislature.

In spite of his firm faith in democracy, Nehru during the 'thirties was not quite sure of the practicability of introducing socialism in a country through democratic means, as he thought that the democratic process would be rejected by those who were opposed to the socialist ideal. For Nehru, who was greatly under Marxist influence then, democracy in a capitalistic structure was little more than the rule of possessing classes for the perpetuation of their own good and as such socialism had no place there.

Nehru's radicalism, however, was toned down when he became the first Prime Minister of free India in August 1947. In the post-Independence period, he had to come to grips with practical problems and it was no longer possible for him to talk merely on the theoretical plane. The Marxist influence on him became noticeably less and he began thinking and speaking like a pragmatic statesman, who, above all, was particular about giving his country what it needed, regardless of 'isms' and political postulates.

It was during this period that Nehru became intellectually convinced about the practicability of introducing socialism in a country by democratic process as capitalism itself had been greatly modified and had become something, 'completely divorced from the old style capitalism'.[35]

Many factors combined together to make Nehru less radical in his approach to national problems. The process of breaking away from the past was by no means an easy matter. The struggle for freedom was over and the common bond which had brought all sections of society together, no longer existed. The sectional economic interests manifested themselves on the political scene of India, pressing their special claims. The partition of the country added to the difficulties; it affected very adversely its integrated economy. Nationalisation and socialisation of the key industries in the country was not a practical proposition, as India lacked the necessary technical personnel and finances. Moreover, there was great opposition to the pursuit of such a policy in the Congress itself. All these factors toned down Nehru's enthusiasm for radical changes and the practical difficulties which his Government had to face, compelled him to follow a go slow policy in all basic matters. Thus Nehru, who in the 'thirties had condemned the reformist approach to the solution of basic problems with which a country was faced, himself followed a policy of 'reformism' in the post-Independence period.

In such adverse circumstances, Nehru could not but follow a policy of gradualism. The fiery enthusiast of the 'thirties became realistic and pragmatic enough to follow a policy of gradual changes, which would lead the country towards progress and prosperity, without affecting in any way its economic structure.

Nehru realized that higher standards for the people of India could be ensured only through a progressive increase in production and since India was essentially an underdeveloped country, with inadequate capital and shortage of technical personnel, it was necessary to allow public as well as private capital to come into play. In the conditions in which India found herself, immediately after freedom it was wise and prudent to support mixed economy rather than go headlong in the socialist direction.

This retreat revealed Nehru as a statesman endowed with wisdom and an open mind. He realized sooner than others that economic advancement of India, demanded, not a complete break with the existing capitalist order but a compromise with it. Any dogmatic or doctrinaire approach, felt Nehru, would only aggravate the conditions, instead of solving any problem. Any method that delivered the goods was to be used, regardless of the 'ism' with which that method and approach was associated. 'I am not enamoured of these 'isms' and my approach is, and I should like to say the country's approach should be, rather a phlegmatic approach in considering the problem and I want to forget the 'ism' attached to it.... Whatever the method may be, the method ... which brings about the necessary changes and gives satisfaction to the masses will justify itself and give hope.'[36]

Notwithstanding his policy of gradualism and moderation, Nehru was slowly leading the country towards socialism, inspite of the opposition from many of his own countrymen. In December 1954, Nehru initiated a proposal in the Parliament in regard to the amendment of a certain part of the Constitution, so that the courts may no longer have the right of determining the amount of compensation for the property confiscated by the state. In the same session, proposals in regard to the nationalisation of the Imperial Bank of India were made known to the Parliament by the then Finance Minister, C.D. Deshmukh.

In this very session of the Parliament, the Lok Sabha passed a resolution as follows: 'This House having considered the economic situation in India and the policy of the Government in relation thereto is of the opinion that (1) the policy of the Government is in harmony with the statement of 6th April 1948, (2) the objective of our economic policy should be a socialist pattern of society, and (3) towards this end the tempo of economic activity in general and industrial development in particular should be stepped up to the maximum extent possible.'[37]

The Congress passed an important resolution in its session at Avadi (January 1955) which took India a step further in the direction of a socialistic state. This resolution, (known as the 'socialist pattern' resolution) which was passed unanimously, envisaged the establishment of a socialistic pattern of society in India, '... planning should take place with a view to the establishment of a socialistic pattern of society, in which the principal means of production are under social ownership or control, production is progressively speeded up and there is equitable distribution of the national wealth ... the public sector must playa progressively greater part, more particularly in the establishment of basic industries.'[38]

Since the Congress passed at its Avadi session (1955), the resolution pertaining to the establishment of a 'Socialistic Pattern of Society' in India, and later when it adopted 'the Co-operative Farming' resolution at its Nagpur session (1959), Nehru was being accused in certain quarters of India, of leading the country, gradually towards totalitarianism, Nehru's critics held the view that the sphere of individual freedom was shrinking progressively and the domain of state activity was enlarging, as a result of Nehru's socialistic policies, and if this trend continued, it could not but result in a totalitarian set up, wherein individual freedom would be completely absent.

The discussion in regard to the question as to how far this criticism was justified would be taken up in a subsequent chapter. However, what has been discussed in this chapter would bring home the point that Nehru's approach vis-a-vis socialism was pragmatic and realistic and not dogmatic and doctrinaire. It would also become clear that it was primarily because of Nehru that gradually the Congress got committed to the socialistic ideal and could take certain steps in the direction of socialism in the post-Freedom period.

NOTES

1. Important Speeches of Jawaharlal Nehru (1922-1945), edited by J.S. Bright, The Indian Printing Works, Kacheri Road, Lahore, 1945, p. 134.
2. *India and the World*, Jawaharlal Nehru, George Allen and Unwin Ltd., London,1936 pp. 82-83.
3. *An Autobiography*, Jawaharlal Nehru, The Bodley Head, London, 1953 p. 182.
4. Ibid., p. 183.
5. Ibid., loc. cit.
6. Ibid. p. 197.
7. A Bunch of Old Letters: Written mostly to Jawaharlal Nehru and some written by him, Asia publishing House, November, 14, 1958, p. 115.
8. Ibid., p. 116.
9. *An Autobiography*, Jawaharlal Nehru, The Bodley Head, London, 1953 p. 557.
10. The History of the Indian National Congress, Volume II, (1935-1947), Dr. Pattabhi Sitaramayya, Padma Publications, Ltd., Bombay, p. 15.
11. *The Mind of Mr. Nehru*, R.K. Karanjia, Allen and Unwin Ltd, London, 1961, p. 57.
12. Ibid., p. 27.
13. *The Discovery of India*, Jawaharlal Nehru, Signet Press, Calcutta, 20, Fourth Printing, September 1948, p. 209.
14. *The Unity of India*, Jawaharlal Nehru, Lindsay Drummond, London, W.C.1, 1948, p. 67.
15. Important Speeches of Jawaharlal Nehru (1922-1945), Edited by J.S. Bright, The Indian Printing Works, Kacheri Road, Lahore, 1945, p. 8 and 11.
16. *An Autobiography*, Jawaharlal Nehru, The Bodley Head, London, 1953, p. 591.
17. *The Discovery of India*, Jawaharlal Nehru, Signet Press, Calcutta-20, Fourth Printing, September 1948, p. 331.
18. Ibid., loc. cit.
19. Ibid., loc. cit.
20. Ibid., loc. cit.
21. Ibid, pp. 335-336.
22. Important Speeches of Jawaharlal Nehru (1922-1945), Edited by J.S. Bright, The Indian Printing Works, Kacheri Road, Lahore, 1954, p. 114.
23. Ibid., pp. 114-15.
24. *The Unity of India*, Jawaharlal Nehru, Lindsay Drummond, London, W.C.1, 1948, p. 408.
25. Ibid., loc. cit.
26. Important Speeches of Jawaharlal Nehru (1922-1945), Edited by J.S. Bright, The Indian Printing Works, Kacheri Road, Lahore, 1945, pp. 163-164.
27. Jawaharlal Nehru's Speeches (1949-1953), The Publication Division, Ministry of Information and Broadcasting, Govt. of India, Calcutta, 1954, p. 480.
28. Ibid., pp, 479-480.
29. Ibid., pp. 480-481.
30. Ibid., p. 483.
31. Ibid., pp. 482-483.
32. Jawaharlal Nehru's Speeches (1953-1957), The Publication Division, Ministry of Information and Broadcasting, Govt. of India, 1959, p. 129.

33. Ibid., loc. cit.
34. Ibid., p. 130.
35. *Independence and After: A Collection of Nehru's Speeches* (1946-1949), John Day and Co., New York, 1950, p. 190.
36. Ibid., loc. cit.
37. *The Hindu*, (Madras), December 23, 1954, p. 1.
38. Indian Approaches to a Socialist State, Fisher, Margaret W. and Bondurant Joan V; (Socialist Pattern Resolution Text, incorporated in Appendix II of the book).

6

THE UNITY OF INDIA

In 1940, the All-India Muslim League demanded a separate state for the Muslims in India, on the grounds that the Hindus and Muslims constituted two different nations. That demand was very strongly opposed by the Congress, which had in its ranks persons belonging to different religious groups, including a large number of Muslims. As opposed to the League, the Congress had always maintained that the people of India constituted a nation inspite of the diversity in religion, language etc.

The resolution demanding the partition of India, was passed by the Muslim League at its Lahore session of 1940. An important part of the resolution stated: '...it is the considered view of this session of the All-India Muslim League that no constitutional plan would be workable in this country or acceptable to Muslims unless it is designed on the following basic principle, viz., that geographically contiguous units are demarcated into regions which should be so constituted, with such territorial readjustments as may be necessary, that the areas in which the Muslims are numerically in a majority as in the North Western and Eastern zones in India, should be grouped to constitute 'Independent States' in which the constituent units shall be autonomous and sovereign'.[1]

In his presidential address to the Lahore Session of the Muslim League in 1940, Jinnah declared that the Muslims in India constituted not only a religious community but formed a distinct nation. He strongly put forward the view that it was not possible to weld the Hindus and the Muslims into a single nation. In fact, he went as far as to say that the evolution of the Hindus and Muslims into a common nationality was nothing short of a dream, as Hinduism and Islam were not religions strictly, but 'different and distinct social orders.' Jinnah further pointed out that the religious philosophies, social customs and literatures were different in the case of the Hindus and the Muslims. They did not inter-marry or inter-dine together as they belonged to 'two different civilisations which are based mainly on conflicting ideas and conceptions'. The Hindus and Muslims derived their inspiration from sources of history that were different and had different epics and different heroes. In fact, in several cases the hero of one community was the enemy of the other. Thus, it was very inadvisable to have one single state for two such nations, specially when one of them constituted a numerical minority and the other majority, as it would necessarily lead to increasing discontent and many other complications. Muslims, stated Jinnah, were 'a nation according to any definition of a nation and they must have their homelands, their territory and their state. ... we wish our people to develop to the fullest, our spiritual, cultural, economic, social and political life in a way that we think best and in consonance with our own ideals and according to the genius of our people.'[2]

The idea of India's partition took birth in 1930, through Sir Mohamed Iqbal's Presidential address[3] to the Allahabad session of the Muslim League. Iqbal expressed the view that the Punjab, North West Frontier Province, Sind and Baluchistan should constitute a single state.[4] It would perhaps not be wrong to infer that what Iqbal had in his mind was not a separate sovereign state for the Muslims but a single unit of North-West areas, constituting an integral part of an All-India federation. A direct suggestion in regard to the partition of the country however came in January 1933, through a leaflet circulated privately by a few young Indians in England titled 'Now or Never'. The authors declared that India was not the name of one single country nor was it the home of one single nation. It was, in fact, the name given to a state created for the first time in history by the British ... 'our national customs and calendars, even our diet and dress are different... (we) demand the recognition of a separate national status.'[5]

At the Madras session of the Muslim League in 1941, Jinnah reiterated the idea of a separate state for the Muslims, incorporated in the Lahore resolution. He stated very categorically that the Muslim League would not rest till the goal of a complete independent state for Indian Muslims was reached. The state, according to Jinnah, was to be in the North West and Eastern zones of India, with full control finally of defence, currency, exchange etc.[6] An independent state would normally imply full control over defence, currency etc. and one wondered as to why Jinnah made a specific mention of them. It might be that through that specific mention he was ruling out the possibility of a confederation between the two sovereign states to be carved out of the Indian territory.

While it is wholly unnecessary to state that Nehru was opposed to the partition of the country, it is very essential to trace the various factors which contributed to his opposition to any such division. It is therefore instructive to find out as to what case Nehru made in favour of the view that India was a nation.

Nehru did not agree with Jinnah's view[7] that the Hindus and Muslims constituted two different nations. In early 'thirties, he wrote, 'so far as India is concerned, not only do I believe that a Unitary Indian nation is possible but that, fundamentally and culturally, it exists in spite of numerous superficial differences.'[8]

In The Unity of India, Nehru dealt at length with the facts pertaining to the basic unity of India inspite of its variety and diversity. Though, political unity of the country was not achieved in the past except perhaps during Ashoka's period (when almost the whole of India was under the king's control, except a small part in South India), it was always the ambition of the kings and emperors to realize political unity of the Indian sub-continent. One major obstacle in the way of achieving political unity of the country was the inadequacy of communications and means of transport. Inspite of the absence of political unity, there always prevailed basic unity amongst the people of India. The history of India ran into thousands of years and there was hardly any nation in the world except China with cultural background so ancient & continuous. As early as five to six thousand years ago the Indus Valley Civilization flourished in India and was even at that stage, highly developed. Since that period of history 'innumerable peoples, conquerors and settlers, pilgrims and students', had come to India from the highlands of Asia and had exerted a certain measure of influence over Indian life, culture and art, but they had always been absorbed and assimilated. Those contacts with outsiders resulted in changing India to a certain extent and yet she remained essentially her own old self. India succeeded in continuing that astonishing process of assimilation and adaption because of the deep-rooted idea of fundamental unity[9] which even the new-comer accepted, and also because its culture was flexible and adaptable.[10]

According to Nehru, the Indian unity and background were essentially cultural. The culture that India represented was 'receptive and adaptable' and not 'exclusive or intolerant'.[11]

Though the people of India belonged to different religions, basically they were the products of the same racial stock. As such the factor of common race, which was considered important from the point of view of the growth of the sentiment of nationality amongst people, was also present in India. 'Hindus and Muslims do not form different races. Thus, though there are various races, they run into one another and on the whole form a definite unit, racially and culturally.'[12]

Then came the vital question of language. Since common language was considered to be one of the important pre-requisites of nationhood, the fact that several languages were spoken in India was cited as an argument against India being a nation. Nehru believed that linguistically speaking India was singularly well knit and that the growth of numerous dialects was the result of the absence of popular education. Moreover, Hinudstani (Hindi or Urdu) was a language that was spoken and understood by a vast number of people in India and was thus a popular medium of communication with one another. Moreover, as Nehru pointed out, even the census of U.S.A. and Germany, which were considered single nations, mentioned large number of languages, the latter's census mentioning more than sixty. Of course most of those languages were spoken by small groups or were dialects. As already stated, India was a singularly unified area from the point of view of languages. In all there were a dozen languages in India and they had intimate association with each other. Those languages could be divided into two groups: 'the Indo-Aryan languages of the North and the Centre and West, and the Dravidian languages of the East and South.' The languages belonging to the Indo-Aryan group were derived from Sanskrit and a person, who knew one, would find it easy to learn another. The languages of the Dravidian group were not derived from Sanskrit and yet each of them contained at least fifty percent words from Sanskrit. Hindustani, of course was spoken by a vast number of people and understood by even a greater number. Thus, though India had to solve numerous difficult problems, the problem of language was not one of them.[13]

The absence of a common religion for the people of India was also considered a strong impediment in the way of India becoming a nation. It was stated that people belonging to the two major religions in India, viz.

the Hindus and the Muslims differed from each other in many vital respects and as such there were bound to be incessant conflicts between them. Nehru held the view that India was known for her tolerance and her history bore testimony to the fact that people professing different religions had lived together for centuries without coming into conflict with one another. 'India was never known in the whole course of her long history for the religious strife that had soaked Europe in blood. The whole background of Indian religions, culture and philosophy was one of tolerance, and even encouragement of other beliefs. Some conflict arose when Islam came, but even that was far more political than religious, although stress is always laid on the religious side. It was the conflict between conquerors and the conquered.'[14]

The suggestion in regard to the division of India on the basis of religion appeared to Nehru impracticable as any such division like the one envisaged by the Muslim League could not be made because the Hindus and the Muslims were spread out all over the country. If areas in which each group was in a majority were separated, even then big minorities belonging to the other group would remain in each area. Instead of solving the minority problem that approach would create many more problems. If it was argued that the majority should prevail in each area, so far as the question of separation was concerned, why should there be any objection to the majority view deciding the question for the whole of India or why should not each tiny area 'decide its independent status for itself and thus create vast number of small states—an incredible and fantastic development. Even so it cannot be done with any logic, for religious groups are intermingled and overlap in the population all over the country.'[15]

Apart from the question of the practicability of any such division, Nehru considered the idea of dividing the country on the basis of religion as a medieval one, which had little relevance to modern conditions.[16]

Nehru was opposed to partition on economic grounds also. Since India was a more or less self-sufficient economic unit, the division of the country, thought Nehru, would inevitably weaken her and render it necessary for her to depend on others. Moreover, Nehru knew it too well that if division of India was made in such a way as to separate the predominantly Hindu and Muslim areas, it would be to the disadvantage of Muslims only as the Hindu areas had in them most of the minerals, resources and industries. Thus, as a result of partition, the Hindu areas would not suffer much, whereas Muslims areas would be economically backward and often deficit areas which could not exist without a great deal of external help. Thus, it would become fairly clear that those who demanded separation, would suffer most from it.[17]

Apart from other considerations, the most powerful factor, in favour of a united India was the trend of world events. The trend throughout the world was towards bigger states, as small states had very little chance of surviving as really independent units. Thus, even granting that India was not a nation, there was a strong case for a united India. If nation– states were carved out in different parts of the world, most of them would be too small either to defend themselves or to look after their needs. Thus, Nehru not only drew the attention of the Muslims in India to the geographical, historical, cultural and economic aspects of Indian unity but also created in them an awareness in regard to the international aspect of the problem.[18]

What factors were responsible for the demand of a separate state for the Muslims? Nehru felt that to a considerable extent, 'the deliberate separatist policy of the British Government'[19] was responsible for that demand. Almost since the beginning of their rule over India, the British followed a policy of 'creating divisions among Indians, of encouraging one group at the cost of the other. That policy was openly admitted in the early days of their rule, and indeed it was a natural one for an imperial power. With the growth of the nationalist movement that policy took subtler and more dangerous forms and, though denied, functioned more intensively than ever.'[20]

It would have been very easy for the people of India to solve the communal problem but for the British in India. The repeated attempts made by the Congress to settle the communal problem failed because the British Government by its subtle moves thwarted all such attempts by playing off one side against the other, by giving special privileges. On many occasions when the settlement was almost in sight the Government took some step to prevent it.[21] To give the people of India the opportunity to solve the communal problem Nehru suggested the convening of the Constituent Assembly. 'Settlement of the communal problem will come about only when everyone realizes that this (the Constituent Assembly) is the final authority, and no outsider can intervene. The pressure of events will then force a solution for the alternative is internal conflict.'[22]

While Nehru considered the British Government responsible for encouraging communalism in India,[23] he did not believe that the problem was deliberately created by the British[24] as such, though to start with it did result out of British rule over India and through the systems of landlordism that they introduced. Bengal where that system was introduced became a province chiefly of Hindu landlords and though they had for their tenants, Muslims as well as the Hindus, the majority of them belonged to the former community. Thus the beginning of the Hindu-Muslims problems were traceable to the landlord system.[25] Whatever might be that problem's point of origin, it was important to know as to why that problem became grave during the twentieth century. That could be understood by finding out as to what happened in the latter half of the nineteenth century, when Sir Syed Ahmed Khan was the leader of the Indian Muslims. Sir Syed tried to turn away the Muslims from the Indian National Congress, because he wanted British help and co-operation, which he was afraid would not be forthcoming, if the Muslims joined the Congress, which in his opinion was aggressive. Sir Syed did succeed to a considerable extent in diverting the Muslims from the political movement. The starting of the Mohammadan Educational Conference resulted in the Muslim middle-class getting attracted to professions and services. However, inspite of the efforts made by prominent Muslim leaders, many eminent Muslims joined the Congress. In consequence, the British policy became pro-Muslim, i.e. in favour of those Muslims who opposed the national movement. And yet, the tendency amongst the younger generation of Muslims to drift towards nationalism and political activity became more pronounced in the beginning of the twentieth century. In order to divert that tendency and to provide a safer outlet to it, the Muslim League was started in 1906. It was started by Aga Khan, a great supporter of the British Government and it of course had the blessings of the British Government. The League had loyalty to the British Government and protection of Muslim interests, as its principal objectives.[26]

Two major trends were noticeable among the Muslim intelligentsia during the early years of the twentieth century. The younger element among them was mostly drawn towards nationalism, whereas the other was, somewhat indifferent to India—past or present, and had great interest in Islamic countries, more particularly so in Turkey, the seat of Khilafat. In India, there was general sympathy for the Sultan about who it was thought that he was equal to the task of meeting the challenge of the intrigues of European powers in Turkey. There were however other Muslims—like Abul Kalam Azad, who very enthusiastically welcomed the young Turks and their promise of constitutional and social reforms. When Turkey was attacked all of a sudden by Italy in 1911, and later in 1912 and 1913, during Balkan wars, it aroused a great deal of sympathy amongst Indian Muslims, resulting in a medical mission going to Turkey, for which even the poor subscribed. During the war period the Indian Muslims could do little else except sending a medical mission to Turkey, but when it ended their pent-up feelings found expression in the Khilafat movement.[27]

In the 'twenties, Muslims joined the national movement, primarily because of the Khilafat. That issue of course, was a purely religious one, and the Hindus and other non-Muslim elements in India had nothing to do with it. However, Gandhi 'adopted it, and encouraged others to do so, because he felt it his duty to help a brother in distress. He also hoped in this way to bring the Hindus and the Muslims nearer each other. The general Muslim outlook was thus one of Muslim nationalism or Muslims internationalism and not of true nationalism. For the moment the conflict between the two was not apparent.'[28]

The general reaction of the Muslims in India to what was going on in Turkey and other places in the Islamic world, showed unmistakably that with them the rallying point was Islam. That should help us in the proper understanding of the whole Indian problem.

Communal leaders both Hindu and Muslim, emerged on the political scene of India once again after the suspension of the non-cooperation movement in 1922. Communal problem once again sprung up and resulted in ill feeling between Hindus and Muslims. The middle-class Muslims felt that all jobs were monopolised by the Hindus and that they were coming in the way of the advancement of Muslims. Thus, they made a demand for 'separate treatment and separate shares in everything. Hence from the political point of view, the Hindu Muslim problem was essentially one of middle-class quarrel over jobs.'[29]

The demand for separate treatment and separate shares led within a few years to the demand for a separate state for the Muslims. The solution to India's minority problem according to Nehru was not the partition of the country but better economic standards of the people. Nehru was confident that the minority problem would be automatically solved when economic standards improved. In fact he went to the extent of saying that few problems in the world were basically so simple of solution as the minority problem, because it was not deep rooted, though it did hamper progress. When real problems of India, such as those of poverty and low standards were tackled effectively, the minority problem would no longer exist. As soon as there was growth in industries, the economic standards of the people would be raised and they (the industries) would also provide the people with new avenues of employment, and there would no longer be the quarrel over jobs amongst middle classes, resulting in demands for reservation of seats in the administration.[30] That the solution of the communal problem lay in the economic betterment of the Indian people and not in the partition of the country, was not realized either by the Muslim middle-class or by the Muslim masses, as their mentality was being shaped during the first two decades of the twentieth century, not only by the events that were taking place inside and outside India but also by the powerful pro-Islamic poetry of the great Urdu poet, Sir Mohamed Iqbal. His poetry particularly influenced the Muslim middle-class and the younger generation. Iqbal, who wrote poems full of nationalistic fervour in the earlier part of his life, turned to Islamic subjects during the Balkan wars—a result of the impact of prevailing circumstances as well as Muslim mass feeling on his mind and that added to mass emotions. Iqbal however was no mass leader he was essentially a poet, intellectual and a philosopher, with feudal order affiliations. By his great Urdu and Persian poetry he supplied to the Muslims intelligentsia a philosophic background and thus diverted its mind in a separatist direction.[31] Iqbal thus fulfilled a need at a time when the Muslim mind was in search of some anchor to hold on to. The old ideal of pan–Islamism had no longer any meaning, as the Islamic countries had started functioning in an intensely nationalist way, caring little for the Islamic world as a whole. Nationalism was the most potent factor in Asia and in India itself the nationalist movement had become very powerful and was shaking the very foundations of the alien rule over the country. Thus, nationalism appealed to the Muslim mind strongly and yet India's nationalism had 'a Hinduised look' about it as it was dominated by them. 'So a conflict arose in the Muslim mind; many accepted that nationalism, trying to influence it in the direction of their choice; many sympathised with it and yet remained aloof, uncertain, and yet many others began to drift in a separatist direction for which Iqbal's poetic and philosophic approach had prepared them....This I imagine, was the background out of which in recent years, arose the cry for a division of India.'[32]

There were of course many reasons for the demand of India's partition, many mistakes on all sides, and particularly there was the separatist policy of the British Government. But there was that psychological background behind all those, which in itself was partly a result of delayed development of a Muslim middle-class in India. The internal conflict in India, according to Nehru, was essentially between 'the remnants of the feudal order and modernist ideas and institutions.'[33] That conflict manifested itself not only on the national plane but was present amongst the Hindus as well as the Muslims. The Congress, which symbolised the national movement represented 'the historic process of growth towards these new ideas and institutions' though it tried to 'adapt these to some of the old foundations'.[34] As a result of this, it succeeded in attracting people of all sorts, holding different opinions on many matters. Though the rigid and exclusive social order amongst the Hindus prevented growth, that social order itself got undermined and thus could not come very much in the growth of the Indian national movement, 'in its widest political and social sense'.[35] That was however not the case on the Muslims side. Feudal elements remained strong and succeeded in influencing the masses, because leadership still remained with them. Since there was a difference of more than a generation in the development of the Hindu and Muslim middle classes, it showed itself in different directions, political, economic etc. and this lagging behind on the Muslim side produced 'a psychology of fear among the Muslims.'[36]

In an essay, written by him in August 1940, Nehru pointed out that communalism in India began by a demand for 'a specified share in services and in representation in the Legislatures.'[37] Then it grew into an anti-national, anti-democratic movement, demanding the division of the country on religious basis. For a number of years it had no programme of its own and it throve on violence and offensiveness. The separate electorates, which were so eagerly sought did not do much good but rather weakened the minority groups. Then it tried to revive the medieval theory of theocratic states and endeavoured to reverse the whole process of history. All this was very surprising, specially in the context of world trend. At a time when nationalism was giving place to internationalism, a creed that was narrower than nationalism was advanced and that found favour and protection with the British authority over India. The talk about splitting India into parts and that too on the religious basis became surprising as well as painful, at a time when the world was gradually moving towards a world federation.[38]

Even Muslim countries like Turkey, Egypt, Iraq, Syria and Persia gave up the theory of theocracy long back. In fact, some of those countries even went to their pre-Islamic days for getting cultural inspiration.[39] In short, almost everywhere the concept of theocracy had been rejected as one amounting to a throw back and being out of keeping with modern trend.

The Muslims in India, however, were not interested in finding out as to what the world trend was. They were made to believe by the Muslims League leaders that in an undivided India, the Muslim minority would be completely at the mercy of the overwhelming Hindu majority. An important part of a resolution passed by the Subjects Committee of the Muslims League ('to be placed before the All-India Muslim League Legislators' Convention on April 9th 1946'), dealt with the Muslim apprehensions in regard to Hindu domination. It stated 'whereas the Muslims are convinced that with a view to save Muslims of India from the domination of the Hindus and in order to afford them full scope to develop themselves according to their genius, it is necessary to constitute a sovereign independent State comprising...'[40]

This resolution reflects the oft-repeated fear expressed by Jinnah and others in the League, in regard to the future of the Muslims in a united India, with a brute Hindu majority. The only solution to this problem according to Jinnah was the partition of the country. Nehru, on the other hand, was convinced of the fact that in a united India Federation, Muslims need have no fears, and though technically a minority, they were too big in number to be ignored or unjustly treated. They numbered eighty millions and were in a majority in five provinces of northern India. Provincial autonomy would enable them to control those five provinces. Moreover, there was a balance in the distribution of population and the administrative areas, which would make it very difficult for the Hindus and the Muslims to ignore each other or to behave unjustly towards each other.[41]

Though wholly convinced about the undesirability of the country's partition, Nehru and the other Congress leaders were compelled by the force of circumstances to agree to the division of the country, as the alternative would have been complete chaos.[42] Lord Ismay, Chief of Lord Mountbatten's staff, described the conditions in India a few months before the partition of the country as analogous to that of 'a ship in mid-ocean with a fire on the deck and ammunition in the hold.'[43] The situation was such that realising the ideal of a United India was well—nigh impossible and the Congress was left with the choice of choosing between partition or a civil war and complete chaos, and understandably enough it chose the lesser evil, viz., agreeing to the partition of the country. As Nehru put it privately that by 'cutting off the head we will get rid of the headache.'[44]

What were the factors which led to a situation wherein partition of India became inevitable? The partition may primarily be attributed to the success of the British policy of 'divide and rule' and, as Nehru pointed out the difference of more than a generation in the development of the Hindu and the Muslim middle-classes. It was perhaps also the result of the over-anxiety on the part of the Congress leaders to accommodate the League view-point as far as possible, in the larger interests of communal amity. It must however be stated that the Congress leaders and Nehru in particular made it perfectly clear that the partition of the country was accepted as a matter of expediency and that it did not amount to the acceptance of the two-nation theory, propounded by Jinnah. In a speech delivered in January 1957 Nehru while making a reference to the Kashmir issue, declared: 'We had never accepted and we do not propose to accept the two nation theory on which Pakistan was founded.'[45] That the Congress leaders did not accept the two nation theory becomes evident when we consider the fact that independent India emerged on the political scene of the world as a secular state and not as a theocracy.

One of the major problems with which India was faced after Independence was the problem of the reorganization of States (federating units) on linguistic basis, for which the demand became very incessant in the post-freedom period, because of the Congress commitment on that matter in the pre-Independence period.

It was at the Nagpur session of the Congress in 1920 that the Congress accepted the redistribution of provinces on the linguistic basis as one of its political objectives. Many years earlier, i.e., in 1905, it had given its indirect support to the principle of linguistic provinces by supporting the demand for the reunification of Bengal, the partition of which had resulted in the division of people who spoke Bengali, into two units. The linguistic principle was once again supported by the formation in 1908 of a separate Congress province of Bihar and in the year 1917, those of Sind and Andhra.

The Nehru Committee (the Chairman of the Committee was Pandit Motila Nehru) of the All Parties Conference, formed in 1928, went into the question of the reorganization of provinces and came to the conclusion that language should be the primary consideration while bringing about any such reorganization. An important part of the Committee Report says: 'If a province has to educate itself and do its daily work through the medium of its own language, it must necessarily be a linguistic area. If it happens to be a polyglot area difficulties will continually arise and media of instruction and work will be of two or even more languages. Hence, it becomes most desirable for provinces to be re-grouped on a linguistic basis. Language as a rule corresponds with a special variety of culture, of traditions and literature. In a linguistic area all these factors will help in the general progress of the province.'[46]

The Congress reaffirmed its faith in the principle of linguistic provinces at its Calcutta session in October 1937,[47] and also in July 1938,[48] through a Working Committee resolution. On the eve of Independence, the Congress reiterated its view through the election manifesto of 1945-46, that as far as possible the re-distribution of provinces should be on linguistic and cultural basis. The relevant part of the manifesto stated that the Congress 'has stood for the freedom of each group and territorial area within the nation to develop its own life and culture within the larger framework and it has stated that for this purpose such territorial areas or provinces should be constituted as far as possible on a linguistic and cultural basis.'[49]

Though the Congress gave its almost unqualified support to the reorganization of provinces in the pre-Independence period, its leaders started getting second thoughts[50] on the advisability of any such reorganization in the context of the partition of the country. Thus, the Dar Commission was appointed, which was asked to go into the question of the desirability or otherwise of creating any of the proposed provinces, viz., Andhra, Karnataka, Kerala and Maharashtra. The Commission was also directed to assess the various consequences of any such creations, such as the financial, economic, administrative etc., in those provinces as well as the adjoining territories of India. It was fairly clear from the terms of reference that the linguistic basis for the redistribution of provinces was no longer taken for granted.[51]

The Dar Commission, which submitted its report in December 1948,opposed the idea of new provinces being formed in the immediate future and suggested that no such reorganization should take place till the Indian States problem was solved, India was physically and emotionally integrated and the national sentiment strengthened.[52] It also stated that when the time came for the formation of new provinces, language should not be exclusively or even mainly the basis, but primarily the emphasis should be on administrative convenience and mainly in the context of the administrative convenience that the homogeneity of language be considered.[53] The Commission also stressed the need of taking other factors into consideration (while forming new provinces) such as history, geography, economy and culture.[54]

A few days after the submission of the report by the Dar Commission, a Committee was appointed by the Congress at its Jaipur session to go into the question of linguistic provinces and review the position in the context of the post-Independence problems and in the light of the Dar Commission Report. The Committee had Jawaharlal Nehru, Vallabhbhai Patel and Pattabhi Sitaramayya for its members and was known as J.V.P. Committee.

Surprisingly enough, the conclusions of the J.V.P. Committee—a Congress Committee, were not very different from those arrived at by the Dar Commission. The Committee admitted that when the principle of linguistic provinces was accepted by the Congress, the various implications and consequence that would flow from its practical application were not considered by the Congress at that time, as it was not faced with the problem of the practical application of the principle. It also stated that language was binding as well as a separating force, as such case for a linguistic province should be carefully and separately considered and the linguistic principle be applied in cases where there was no danger of serious administrative dislocation or mutual conflicts which jeopardize the political and economic stability of the country. The report also stated that a beginning could be made by the creation of Andhra.[55]

At the end of 1953, the Government of India appointed the States Reorganization Commission so that the whole question of reorganization of the states may be examined, 'objectively and dispassionately.'[56] The Commission was headed by Sayid Fazal Ali and had H.N. Kunzru and K.M. Pannikar for its other members. The resolution appointing the Commission also indicated the broad principles, which the members of the Commission were to bear in mind. While examining the question of reorganization of states para 4 of the resolution stated: 'The language and the culture of an area have an undoubted importance as they represent a pattern of living which is common in that area. In considering a reorganization of states, however, there are other important factors which have also to be borne in mind. The first essential consideration is the preservation and strengthening of the unity and security of India. Financial, economic and administrative considerations are almost equally important, not only from the point of view of each state, but for the whole nation. India has embarked upon a great ordered plan for the economic, cultural and moral progress. Changes which interfere with the successful prosecution of such a national plan would be harmful to the national interest.'[57]

The States Reorganization Commission after interviewing 'members of political parties, public associations, social workers, journalists, municipal and district board representatives and other people representing cultural, educational, linguistic and local interests',[58] 'and after studying about 2000' well-considered memoranda,[59] prepared its report and submitted it to the Government in October 1955.

A few days after the submission of the Report, Nehru in a broadcast to the nation (October 9, 1955), urged the people of India to consider the Report (which was to appear in the newspapers the next morning), 'not only in its separate parts dealing with special problems but even more so as a whole because of the interrelation of each of these separate problems and areas. Above all, we have to consider these questions from the point of view of the unity, strength and prosperity of India'.[60] About two months later, Nehru, in his speech during the debate on the S.R.C. Report, emphasised the necessity of facing separatist forces and diverting the attention of the people from local, parochial, state and provincial problems to those concerning India at large.[61] It became necessary for Nehru to stress the importance of taking a broader view of problems, as the publication of the S.R.C. report gave rise to numerous quarrels and conflicts in regard to the propriety of certain areas going to this or that linguistic state. In his speech in the Lok Sabha on February 23, 1956, Nehru while tracing development of the Congress outlook on the subject of linguistic provinces, stated that since the 'twenties the Congress was greatly in favour of all work being done in the language of the area so that the local people might play their part satisfactorily. But the importance of the development of the language should not be mixed up with linguistic boundaries as they were two different matters. Nehru drew the attention of the House to the Congress resolutions of the previous three or four years, in which it was stated clearly that not only language was an important factor but other factors also had equal importance, such as the economic, geographical and developmental factors. Above all, the most important factor obviously was that of perpetuating the unity of India and in the context of the happenings in India since the publication of the States Reorganization Commission Report, it had become all the more important to lay greater stress on the factors that were conducive to unity.[62]

Thus, though Nehru attached a great deal of importance to language, he did not like the idea of associating it necessarily with a state.[63] In areas, where there were two languages it was better to have a bilingual state and if more than two even a multi-lingual state. Nehru told the Lok Sabha that on his part, he would prefer bringing up his children in bilingual or trilingual areas as that was more conducive to the gaining of a 'wider culture and a wider understanding of India and of the world'. In this connection, Nehru told the House as to how he had sent his daughter to a school not in U.P. but in Poona (where Marathi was spoken) and that too a Gujrati school, so that she might learn the Marathi and Gujarati languages and be influenced by them. Later he had sent her to Shantiniketan where she might understand the background of the Bengali language and culture.[64]

The debates in the parliament on the S.R.C. Report revealed not only Nehru's views on linguistic states but also the important change that came over in his thinking in regard to the size of the various administrative units in the country. In a speech delivered in the parliament (July 7, 1952), on the question of the reorganization of states on linguistic basis, Nehru had stated that he was never 'very enthusiastic about linguistic provinces'[65] and that his views on the provinces of India were rather 'peculiar'. Nehru had then suggested that the provinces ought to be smaller in size than those that existed. He thought that it was not necessary to have a Governor, a High Court and so on for every province.[66] It was interesting to see as to what Nehru had to say on the question of the size of different administrative units in India about three and half years later. Speaking in the Lok Sabha on December 21, 1955, Nehru admitted that he was being attracted more and more to something which he had rejected previously and that was the idea of dividing the whole of India into four, five or six major groups, irrespective of language considerations, but at the same time giving great importance to the languages in those areas. He agreed of course that the country had gone too far in the opposite direction to make that possible.[67]

The change in Nehru's views in favour of larger units was a result of the thinking done by him in the context of India's Five Year Plans. The success of national development plans requires a great measure of coordination in work which is greatly facilitated when there are few big units rather than many small ones. Since bigger multi-lingual units were no longer possible, Nehru suggests 'a rather feeble imitation of that',[68] viz., Zonal Councils. A Zonal Council was described by Nehru as a common Council, 'for a group of three, four, or five states'.[69] It should 'to begin with...an Advisory Council. Let us see how it develops...Centre also should be associated with it for dealing with economic problems as well as multitude of border problems or other problems that arise....In the main I want the states to develop the habit of cooperative working.'[70]

The numerous controversies that took place in the period following the publication of the S.R.C. Report and the passions that were roused were partly due to the vacillating attitude of Nehru towards the question of the Report's implementation. This however was not due to any confusion in his mind in regard to the procedure to be adopted but was rather the result of his anxiety to accommodate every point of view and to follow the method of democracy, i.e., of 'discussion, argument, persuasion and acceptance of that decision even though it might go against our grain.'[71] This approach however landed the Government into difficulties and at a later stage Nehru himself came to the conclusion that however desirable it might be to evolve a formula acceptable to all, in practice it was almost impossible to arrive at an agreement wholly acceptable to the concerned parties. In a broadcast to the nation on January 16, 1956, Nehru pointed out as to how the Government were anxious to take the people into confidence and how with that aim in view they arranged for the publication of that Report within ten days of its submission to the Government. He further pointed out as to how in their anxiety to follow democratic procedures to the maximum, possible extent, they had consulted a very large number of representatives from different parts of India and listened to their view-points. The arguments that were put forward by those representatives had force in them though in certain cases they were opposed to each other. The Government went a step further and consulted State Governments and State Assemblies and the Parliament of course discussed the Report at very great length. After giving a great deal of thought to that question, the Government arrived at the conclusion that the right policy on their part would be 'to accept broadly the recommendations of this Report which had been prepared after great thought by three eminent and impartial men. It was obvious that in regard to almost every recommendation, there was dissatisfaction somewhere and some reason for it. It was impossible to evolve something that was acceptable to all.'[72]

Nehru's anxiety to respect the wishes of the people as far as possible, had revealed itself even earlier when the people in different parts of the country started clamouring for the formation of linguistic states. Though Nehru was not very enthusiastic or keen about the reorganization of states he bowed to the wishes of the people and proceeded in the matter. It would however be erroneous to conclude that he succumbed to public pressure and agreed to things even when they were injurious to national interests. Though his attitude towards the reorganization of States was ambivalent, he did not share the apprehension with many others that the linguistic States would lead to the Balkanisation of the country. When the author asked Nehru (during the author's first interview with Nehru – October 16, 1959) about this fear in regard to the Balkanisation of the country, Nehru pointed out that the basic unity in India was strong enough to counteract centrifugal tendencies. Moreover, the trend all over the world was towards bigger States as smaller States had no future and this also according to Nehru would prevent any such eventuality.

Nehru, with his tremendous influence over the people of India, could have postponed the issue of the reorganization of States, thereby enabling the nation to settle down and devote itself to tasks that were more urgent and which demanded priority. However, it must be stated that the Congress under Nehru's leadership did its best to ensure the reorganization of States in such a way as not to affect adversely the unity of India as it is clear from the terms of reference to the States Reorganization Commission. It also did not ignore the administrative, financial and economic aspects of the proposed redistribution, as is evident from the terms of reference to the States Reorganization Commission as well as from the Congress Election Manifesto[73] of the 1951 General Elections.

A major achievement of Nehru during the post-freedom period was making India a secular state. There is nothing very unique or remarkable about the acceptance of the secular ideal by a state as in our times a secular state is rather a rule than exception. Moreover, it could be argued that it was little more than a mere corollary of Nehru's oft-repeated stand that India was a nation. However true this argument might appear, it has to be remembered that but for Nehru's unshakable faith in Secularism (a result of his childhood environment as well as education at England in subsequent years), it would have been difficult to render India a Secular State, after the country's partition and the severe communal riots that preceded and followed it. Hardly four days after he became the Prime Minister of the country, Nehru, through a broadcast to the nation, gave stern warning to the communalists in India and declared, 'Communal troubles...are not going to be tolerated in the future. So far as the Government of India are concerned, they will deal with any communal outbreak with the greatest firmness. They will treat every Indian on an equal basis and try to secure for him all the rights which he shares with others.'[74]

Nehru's support for the secular ideal was not merely verbal. During the fierce communal riots that broke out in various parts of India immediately after India's independence, Nehru not only made every attempt to crush those riots but personally took the lead in helping the minority community. On one occasion he saved two Muslim children who were about to be murdered by a mob. On yet another occasion, he rushed unarmed into a furious mob which was looting Muslim shops in Connaught Circus and tried to bring the situation under control. As a last resort, he ordered the Police to open fire on the Hindu looters and shoot them down.[75] Who else but a convinced secularist would order the shooting down of his co-religionists when they were misbehaving? Nehru was perhaps the only person at that time who spoke and acted as a devout secularist.[76]

Secularism was almost an instinct with Nehru and his thinking and approach to problems was always wholly on secular lines.[77] As already mentioned, Nehru considered theocratic states in our times as a throwback —a medieval idea which did not fit in with modern trends. Early in 1948, Nehru declared: 'As far as India is concerned, I can speak with some certainty. We shall proceed on secular and national lines in keeping with the powerful trends towards internationalism. Whatever confusion the present may contain in the future, India will be a land, as in the past, of many faiths equally honoured and respected.'[78] Late in 1948, Nehru reiterated his complete faith in the secular ideal and also explained some of the implications of secularism. In a broadcast to the nation on Gandhi's birthday anniversary, Nehru stated:' We will not tolerate any communalism in this country...we are building a free, Secular State, where every religion and belief has full freedom and equal honour, where every citizen has equal liberty and equal opportunity.'[79]

The implications of this statement are obvious; they are: (1) the State will not come in the way of the promotion and practice of any religion; and (2) whatever be the religious group to which a citizen may belong, he will be entitled to and would be treated on a footing of equality with others in matters of rights and privileges.

Three clauses of the resolution on Fundamental Rights and Economic Programme,[80] drafted by Nehru and passed at the Karachi Congress of 1931, merit attention from the point of view of his support to the basic principles of secularism. The clauses are as follows: (ii) Every citizen shall enjoy freedom of conscience and the right freely to profess and practice his religion, subject to public order and morality. (v) No disability attaches to any citizen by reason of his or her religion, caste...in regard to public employment, office of power or honour, or in the exercise of any trade or calling. (ix) The state shall observe neutrality in regard to all religions.[81]

In the light of the Karachi resolution on Fundamental Rights and in the context of Nehru's very consistent support to the secular ideal, it could be safely said that India's emergence on the political scene of the world as a secular State, was a personal triumph of Nehru.

The Constitution of India has rendered India a secular state, by guaranteeing to its citizens those rights which the citizens of any secular state usually enjoy. Part III of the Indian Constitution, which deals with Fundamental Rights, incorporates such rights. The relevant Articles are: Articles 14, 15, 16, 25, 26, 27, 28, 29 and 30. Article 14 says: 'The state shall not deny to any person equality before the law or the equal protection of laws within the territory of India. Article 15(1) states: 'The State shall not discriminate against any citizen on grounds only of religion, race, caste.... As per Article 16(1), 'There shall be equality of opportunity for all citizens in matters relating to employment or appointment to any office under the State, whereas, as per Article 16(2): 'No citizen shall, on grounds only of religion, race, caste...be ineligible for, or discriminated against in respect of employment or office under the state. As per Article 25(1), all persons are equally entitled to freedom of conscience, the right freely to profess, practice and propagate religion, subject to the requirements of Public Order, mortality and health. Article 26 confers on religious denominations the right of establishing and maintaining institutions for religious purposes, of acquiring, owning and administering its properties. As per Article 27, no one may be compelled to pay taxes, the proceeds of which are earmarked for the support of any religion or denomination. As per Article 28, no religious instruction is to be imparted in schools maintained by the State; whereas as Article 29(1) gives assurance to the minority in regard to the preservation of their language, script and culture. Article 29(2) lays down that there will not be any discrimination in regard to admission to educational institutions maintained by the State or receiving aid from State funds on grounds of religion, race, caste.... The State has however been authorized (First Amendment) to make special provision for the educationally backward and Schedule Caste (Article 15(4)). Article 30 of the Constitution bestows on every religious and linguistic minority the right of establishing and administering educational institutions of their own and prohibits the State from discriminating against them on the ground that they are managed by minority.

Secularism demands that a citizen's caste or religion should not prevent him from getting equal rights and privileges from the State. Moreover, the State would not be truly secular where a citizen's social status is adversely affected because of his caste or any religious divisions. Speaking in the Parliament on May 29, 1961 Nehru said: 'We want to put an end to all those infinite divisions that have arisen in our social life; I am referring to the caste systems and other religious divisions, call them by whatever name you like....It is thus one of our objectives to get rid of these and to give every individual in India an opportunity to grow as also to build up a united nation where the individuals do not think so much of their particular group or caste but of the community at large.'[82] Of course, Nehru was wholly aware of the fact that this ideal could not be reached within a few years and that the State would have to go slowly in that direction, keeping always in view the existing realities as well as the ideal to be sought. Nehru, therefore, was in favour of giving special concessions and privileges to those belonging to the backward classes for a specified number of years, so that they may catch up with other sections of the society.[83]

Secularism requires that the people in the country, should be governed by the same set of laws. In India, however, in many matters, Hindus are governed by the Hindu Law and the Muslims by the Muslim Law. Since this is not quite consistent with the secular nature of the State, it was Nehru's endeavour to have a uniform civil code for the whole of India.[84] In fact, Article 44 of the Constitution (Part IV. Directive Principles of State Policy) states: 'The State shall endeavour to secure for the citizens a uniform civil code throughout the territory of India.'

Even as for Hindu Law, there is hardly any uniformity throughout the country. It was because of that, that Hindu Law had to be codified and in order to ensure uniformity in certain basic matters, modifications were also made in it. It was Nehru who took the initiative in this matter and saw to it that the bill was passed inspite of severe opposition from many quarters in the country. Nehru took the lead in this matter because of his firm belief that no revolution was complete unless the people in a country were emancipated from social tyranny. Speaking in the Parliament on May 22, 1954, Nehru emphasised the importance of social and economic changes. He pointed out that people had come to believe that economic changes were necessary as political changes, but somehow in matters of social changes, in a narrower context, they thought that it was a different matter altogether and that it could be kept a 'cold preserve'. That outlook, thought Nehru, was not a right one as life was an integrated whole. A true revolution in a country would involve changes not only in the political and economic domain but also in the social one. On the question of untouchability, many held the view that the sacred books had enjoined it on them. Nevertheless Gandhi and others came to the conclusion that it should be done away with not only because it was undesirable and unjust but also because such a step was necessary for the very survival of Hindu Society. That was the way in which every problem of human relationship was to be considered, as the biggest problems of the world were those of human relationships, whether they may be of one individual with another, or an individual with a group, or one group with another group for that matter.[85]

It must however be remembered that Nehru did not want to single out only Hindu community for social legislation as his critics believed. He wanted that the process should be extended to other groups also, the time however, thought Nehru, was not ripe for it.[86]

Thus, Nehru's role as a secularist was almost the role of a social reformer. By rooting out the chronic evils from which the Indian society suffered, Nehru wanted to strengthen its fabric and thereby contribute to social advancement and greater social unity.

Though India was politically united, the need of the hour was the emotional integration of the country. Since independence, the forces of sub-nationalism had manifested themselves on several occasions and it had become essential to take steps towards the emotional integration of the Indian people, so that the political unity of the country might not be undermined. If the people of the country did not do away with provincial, caste, communal or religious barriers, it would not be a unified India in the real sense of the term. Nehru stated that he would rather lose all elections than win them by appealing to the religious and caste feelings of the people. He made a fervent appeal to the Newspaper Editors (whom he was addressing), to create an atmosphere conducive to the emotional integration of the country. The prerequisite for the integration of minds stated Nehru, was the absence of communal and caste feelings, which ought to be discouraged by every Indian, who had India's interest at his heart.[87]

The emotional integration of the country is absolutely essential not only in the context of present day conditions in India but also in the context of India's past, which is one of defeats due to factions and divisions amongst Indian people. In fact, the incapacity to stand together and to face the enemy has been the greatest drawback of the Indian people and as such no amount of stress on the emotional integration of the country could be too much. Speaking about the necessity of emotional integration, Nehru referred to India's past history and said: 'You are acquainted somewhat with the history of India. It has been our misfortune through long periods of history to be very factious, to be liable to separation, with the result that the great strength of India has been wasted in inner conflict, in inner argument and in fissiparous and separatist tendencies.... We have produced great men in every field of human endeavour, in thought in action, in art, in literature, in music. Yet we have failed to take advantage of this greatness because of the tendency amongst us to disrupt, to go our individual ways. Hence, we have been weak, and often subjugated and dominated by foreigners who have come here. I think it is correct to say that foreigners who came here hardly ever really conquered India. Certainly the British did not, in spite of their superior arms. They simply took advantage of the divisions in India. Others who came did the same thing. That is the big lesson of Indian history. And therefore, we must learn to hold together.'[88]

Nehru's role in the emotional integration of the country had been an important one. To start with, his own personality had been an integrating force of immeasurable importance. When the author asked Nehru (during the authors first interview with Nehru—New Delhi, October 19, 1959) as to whether he would feel embarrassed, if it was stated that he was the only emotional factor binding the people of India together, Nehru replied: 'I am a cementing force...' However, he thought that there were more important factors responsible for the unity of the Indian people, and in this connection he referred to the basic unity prevailing in India throughout the ages, inspite of diversity.

The way in which the whole nation responded to Nehru's call and rallied round him during the crisis (after the Chinese invasion over the Indian territory), was indicative of the extent to which, Nehru was an integrating force in India. It is highly doubtful as to whether the people, with all their patriotism, would have responded so enthusiastically to anybody else's call.

Nehru's language policy has contributed greatly to the creation of an atmosphere, which is conducive to the emotional integration of the country. But for Nehru's repeated assertions that all major languages of India would be given the same importance (which later took the form of constitutional provisions)[89] and, his go-slow policy in regard to the introduction of Hindi, as the official language of India, it is conceivable that language would have become a major disrupting factor and would have greatly added to the divisive tendencies in the country.

After independence, Nehru did his utmost to encourage even tribal languages. Nehru's was keenly aware of the fact that language was an important integrating factor and as such believed that the languages spoken in various parts of the country should be encouraged and allowed to flourish. In a speech delivered at the opening session of the Scheduled Tribes and Scheduled Areas Conference (New Delhi, June 7, 1952), Nehru while emphasising the importance of encouraging and fostering tribal languages, stated as to how the language problem was extremely important from the psychological point of view. In that connection, he made a mention of the way in which Lenin and others brought about the emotional integration of the Russian people by following a policy of encouraging different languages. In order to win the goodwill of the people, they went out of their way to encourage not only their languages but also hundreds of dialects, by compiling dictionaries and even by evolving new scripts. By pursuing that policy they succeeded in creating the impression that the people were free to live as they wished to live.[90]

While suggesting that Hindi should become the official language of India, Nehru took care to emphasise the fact that Hindi was being chosen not because it was in any way superior to any other language of India but because it was spoken and understood by maximum people in India. That was the reason as to why it was a suitable all-India language, though other languages of India were equally great.[91]

However, Nehru had constantly advocated a go-slow policy in regard to the introduction of Hindi as the official language of India as he was sensitive to the public opinion in the non-Hindi speaking areas of South India. He was well aware of the fact that any haste in that matter would be harmful to the emotional integration of the country and would have far reaching consequences. Speaking before the members of the Congress Party in Parliament on May 7, 1954, Nehru said that even in a country like Yugoslavia, which had an authoritarian government, no attempt was made to impose any language on the people, though it could easily do so. The Government there very wisely decided to encourage all the three languages fully, without making any of them compulsory. He stated that he had given the example of Yugoslavia in order to emphasise the fact as to how cautious was the manner in which wise countries proceed in those matters. Though maximum effort had to be made to encourage the regional languages as well as the all-India language, Hindi, it should be so done as not to create the impression of opposition to any other. If that was not done difficulties and complications would inevitably arise.[92]

There was of course, according to Nehru, a vast measure of agreement on that issue. He urged the Congress members of the Parliament to look at that matter in perspective, bearing in mind the amount of agreement and not disagreement, something which was unparalleled in history, for a country so big as India and with so many languages. And yet it was necessary that whatever the steps that the Government might take, on no account should they create the impression that they were placing the people of the South at a disadvantage. It was necessary that the apprehensions in the minds of the people belonging to the South should be removed in regard to they being handicapped in service, in business and in politics on account of their inadequate knowledge of a certain language.[93]

Nehru's policy of going slow in the matter of replacing English by Hindi was reflected in the Government's decision to give English an Associate status in the Constitution. The supporters of Hindi felt very unhappy about the Government's decision and started an agitation against giving English an associate status. Addressing a public meeting on 2nd October 1962, Nehru referred to the agitation started by the 'lovers of Hindi', and declared, 'Let them be under no illusion. The pledge we gave on the floor of Parliament to the people of South India that nothing would be done against their wishes in the matter of English will be fulfilled. This is crystal clear.'[94] Nehru then stated that he had made the proposal of giving English the status of an associate language, two years earlier, as the people in the South had urged him to retain English for sometime more. The Government had agreed to it as it did not want to impose Hindi on half or one fourth of the country, against the wishes of the people there. Sounding a note of warning to the 'lovers of Hindi' Nehru in an obvious reference to the activities of *Dravida Munnetra Kazhgam*, a political party, which was advocating the secession of Madras State from the Indian Union, said: 'There is a party in Madras which is propagating secession of that State from India. These demonstrations against English will only strengthen the hands of those who are demanding secession'.[95]

Nehru desired the continuance of English in India, not only in the context of the emotional integration of the country but also because it served as a 'window to the outside world and knowledge'.[96] English was necessary also for the purposes of higher studies and they would always require study of books, other than text books, and it would be impossible to translate all the literature in the world in the Indian languages. Hence, it was essential to know foreign languages and more particularly so English, which was very rich in every type of literature.

In most of the European countries the trend of the people is that of learning more and more foreign languages. There is a big move in Britain for people to learn French, German and Russian because they feel that they are remaining behind in science and other matters by not being in a position to read the various books and scientific literature coming out in other languages. Even in Egypt, learning of English and one additional foreign language has been made compulsory. Thus, if India is not to lag behind, not only is it essential to retain English but also to learn other foreign languages.[97]

Thus, Nehru's approach towards various languages spoken and understood in India, was extremely desirable. His language policy would not only help the process of the emotional integration of the Indian people, but would also help India to keep pace with the more advanced countries of the world in the domain of science and technology.

What are the positive ways in which the emotional integration of the people could be brought about? According to Nehru that could be done in various ways, but more particularly so, by creating amongst the people an awareness in regard to their common heritage and also by creating in them an emotional awareness, in regard to India's present problems, by putting the idea behind planning in India in perspective.[98] In a speech delivered in December 1955 (at Trichur), Nehru while emphasising the aspect of the common heritage of the Indian people as a whole, said: 'the whole of India from the North to the South is the common heritage of every Indian, and all India's history, from thousands and thousands of years till today, is our common heritage. All the culture of India, whether it comes from the North or the South or anywhere else, is our common heritage, and what is more, the great future that spreads out before us is going to be our common heritage.'[99]

While speaking in the Parliament on Demeber 15, 1962, Nehru described the First Five Year Plan as 'the first attempt in India to integrate the agricultural, industrial, social, economic and other aspects of the country into a single framework of thinking.'[100] It was because of the plan that the people of India began to think of the country as a whole. Nehru further stated that it was highly essential that India which was politically united should also become united mentally and emotionally. That he thought could be partly accomplished through planning as it helped in the creation of an emotional awareness in regard to the problems facing India as a whole.[101]

Nehru did not desire the emotional integration of the country at the expense of its diversity. As profound student of Indian history he knew it too well that India had always sought unity through diversity. 'I am after (the) emotional integration of the Indian people so that we might be welded into one strong national unit, maintaining at the same time all our wonderful diversity. I do not want this diversity to be regimented and taken away.'[102]

It must also be mentioned that Nehru's constant endeavours to render Indian a Secular State in the very spirit of the word, has also been an important factor in the emotional integration of the country. If Nehru's policy is meticulously followed by his successors too, there is every reason to believe that India will become in the near future, one integrated emotional unit.

When the author asked Nehru (26th October 1960, New Delhi) as to whether he was in favour of a common script for all the Indian languages so as to facilitate the emotional integration of the country, Nehru had shown himself in favour of such an idea and had expressed the view that it would be a good thing, if it could be done.[103]

Nehru's intense desire to find ways and means of bringing about national integration reflected itself in the appointment of the National Integration Committee at the Bhavnagar session of the Congress (1960), with Indira Gandhi as its Chairperson. The recommendation of that Committee, which were issued on 1st June 1961 were in harmony with Nehru's views on that very vital question.[104]

To conclude, Nehru who strove for a united free India in the pre-Independence period, tried his utmost in the post-Independence era, to create proper conditions for the perpetuation of the political unity of the country, through the emotional integration of its people. There could hardly be two opinions about the fact that Nehru's approach to the problem of the emotional integration of the country was a right one, whatever might be the measure of success with which it has met so far.

NOTES

1. The Indian Annual Register, 1940, G.C. University Library, Lahore, p.312.
2. The March of a Nation: a collection of the most important speeches of Qaid-i-Azam, M.A. Jinnah, F. Akhtar, Malik Book Depot, 1945, Delhi, Lahore, pp.60-61.
3. As for Iqbal's advocacy of a separate state for the Muslims, Nehru wrote in *The Discovery of India*: 'Edward Thompson has written that, in the course of a conversation, Iqbal told him that he had advocated Pakistan because of his position as the President of the Muslim League session, but he felt sure that it would be injurious to India as a whole and to Moslems specially. Probably he had changed his mind, or he had not given much thought to the question previously, as it had assumed no importance then. His whole outlook on life does not fit in with subsequent developments of the idea of Pakistan or division of India'.

   (*The Discovery of India*, Jawahrlal Nehru, Signet Press, Culcutta-20, Fourth Printing, 1948, p.293)
4. Presidential address, All India Muslim League, Allahabad Session, December 1930, printed at Muslim League Printing Press, Daryaganj, Delhi, 1945 edition, p.12.
5. *The Indian Problem* (1836-1942), R. Coupland, printed in Great Britain by Richard Clay and Company Ltd., p.199.
6. The March of a Nation: A collection of the most important speeches of Qaid-i-Azam, M.A. Jinnah, F. Akhtar, Mulik Book Depot,1945, Delhi, Lahore, p.101.
7. The following question and answers reveal Jinnah's basic stand about Hindus and Muslims constituting not one single nation but two. These questions and answers form a part of a conversation between Edward Thompson and Jinnah:

   Edward Thomson: 'Two nations Mr. Jinnah? Confronting each other in every province? Every town.Every Village.

   Jinnah: 'Two Nations. Confronting each other in every Province.Every Town.Every Village. That is the only solution.

   Edward Thomson: 'That is very terrible solution Mr. Jinnah?

   Jinnah: It is very terrible solution, but it is the only one.'

   (This conversation has been quoted by M.G. Nena and S.M. Barde, in their book 'India in Transition' printed at Shivaji Printing Press, Bombay, 1948, p. 252).
8. *Recent Essays and Writings*, Jawaharlal Nehru, Kitabistan, Allahabad, 1934, p .65.
9. In the Unity of India, Nehru quoted Vincent Smith from the Oxford History of India and Frederick Whyte from the Future of East and West, in favour of his view in regard to India's fundamental unity. According to Vincent Smith: 'India beyond all doubt possesses a deep underlying fundamental unity far more profound than that produced either by geographical isolation or by political suzerainty. That unity transcends the innumerable diversities of blood, colour, language, dress, manners, and sect'. Frederick Whyte after making a reference to the tremendous diversity of India stated, 'the greatest of all the contradictions in India is that over this diversity is spread a greater unity, which is not immediately evident because it failed historically to find expression in any political cohesion to make the country one, but which is so greatly a reality, and so powerful, that even the Mussalman world in India has to confess that it has been deeply affected by coming under its influence.'

   (The Unity of India, Jawaharlal Nehru, Lindsay Drummond, London, W.C.1, 1948, pp. 14-15).
10. Ibid., loc. cit.
11. Ibid., p.15.

12. *India and the World,* Jawaharlal Nehru, George Allen and Unwin Ltd., London, 1936, p. 187.
13. *The Unity of India,* Jawaharlal Nehru, Lindsay Drummond, London, W.C. 1,1948, pp. 20-21.
14. *Eighteen Months in India,* Jawaharlal Nehru, Allied Publishers, Bombay, 1962, p. 188.
15. *The Discovery of India,* Jawaharlal Nehru, Signet Press, Calcutta-20, Fourth Printing, September 1948, p. 447.
16. Ibid., loc. cit.
17. Ibid., loc. cit.
18. Ibid., p. 449.
19. Ibid., p. 292.
20. Ibid., p. 253
21. *The Unity of India,* Jawaharlal Nehru, Lindsay Drummond, London, W.C.1, 1948, p. 367.
22. Ibid., loc. cit.
23. 'We have some knowledge of how the communal question....was nurtured and grew under the benign influence of successive Viceroys and Governments. It is evident that the old tradition still holds and finds expression in British Govt. Policy in India. (Ibid. p. 347).
24. 'To say that the British Government created the Hindu-Muslim problem would be patently wrong, but it would be equally wrong to ignore their continuous effort to keep it alive and to discourage the coming together of the communities. (*Glimpses of World History,* Jawaharlal Nehru, Lindsay Drummond Ltd, London, W.C.1., Fourth Edition, January 1949, p. 721).
25. *The Discovery of India,* Jawaharlal Nehru, Signet Press, Calcutta-20, Fourth Printing, September, 1948, p. 228.
26. Ibid., loc. cit.
27. Ibid., pp. 228-29
28. *Glimpses of World History,* Jawaharlal Nehru, Lindsay Drummond Ltd, London, W.C., Fourth Edition, January, 1949, p. 270.
29. Ibid., p. 721.
30. Important Speeches of Jawaharlal Nehru (1922-1945), Edited by J.S. Bright The Indian Printing Works, Kacheri Road, Lahore, 1945, p. 195.
31. *The Discovery of India,* Jawaharlal Nehru, Signet Press, Calcutta-20, Fourth Printing, September, 1948, p. 292.
32. Ibid., loc. cit.
33. Ibid., p. 293.
34. Ibid., loc. cit.
35. Ibid., loc. cit.
36. Ibid., loc. cit.
37. *The Unity of India,* Jawaharlal Nehru, Lindsay Drummond, London, W.C.1, 1948, p.387.
38. Ibid., pp. 387-388.
39. Ibid., pp. 388.
40. *The History of the Indian National Congress,* Volume II, (1935-1947), Dr. Pattabhi Sitaramayya, Published by Navjivan Publishing House, 1969, Appendix IV.
41. *Recent Essays and Writings,* Jawaharlal Nehru, Kitabistan, Allahabad, 1934 p.365.

42. Allan Campbell-Johnson writes in his book ' Mission with Mountbatten' that the moment Mountbatten's party set foot in India (March 1947), it was 'faced by rapidly rising Hindu-Moslem tensions. 'Direct Action' had been launched by the Muslim League in August 1946, there were riots and reprisals for riots. This set off the spark and disturbances of great intensity took place in Bengal and Bihar. The trouble spread to Lahore and the North-West Frontier Province. In his first talks with Lord Mountbatten the Muslim League leader, Mr. Jinnah gave a frank warning that unless an acceptable political solution was reached very quickly he could not guarantee to control the situation from his side.' (Robert Hale Ltd, London, 1951).
43. Ibid., loc. cit.
44. Ibid., loc. cit.
45. Jawaharlal Nehru Speeches (1953-57), The Publication Division, Ministry of Education and Broadcasting, Govt. of India, Calcutta, Delhi, 1959, p.234.
46. Report of the Nehru Committee, All Parties Conference, 1928, Author: Motilal Nehru, Publisher: Allahabad: All India Congress Committee, 1928, p.62.
47. *The History of the Indian National Congress*, Dr. Pattabhi Sitaramayya, Vol. II, 1947, Published by Navjivan Publishing House, 1969, p.67.
48. Ibid., p. 89.
49. Ibid., Appendix I, pp. I-II.
50. In November 1947, Mahatma Gandhi wrote: '...the reluctance to enforce linguistic redistribution is perhaps justifiable in the present depressing atmosphere. The exclusive spirit is ever upper most. Everyone thinks of himself and his family. No one thinks of the whole of India. The centripetal force is undoubtedly there, but it is not vocal, never boisterous; whereas the centrifugal is on the surface and in its very nature makes the loudest noise demanding the attention of all...The history of the quarrel between Orissa and Andhra, Orissa and Bihar and Orissa and Bengal is fresh in our minds. The whole of it has not died out even now.' (*Harijan*, 30-11-1947).
51. Report of the States Re-organisation Commission, Delhi: Manager of Publications, 1965, p. 15.
52. Report of the Linguistic Provinces Commission, Manager, Govt. of India Press, Delhi, 1948, paras 138 and 152 (3).
53. Ibid., para 131.
54. Ibid., para 147.
55. Ibid., pp. 2, 7, 15, 16.
56. Report of the States Reorganisation Commission, Delhi: Manager of Publications, 1965, Appendix A, p. 264.
57. Ibid., loc. cit.
58. Ibid., p. 11.
59. Ibid., loc. cit.
60. *Jawaharlal Nehru's Speeches* (1953-57), The Publication Division, Ministry of Information and Broadcasting, Calcutta, Delhi, 1959, pp. 168-169.
61. Ibid., p. 171.
62. Ibid., p. 193.
63. Ibid., p. 175.
64. Ibid., loc. cit.
65. *Jawaharlal Nehru's Speeches* (1949-53), The Publication Division, Ministry of Information and Broadcasting, Govt. of India, Calcutta, 1954, p. 54.

66. Ibid., loc. cit.
67. *Jawaharlal Nehru's Speeches* (1953-57), The Publication Division, Ministry of Information and Broadcasting, Calcutta, Delhi, 1959, pp 182-183.
68. Ibid., p.183.
69. Ibid., loc. cit.
70. Ibid., loc. cit.
71. Ibid., p. 178.
72. Ibid, pp. 184-185
73. The relevant part of the Congress Manifesto states: 'the demand for a redistribution of Provinces on a linguistic basis has been persistently made in the South and West of India. The Congress expressed itself in favour of linguistic provinces many years ago. A decision on this question ultimately depends upon the wishes of the people concerned. While linguistic reasons have undoubtedly a certain cultural and other importance, there are other factors also, such as economic, administrative and financial, which have to be taken into consideration.'

    (*Jawaharlal Nehru's Speeches*, 1949-1953, The Publication Division, Ministry of Information and Broadcasting, Govt. of India, Calcutta, p. 55)
74. Independence and After, A collection of the more important speeches of Jawaharlal Nehru, from September 1946 to May 1949, The Publication Division, Ministry of Information and Broadcasting, Govt. of India, Calcutta, 1954, p.45.
75. *Nehru: A Political Biography*, Michael Brecher, Oxford University Press, London, New York, Bombay, Toronto, 1959, pp. 355-356.
76. Campbell–Johnson who saw Nehru from close quarters during communal riots in New Delhi, writes: '...to see Nehru at close range during this ordeal is an inspiring experience. He vindicates one's faith in the humanist and the civilised intellect. Almost alone in the turmoil of communalism, with all its variations, from individual intrigue to mass madness, he speaks with the voice of reason and sanity.'

    (Mission with Mountbatten, Cambell–Johnson, Robert Hale Ltd., London, 1951, p. 189).
77. Vincent Sheean in his book, 'Nehru: The Years of Power' writes: '...as for his (Nehru's) intellect I have never found anything but secular, purely secular. I do not discover, in his printed work or in any talk I have had with him during the past twelve years, one vestige of the religiosity which otherwise obsesses Hindu Culture. This is truly extraordinary in India. I have never met any other person who could sustain a closely knit conversation for two or three hours at a stretch without bringing into it something of religious nature, some concept which originates in religion. This is just true of Muslims and Christians as of Hindus; all Indian are steeped in it. It may only be a reference or a quotation; it may be oblique or obscure, but religious concept always creeps in. Not so with Mr. Nehru."

    (Nehru: The Years of Power, Vincent Sheean, London, Victor, Gollanez Ltd., 1966, p. 22).
78. *Jawaharlal Nehru's Speeches* (1946-1949), The Publication Division, Ministry of Information and Broadcasting, Government of India, Calcutta, 1958, p. 339.
79. Ibid., p. 60.
80. Though these clauses have already been quoted along with a few others in chapter 5, they needed mention once again in the context of Nehru's views on secularism.
81. The Unity of India, Jawaharlal Nehru, Lindsay Drummond, London, W.C., 1, 1948, p. 406.

82. *Jawaharlal Nehru's Speeches* (1949-1953), The Publication Division, Ministry of Information and Broadcasting, Govt of India, Calcutta, 1954, pp. 518-519.
83. Ibid., Loc cit.
84. *The Times of India*, September 16, 1954, p. II.
85. *Jawaharlal Nehru's Speeches* (1953-1957), The Publication Division, Ministry of Information and Broadcasting, Govt. of India, Calcutta, Delhi, 1959, pp. 441-442.
86. *The Times of India*, September 16, Bombay, 1954, p. II.
87. Ibid., Loc cit.
88. *Jawaharlal Nehru's Speeches* (1953-1957), The Publication Division, Ministry of Information and Broadcasting, Govt. of India, Calcutta, Delhi, 1959, p.31.
89. The principal languages of India have been enumerated in the Eighth Schedule of the Constitution. These are Assamese, Bengali, Gujarati, Hindi, Kannada, Kashmiri, Malayalam, Marathi, Oriya, Punjabi, Sanskrit, Tamil, Telugu and Urdu. Sanskrit though not a living language has been included in the list, because of its supreme cultural significance in Indian life.
90. *Jawaharlal Nehru's Speeches* (1949-53), The Publication Division, Ministry of Information and Broadcasting, Govt. of India Calcutta, 1954, pp. 46-47.
91. *Jawaharlal Nehru's Speeches* (1953-57), The Publication Division, Ministry of Information and Broadcasting, Govt of India, Calcutta, Delhi, 1959, p.398.
92. Ibid. p.395.
93. Ibid. loc. cit.
94. *The Deccan Chronicle*, Hyderabad, October 4, 1962, p. 1.
95. Ibid., loc. cit.
96. Ibid., loc. cit.
97. To a public meeting on October 2, 1962, *The Deccan Chronicle*, Hyderabad, October 4, 1962, p. 1.
98. To the author, 16th October 1959, New Delhi.
99. Jawaharlal Nehru's Speeches, 1953-1957, The Publication Division, Ministry of Information and Broadcasting, Govt. of India, Calcutta, Delhi, 1959 pp. 37-38.
100. Jawaharlal Nehru Speeches-1949-1953, The Publication Division, Ministry of Information and Broadcasting, Govt. of India, Calcutta, 1954 p. 97.
101. Ibid., loc. cit.
102. Jawaharlal Nehru Speeches, 1953-57, The Publication Division, Ministry of Information and Broadcasting, Govt. of India, Calcutta, Delhi, 1959, p. 35.
103. The 12-member Emotional Integration Committee, appointed by the National Integration Conference, submitted, its report to the Union Govt. in September. According to one of its Members—A.F. Fyzee, the Committee has suggested the use of Latin script where there were difficulties in popularising the language in the Devanagari script. According to Mr. Fayzee, almost all the witnesses who appeared before the Committee had stressed the difficulty of teaching three languages in three different scripts. Therefore the Committee said that the three languages (the third is the regional language) should be taught in two scripts and this to begin with, should be tried on an experimental basis. (*The Deccan Chronical*, Hyderabad, September 13, 1962, p. 1).
104. The recommendations made by the National Integration Committee appointed at the Bhavnagar Session of the Congress, Appendix 'C' of the authors thesis on 'Nehru's Ideas on Nationalism, Democracy and Socialism', pp. xxiv, xxxi, OU Library, Thesis section, Hyderabad.

7

POLICIES AND DECISIONS IN PERSPECTIVE (I)

[*Note:* In this chapter I have tried to show as to how many of the important resolutions passed in the various sessions of the Congress bear the stamp of Nehru's ideas on social, economic and political matters. Nehru's policy towards the Princely States in pre-Independence period has also been discussed. Some of the controversies revolving round Nehru's policies and decisions during that period have also been subjected to a close examination.]

From 1929 onwards, almost upto 1959, there was a progressive increase in Nehru's popularity. His popularity in India upto 1947 was second only to that of Gandhi. In the post-Independence period, in fact till his passing away in May 1964, Nehru was far more popular than anyone else on the political scene of India. His position in Indian politics was unchallenged upto the year 1962—the year in which China's aggression over India took place. India's humiliation at the hands of China affected Nehru's popularity very adversely and from that time onwards to the date of his passing away, Nehru's popularity was at a low ebb and was hardly comparable to the one that he enjoyed before 1962.

From 1929 onwards, Nehru strode over the Indian political scene like a colossus. After the passing away of Subhash Bose, Gandhi and Vallabhbhai Patel, Nehru became indispensable for the country and so all-pervasive was his influence in the post-Independence period that Jaya Prakash Narain, once while describing Nehru stated that he (Nehru) was like a huge banyan tree under which nothing grew. It was therefore but natural that people started wondering as to what would happen to India after Nehru's passing away. Thus people started discussing the question as to what after Nehru and who after Nehru?

Nehru's popularity gradually started waning from the late fifties due to a variety of reasons, which would be discussed presently. As stated earlier, India's debacle in the Sino-Indian conflict made things worse for Nehru. And, after Nehru's passing away, a number of books came out-books that held Nehru partly or mainly responsible for many supposedly wrong policies and actions of the Indian Government headed by Nehru. The image of Nehru that emerged through these books was one of an inept administrator an idealist who lived in a dream world of his own (and as such couldn't come to grips with realities), and one who proved a failure in solving the manifold problems of the country.

Paradoxical though it may seem, educated people in India by and large had started thinking more or less on the same lines (since late 'fifties), inspite of the fact that they held Nehru in high esteem and had great affection for him. As such, the books that were critical of Nehru's role as India's Prime Minister (published after Nehru's passing away), made them feel to a greater degree still that Nehru was a failure as the Prime Minister, though his role as an agitator for India's freedom was laudable.

The books that criticised Nehru for his alleged failures were useful and informative in their own way. However, it must be pointed out that the authors of those books did not refer to certain important matters (which they obviously knew), probably because those facts did not suit their argument or help them to build up their case. Moreover, for obvious reasons they were not in possession of all relevant facts, which is a pre-requisite for just and correct conclusions.

As ill-luck would have it, Nehru's autobiography covers less than half of his political life. Had destiny spared Nehru for a few more years and, if it had been possible for him to relinquish his office and lead a retired life, he would probably have come out with the second volume of his autobiography, one which would have greatly contributed to the better understanding of the circumstances in which he had to take different decisions and the propriety of such decisions, as he alone had the entire picture before him.

Ironically enough, the image of Nehru as projected by Gandhi in the pre-Independence period—the one which greatly contributed to Nehru's popularity during that period, was responsible, partly, for the growth of scepticism in the minds of the people about his political wisdom, in the post-Independence period. This somewhat enigmatic statement calls for some explanation.

Nehru was elected as the President of the Lahore session of the Congress (1929), because of Gandhi's support for his candidature. While justifying his choice, Gandhi had publicly stated: 'In bravery he (Nehru) is not to be surpassed. Who can excel him in the love of the country? He is undoubtedly an extremist thinking far ahead of his surroundings.... He is pure as a crystal, he is truthful beyond suspicion. The nation is safe in his hands'. While Gandhi in his statement had also referred to Nehru's prudence as a statesman, the image that emerged of Nehru (through Gandhi's words) was more of an idealist and a nobleminded soul than that of a person endowed with political acumen. Not only on this, but on subsequent occasions also, Gandhi had praised Nehru's breadth of vision, magnanimity etc., and his approbation of Nehru had greatly added to Nehru's popularity and had enhanced his prestige in the minds of the people. However, in the post-Independence period, Nehru's constant emphasis on peaceful approach to problems and friendly relations with all countries (inspite of provocations from them), gradually made the people feel (in late 'fifties), that this noble person (hadn't Gandhi described him as truthful beyond suspicion and pure as a crystal!), though good in the role of a nationalist fighting for his country's independence was too noble and sincere to be effective in the role of a shrewd statesman.

In the post-Independence period, some of those who were opposed to the Congress, put forward the thesis that the process of the spectacular victories of the Congress at the polls, could be arrested only by altering the public image of Nehru, which atleast for one decade after freedom was that of a man of vision and one who was endowed with the qualities of a great statesman. They felt, rightly of course, that the moment Nehru went down in public esteem, Congress victories at the polls would come to a halt, as Congress swept the polls during that period almost exclusively due to Nehru's tremendous popularity. In order to alter the public image of Nehru, not only efforts were made to prove that Nehru's policies were entirely devoid of realism, but what was worse, efforts were made to tarnish Nehru's image of a man of unquestionable character and integrity. Though propaganda of such type did not immediately affect Nehru's popularity, it had its adverse effect on his popularity in the long run and the public image of Nehru altered slowly and imperceptibly.

Partly, Nehru was responsible for the gradual change in the attitude of the people towards him. Leave alone his public speeches, even his speeches in the Parliament were such, as to give the impression that the Prime Minister was more of an idealist than a realist. Of course, in his speeches in the Parliament he took care to give some hints to the members about the manner in which his mind was working on a certain problem. But what remained unstated was always considerably more than what was stated by him. Moreover, much of what he said was clothed in such pious sentiments that the pragmatic implications of his statements were not grasped by a great many. When he talked about India's desire for very friendly relations with China and Pakistan, he, actually had in mind the fact that India couldn't afford a war with her neighbours, at least not during that stage of India's economy. As ill-luck would have it, people who listened to him revealed little or no capacity to read between the lines and to sense the realism concealed in those pious statements. Those who wanted to distort the image of Nehru took the fullest advantage of Nehru's vague statements clothed in the fabric of noble sentiments, and tried to project a different image of Nehru, the one of a dreamer and one who was more concerned about ideals like international peace, co-operation and friendship than the requirements of his own country.

It is true that the Prime Minister of a country cannot reveal to the people all that he has in his mind and as such he is likely to be misunderstood. However, Nehru could have created a machinery through which his essentially pragmatic approach to problems was made known to the people. The fact that even those who were fairly near to him could not sense the pragmatism in his approach proves that his efforts to make his policies understood proved thoroughly inadequate. The overall effect of this has been the prevalence of notions till today about Nehru's lack of realism and political sagacity.

While assessing the role of Nehru as the Prime Minister the facts mentioned above must be borne in mind. Moreover, our assessment will go wrong, if we do not take into account the innumerable difficulties that he had to face and the limitations under which he had to function. It would be a mistake to measure Nehru's achievements in arithmetical terms, that is, in terms of the number of problems solved by him and the number of those which he couldn't. Such an approach would lead us to as erroneous a conclusion as the one reached by an expert in statistical averages, who once opined that if a person had one of his hands in a refrigerator and the other on a stove, on an average he would be comfortable !

It is essential to remember in this connection the magnitude of different problems that Nehru had to face as the first Prime Minister of free India. People expected him to solve in a short period the problems which had accumulated during one hundred and fifty years of British mis-rule over India—a fantastic task! Nehru, who had started applying his mind to all such problems in the pre-Independence period itself, knew it too well that they could not be solved in a short period and that only long term planning could result in their solution.

Nehru could not expedite the process of India's progress because of several reasons. The party which he led was not really suited for Independent India's requirements, as it was far from homogenous. The Congress was essentially a heterogeneous organization, having within its fold people of all shades of opinion. It was however quite understandable that it should be so, as it was primarily intended to serve the purpose of winning freedom for the country, and all those who broadly agreed with the Congress strategy to win freedom, became its members. Their views on other political matters, being not of immediate relevance, diversity in them did not very much matter during that period. To take the country quickly in the direction of progress through the instrumentality of such a party was not easy, as groups within Congress pulled in different directions.

It is very important to remember that the task of the first Prime Minister of a newly independent country is far more difficult than that of his successors. He has to do the pioneering work in every sphere and lay down traditions and practices which his successors could follow with advantage. Nehru had to face the added difficulty of brining about changes in a static and tradition bound society. As if all this was not enough, immediately after assuming office, he had to face the tremendous refugee problem, which shook the economy of the newly independent country to its very foundations. It should also be remembered that Nehru had to function in the framework of democracy, the processes of which are essentially very slow.

While assessing Nehru's role in Indian politics, certain important facts must be borne in mind. To begin with, his role as a whole should be considered, instead of dividing it into two water-tight compartments—the pre-Independence role and the post-Independence role. Such an approach would be basically wrong, as Nehru during the pre-Independence period did not merely strive for India's liberation but also made every endeavour to lay down the ideological foundations on which the super-structure of

Independent India was to be raised. Thus, in the post-Independence period Nehru continued the work, which he had started years earlier.

Nehru, because of his profound knowledge of India's history, as also because of his education in England (which made him acutely conscious of India's backwardness in different ways) and awareness of international trends, could know precisely as to what was to be done in order to make India a modern, prosperous and politically strong country. As such, while striving ceaselessly for the achievement of freedom for the country, Nehru also applied his mind to the problems—social, economic and political that would have to be faced by independent India and tried to find solutions to them. It was Nehru, more than anyone else in the Congress, who was responsible for creating an awareness in the rank and file of the party in regard to the fact that the achievement of the country's independence would hardly have any significance unless the country was ready with a blue-print of the policies that would be pursued in the post-Independence period for the overall betterment of the people as independence of the country was not an end in itself but essentially a means towards an end.

The blue-print of independent India's policies and programme gradually emerged through the resolutions that Nehru drafted, moved and eventually got approved in the various sessions of the Congress.

The resolution on Fundamental Rights and Economic Policy (drafted by Nehru) adopted by the Karachi Congress of 1931, constituted an important part of the blue-print that Nehru was preparing. The introductory part of the resolution had stated that any Constitution that was agreed to on behalf of the Congress 'should provide or enable the Swaraj Government to provide, for the following'. Some of the more noteworthy clauses of Article one incorporated in the first section were as follows:

(i) Every citizen of India has the right of free express ion of opinion, the right of free association and combination, and the right to assemble peacefully and without arms, for purposes not opposed to law and morality.

(ii) Every citizen shall enjoy freedom of conscience and the right freely to profess and practice his religion, subject to public order and morality.

(iii) The culture, language and script of the Minorities and of different linguistic areas shall be protected.

(iv) All citizens are equal before law, irrespective of religion, caste, creed or sex.

(v) No disability attaches to any citizen, by reason of his or her religion, caste, creed or sex, in regard to public employment, office of power or honour, or in the exercise of any trade or calling.

(vi) All citizens have equal rights and duties in regard to wells, tanks, roads, schools and places of public resort...maintained for the use of the general public.

(vii) The state shall observe neutrality in regard to all religions.

(viii) The franchise shall be on the basis of universal adult suffrage.

(ix) Every citizen is free to move throughout India and to stay and settle in any part thereof, to acquire property and to follow any trade or calling, and to be treated equally with regard to legal prosecution or protection in all parts of India.

Clauses two, four and five are important from the point of view of Nehru's basic support to secularism. The others, like the third and the fifth have influenced the Directive Principles of State Policy in the Constitution. Part III of the Constitution (on Fundamental Rights) has been considerably influenced by many of the clauses included in this section, in addition to the second, fourth and fifth. This section not only reveals Nehru's great faith in the value of individual liberty in particular and democratic way of life in general, but is also indicative of his great desire to prepare the country for the acceptance of a political set up that is based on the firm foundations of democratic principles.

Many of the Articles in section two and three of the resolution were on socialistic lines. Three such Articles merit attention from this point of view. They are Articles 7, 8 and 15. They are as follows:

7. The system of land tenure and revenue and rent shall be reformed and an equitable adjustment made of the burden on agricultural land, immediately giving relief to the smaller peasantry, by a substantial reduction of agricultural rent and revenue now paid by them, and in case of uneconomic holdings, exempting them from rent so long as necessary, with such relief as may be just and necessary to holders of small estates affected by such exemption or reduction in rent, and to the same end, imposing a graded tax on net incomes from land above a reasonable minimum.

8. Death duties on a graduated scale shall be levied on property above a fixed minimum.
15. The State shall own or control key industries and services, mineral resources, railways, waterways, shipping and other means of public transport.[1]

The resolution as a whole was framed in the context of India's problems —social, economic and political. Its acceptance by the Congress was in the nature of a pledge in favour of socialism. This resolution not only influenced certain provisions of the Indian Constitution but also helped the central and the state governments in independent India to take appropriate steps for the overall betterment of the people.

It has already been pointed out in the chapter 5 as to how Nehru during late 'twenties and 'thirties constantly spoke and wrote about the problem of landlordism in India and, how his views influenced some of the Congress resolutions on this problem during that period. Nehru's resolution on Agrarian Programme adopted at the Lucknow session of the Congress (already referred to in the previous chapter) constituted yet another important part of his blueprint of Independent India's economic policy.

The work that Nehru did as the Chairman of the Planning Committee appointed by the Congress in 1938, was very much to his liking as he was greatly desirous of reaching important conclusions about the strategy to be adopted to solve India's manifold problems, mainly economic, so that achievement of freedom may be immediately followed by the pursuit of appropriate policies based on conclusions already reached.

Nehru was the chief architect of India's foreign policy in the post-Independence period. A close look at some of the resolutions(drafted by Nehru) adopted by the Congress and his speeches during the pre-Independence period would reveal that Nehru had started applying his mind seriously to free India's foreign policy, from that period itself.

Nehru, through the resolutions that he drafted (on foreign affairs), always emphasised the fact that India wanted to have friendly relations with her neighbours and would not like to participate in any 'imperialist war'. The resolution on the War Danger (Madras Congress, 1927) in part stated: 'The Congress declares that the people of India have no quarrel with their neighbours and desire to live at peace with them'.[2] A resolution passed at the Lucknow Congress (1936) referred to the possibility of 'an imperialist war' and stated: 'In such a war an attempt will inevitably be made to drag in and exploit India to her manifest disadvantage, and for the benefit of British imperialism. The Congress...declares its opposition to the participation of India in any such war'.[3] Similar resolutions were passed at the Faizpur (December 1936), Haripura (1938) and Tripuri (1939) sessions of the Congress.

Even in the pre-Independence period, Nehru was keenly aware of the fact that independent India should necessarily have friendly relations with her neighbours, so that her security may not be jeopardized. In his book Soviet Russia, (actually a collection of articles on Soviet Russia), written after his visit to U.S.S.R. in 1927, Nehru lays stress on the fact India could not afford to ignore Russia 'because she is our neighbour, a powerful neighbour, which may be friendly to us and co-operate with us, or may be a thorn in our side.... We have to know her and understand her and shape our policy accordingly.'[4] It is hardly necessary to point out that India's policy of friendly relations with the U.S.S.R. in the post-freedom period, was considerably motivated by considerations in regard to the perpetuation of India's sovereignty and territorial integrity matters about which Nehru had started thinking almost two decades before India attained her freedom.

Nehru's role vis-a-vis the preparation of the blue-print of free India's policies was three-fold. Firstly, as has already been pointed out, he drafted, moved and got adopted resolutions in Congress sessions, resolutions that would form the basis of independent India's policies. Secondly, while doing so, he had to take care not to precipitate a crisis in the Congress. The Congress, as has been stated earlier in this chapter, was essentially a heterogeneous organization, having within its fold people with divergent views on different matters, and more particularly so on economic matters. Since all such people desired freedom for India and approved of the Congress Programme to achieve it, they had come under the banner of the Congress.

Many of the top leaders of the Congress, like Rajaji, Rajendra Prasad, Vallabhbhai Patel and others did not look with favour at Nehru's efforts to make the Congress accept a programme based on socialistic ideas. Apart from their Rightist moorings, there was a practical consideration also behind their opposition to Nehru's ideas. They felt that the prime objective before the Congress was the one of liberating the country from foreign yoke and that the objective could only be reached by perpetuating the solidarity of the Congress. A talk about socialism, they felt, may result in certain groups withdrawing from the Congress, rendering the Congress less effective.

Nehru on the other hand felt that the Congress will not be able to do anything worthwhile in the post-Independence period unless it committed itself to a certain economic programme in the pre-Independence period itself. It must however be said to Nehru's credit that he did not force the pace of the Congress acceptance of a socialism-oriented programme because that would have resulted in a split in the Congress. Nehru's policy during that period was one of leading the Congress in the direction of socialism, without jeopardizing the unity in the Congress.

Inspite of being a socialist, Nehru retained his identity as a national leader instead of becoming a member of the Congress socialist group in the Congress—one important reason for this policy being his desire to take the Congress as a whole towards the objective of socialism, though he knew the process would inevitably be slow.

Apart from drafting and getting important resolutions passed in the Congress sessions, Nehru constantly spoke and wrote about them so that people may realize the significance of such resolutions. Nehru was conscious of the fact that people take to new ideas very slowly and therefore, he felt that the process of creating a climate for the implementation of socialistic measures in the post-Independence period, should begin in the pre-freedom period. This was the third dimension of his role vis-a-vis the preparation and acceptance of a blue-print of independent India's policies and programme.

Ironically enough, not many amongst the top leaders of the Congress, were conscious of the historic importance of what Nehru was doing. They did not attach much importance to these resolutions, as the contents of these resolutions were not of immediate relevance and they seemed to lack the capacity of projecting their minds into the future in order to sense the requirements of the years to come.

Nehru gave an international dimension to the national movement, which it previously did not possess. He believed that India's battle for freedom, should be waged on the national as well as international plane. Before 1920, the Moderates in the Congress had made repeated attempts to create strong public opinion in England in favour of the demands of the Congress. Nehru, by putting India's demand for freedom on an ideological plane sought support to it from all countries that were wedded to democracy, as also from those which were under foreign domination. As such his strategy covered a wider canvas, as compared to that of the Moderates.

Nehru believed that a simultaneous effort on the part of different colonial countries to throw off their respective foreign yokes would result in the end of imperialism at an earlier date. In 'thirties itself he had expressed the view that India's freedom would be followed by the liberation of other countries in Asia and Africa. In this, he indeed proved very prophetic as future events showed.

Time and again, Nehru raised his voice against the Nazi regime in Germany and the Fascist one in Italy and condemned their anti-democratic actions and imperialistic designs, and also in the case of the former, its intense racialism. He avoided meeting Mussolini in 1936, even when he was assured by Mussolini's personal representative that nothing would appear in the press and that he wanted to see him for a few minutes, just in order to convey personally his condolences at his (Nehru's) wife's death.[5] Again in 1938, Nehru turned down an invitation from the Nazi Government in Germany to visit that country, either as their guest or privately, in his name or incognito.[6] Nehru wanted to have no truck with countries which stood for suppression of individual liberty at home and imperialism abroad, and thus did not look forward to the support of countries like Italy and Germany for India's cause of freedom.

It is possible to argue that Nehru's refusal to have any link with countries which did not stand for democracy resulted in the Indian freedom movement losing the support and sympathy of the people in those countries. However, it should be remembered that Nehru's crusade for the cause of democracy and freedom, won for India, friends in all such countries which stood for democracy, and thus more than compensated for the lack of sympathy for India's cause in Fascist countries, which were the target of Nehru's constant hostile criticism. As a result of the Congress image that Nehru projected on the international plane—the one of an organization which stood as much for democracy as for the freedom of India, eminent persons like President Roosevelt got interested in India's movement for freedom and brought pressure on the British Government to solve the Indian problem.[7]

NEHRU AND THE PRINCELY STATES

The role of Sardar Patel in the consolidation of the newly won freedom, through the integration of the Indian States, has been acclaimed on all sides, and rightly so. However, not many are aware of the very important role played by Nehru in the pre-Independence period, in awakening the people living in the Indian States, through the instrumentality of the All-India States Peoples' Conference.

Nehru was very keen on extending the national movement for freedom beyond British India and into the Indian States, which were extremely backward and had very autocratic rulers. He looked at them as the products of a vicious circle that would ultimately have to go. His was the most important role in shaping the Congress attitude towards the princes and he took the most active part in the All-India States Peoples' Conferences and the struggle for responsible government in the princely domains, for well over fifteen years preceding independence. He was extremely critical of the suppression of even elementary rights of the people by the rulers of the various States and he saw to it that the Congress stood for them. Thus, naturally enough, he did not like the policy fathered by Gandhi—that of non-interference in the internal administration of the States, inspite of the fact that very painful events occurred in the States and Governments of those States made attacks on the Congress, without there being the slightest provocation for them. Apparently, Gandhi did not want the Congress to be critical of the happenings in the States as he feared that it would hurt the rulers and would thus render their conversion more difficult. In a letter that Gandhi wrote to N.C. Kelkar, the President of the States Subjects Conference (July 1934), Gandhi gave expression to his conviction that the policy of non-interference was wise as well as sound as the States were independent entities under British law. The British India had no power to shape the policy of the States and those were as independent of the control of British India as were Afghanistan and Ceylon.[8]

In his letter to N.C. Kelkar, Gandhi further stated that he desired the States to grant autonomy to their subjects and he expressed his hope that the Princes would consider themselves and be in fact trustees for the people, who were their subjects.[9]

Nehru, as already stated, disagreed entirely with Gandhi's approach to the problem of Indian States. He considered Gandhi's view in regard to the legal and constitutional position of the Indian States 'most extraordinary'. He was thus not surprised when exception was taken to Gandhi's views and advice even by the Indian States Peoples' Conference-which was a moderate body on the whole and led by the Liberals.[10]

Gandhi's advice to the rulers of the States to act as trustees for their subjects exasperated Nehru. If there was anything in that idea of trusteeship, Nehru saw no reason as to why anyone should object to

British Government's claim that they were trustees for the Government of India.[11]

It is hardly necessary to stress the fact that but for the continuous and intense efforts of Nehru, there wouldn't have been the necessary measure of awakening in the people residing in the Indian States. The task of Sardar Patel in the post-Independence period was rendered easier because of the pressure that was brought by the people in the Indian States on their respective rulers to accede to the Indian Union-the pressure being the direct result of the efforts made by the Indian States Peoples' Conference—Nehru being the moving spirit behind this organization.

Gandhi, who Nehru had accepted as his master, was a great man and a great political leader. However, many of his political and economic ideas, had little relevance to a modern state. He reacted against the capitalist industrial civilisation of the West as embodied in the big machine. As such, he was opposed to big industries. On the political plane, he talked about a state wedded to non-violence and so on. All this introduced an element of confusion in the minds of the people and in consequence they could not clearly visualize the economic and political set up in a free India. While many of the important leaders of the Congress felt that many of the Gandhian ideas were impracticable, it was Nehru more than anyone else, who publicly disagreed with many ideas of Gandhi on economic and political matters, and tried to place before the people his own ideas on all such matters.

Nehru knew that it was not possible to have a political set up in India, such as the one that Gandhi visualized, in a world that was making rapid strides in the direction of industrial, technological and scientific advancement. At the same time, he was conscious of the fact that some of the Gandhian ideas were peculiarly suited to Indian requirements, whereas a few others needed universal acceptance. As such, Nehru accepted such of the Gandhian ideas as could be profitably fitted in the framework of modernity.

The picture of Independent India that emerged through Nehru's resolutions (moved in Congress sessions), writings and speeches was that of a modern industrialized India, wedded to science and technology. However, he knew the importance and significance of some of the Gandhian ideas, economic, social, political and ethical, and all such basically relevant ideas were woven by him in the fabric of his own thought.

How Nehru tried to put things in perspective by removing the confusion in the minds of the people about Gandhian ideas vis-a-vis Princely States, has already been described in an earlier chapter.[12] In fact, one way of appreciating the role of Nehru is to imagine India with Gandhi and without Nehru. While it is difficult to say as to what would have happened if that had been the case, it is safe to infer that it wouldn't have resulted in that harmonious proportion between the Gandhian ideas and the requirements of the Age of Science and Technology, as was maintained by Nehru.

DOMINIAN STATUS—COMPLETE INDEPENDENCE

One of the controversies in which Nehru played a leading role in the pre-Independence period was that over the issue of Dominion Status versus complete Independence. From the fag-end of 1927 to the end of 1929, Nehru fought a battle royal with his senior colleagues in the Congress, and ultimately made them accept the objective of complete Independence for the country, instead of the one of Dominion Status.

At the Madras session of the Congress (1927), Nehru put forward the resolution on Independence and to his surprise, it was unanimously adopted. However, Nehru had the uncomfortable feeling that the resolution was not understood for what it was or was distorted to mean something else.[13] Gandhi attended the open session of the Congress, but took no part in shaping of policy, that broadly being his attitude in the Congress since the dominance of the Swaraj Party. However, Nehru could sense that Gandhi did not like that resolution.

That Nehru's resolution was not taken seriously became obvious in connection with the adoption of another resolution, through which the Simon Commission was condemned and an appeal was made to boycott it. 'As a corollary to this it was proposed to convene an All Parties Conference, which was to draw up a Constitution for India.'[14] It was not difficult to foresee that this Conference would support the objective of Dominion Status and not that of complete Independence, as the parties invited were known for their moderation.

The All-Parties Conference appointed a sub-committee for the purposes of drafting a constitution and making a full report on the communal issue, with Motilal Nehru as the Chairman. Jawaharlal was not a member of this Committee, but acted as the Secretary of this Committee, which came to be known as the Nehru Committee. The Committee as such, was not bound by the Congress resolution on Independence, and as was anticipated, it supported the objective of Dominion Status, when it submitted its report on the proposed constitution.

It is not necessary to go into the details in regard to subsequent developments. Since Nehru, Subhash and others were greatly agitated over the support for the objective of Dominion Status by the Nehru Report, a resolution was adopted by the Congress at its Calcutta session, which avoided a split in the Congress on the issue of Dominion Status versus complete Independence. This resolution accepted the All-Parties Report 'but intimated that if the British Government did not agree to that constitution within a year, the Congress would revert to Independence.'[15]

The resolution on Independence was unanimously adopted a year later at the Lahore session of the Congress (1929), of which Nehru was the President. Since Nehru was the person who was primarily responsible for committing the Congress to the goal of complete Independence, it becomes necessary to find out as to what considerations prompted him to place this objective, before the nation.

The desirability of the objective of complete Independence for the country, took roots in the mind of Nehru during his sojourn in Europe in 1926-1927. During that period, he got the opportunity of reading a large number of books on current affairs and politics, and also got the time to study carefully the vast political, economic and cultural changes that were taking place in Europe, America and Soviet Russia. As a result of all this, his outlook became wider and he came to the conclusion that achieving independence for the country was only a step in the right direction, and by itself independence would be of little use, unless it was followed by 'social freedom and a socialistic structure of society and the state,'[16] without which neither the individual nor the nation could develop much. Moreover, his study of books and events that were taking place in different parts of the world, convinced him of the fact that India's movement for freedom could not be treated as an isolated phenomenon, but had to be looked at as a part of a wider movement against colonialism and imperialism.

The acceptance of a socialistic structure for the country was, according to Nehru not only desirable from the narrow nationalistic point of view, but also from a global point of view. The acceptance of capitalism instead of socialism not only led to the exploitation of one man by another, one group by another but also to that of one country by another.[17] As such, if India accepted a capitalistic structure, it would itself become an imperialist power sooner or later, as capitalism inevitably led to imperialism.

There were two ways of preventing the growth of imperialism on the international plane. One was to accept a socialistic structure on the national plane and the other was to oppose all countries which stood for imperialism. Nehru opposed the objective of Dominion Status for India because Britain and the self-governing dominions were exploiting India, parts of Africa, Malaya and other parts of the world. By associating itself with imperialist countries thought Nehru, free India would lose all its initiative to work for the liberation of other dependent countries and would in fact be a party to the exploitation of different nations by Britain.

During the course of his speech at the All-Parties Conference at Lucknow (29th August, 1928), Nehru asked the people not to remain under the false impression that Dominion Status would be their's for their asking, whereas independence would be obtained only after struggle or, after an appeal to arms and force. Those Indians, he pointed out, who believed that Dominion Status could be obtained by sweet reasonableness and logic were indeed very credulous. Neither Independence nor Dominion Status would come to India without sanctions, so why shouldn't one strive for the former.[18] The manner in which the Nehru Report was ignored by the British Government proved that Nehru was right in thinking that even Dominion Status wouldn't be obtained without a struggle.

As stated earlier, it was during his sojourn in Europe in 1926-27 that Nehru came to the conclusion that complete independence should be the objective that India should strive to reach. After his return from Europe, he ceaselessly strove to place the national movement in the ideological frame-work of Socialism and complete Independence, because that was the only way in which nationalism and internationalism could be harmoniously blended.

THE 1937 CONTROVERSY

Nehru's refusal to have a Congress-League Coalition ministry in U.P. in 1937, led to a great deal of controversy. Nehru has been held responsible for the immense increase in the power of the League thereafter. In fact, many go to the extent of saying that this mistake of Nehru paved the way for the partition of the country.

Before any attempt is made to deal with this criticism, it becomes absolutely essential to have some idea about the results of the elections that took place in February 1937. Of the 1,585 seats, the Congress won 711 seats.[19] In so far as separate Muslim constituencies were concerned, the Congress contested only 58 seats out of 482, and won 26. In five of the eleven Provinces in British India, the Congress obtained an absolute majority, whereas, it was the largest party in three others. The Muslim League on the other hand succeeded in securing only 51 of the total of 482 seats, reserved for the Muslims in Provincial assemblies. In terms of votes, the Muslim League could secure only 4.8 percent of the total Muslim votes. In none of the four Muslim majority provinces, could the League win a majority of seats.

It is clear from the figures given above that while the Congress did very well at the polls, the League fared very badly. Of course, the Congress also fared badly in so far as the seats reserved for the Muslims were concerned.

According to Kanji Dwarkadas, Jinnah was infuriated by two happenings in 1937; they being (1) the refusal of Nehru to include two Muslim Leaguers in the U.P. Ministry, and (2) Chief Minister, designate of Bombay, B.G. Kher, being taken to task by the Congress high Command particularly by Sardar Patel, for having requested Jinnah to suggest the names of two Muslim Leaguers, who could be included in the Bombay Ministry. 'The arrogance and lack of foresight' of the Congress leaders in July 1937, was, according to Kanji Dwarkadas, one of the reasons for the partition of country in 1947.[20]

The account of 1937 happenings by Kanji Dwarkadas has been given, in order to drive home the fact that Jinnah was sore not only over the happening in U.P. but also over those that took place in Bombay. Whether there was anything to be sore about is yet another matter. And according to Kanji, the person who was primarily responsible for what happened in Bombay was Sardar Patel and not Nehru.

In U.P. the Congress secured an absolute majority in the Provincial Assembly. The Muslim League secured only 26 seats in a House of 228 members. The number of seats obtained by the League would have been smaller still, if it had not been supported by the Jamiat-ul-Ulema-i-Hind. The Jamiat supported the League under the impression that it (the League) would work in co-operation with the Congress in the post-election period.

The leaders of the Muslim League in U.P. at that time were Chandhari Khaliquzzaman and Nawab Ismail Khan. According to Maulana Azad, these leaders expected 'some share' in the new Government. Moreover, according to Maulana, 'the local position was such that neither of them could enter the Government alone. Either both would have to be taken or neither."[21] Maulana held out hopes to them that both would be taken in the Government. However, Nehru did not agree and he wrote to Chandhari Khaliquzzaman and Nawab Ismail Khan that only one of them could be taken in the Ministry, and it was for the Muslim League to decide as to who should be included. Maulana writes that this was a very unwise move on the part of Nehru (who at times 'was apt to be carried away by his feelings'), as'Mr. Jinnah took full advantage of the situation and stated an offensive which led to Pakistan.'[22]

The Maulana however admits that Gandhi approved of Nehru's move! It may be that Nehru was impetuous and was 'carried away by his feelings', but how was it that the cool and calculating Gandhi agreed with Nehru's move! Maulana is discreetly silent on this point.

Now let us subject what Maulana has written, to some close scrutiny. According to the Maulana, because of local conditions, it was not possible for either of them (the two League leaders) to enter the Government alone. Either both would have to be taken or neither.

If this be true (and Maulana should know, as he carried on the negotiations with the League leaders), then it means that the demand for two seats in the Ministry was not based on considerations of adequate representation, but had for its basis, what Maulana calls the 'local position'. This clearly implies that but for the difficulty of 'local position', the League wouldn't have had any objection to only one League member being included in the Ministry. If this was so, did Jinnah's offensive have any genuine basis? If one of the two leaders of the League couldn't get into the Ministry, that was League's headache, with which the Congress was not concerned.

Why did Nehru offer only one seat to the League? The Ministry was to be of seven members and Nehru rightly felt that the League, which had captured only 26 seats out of 228, need not be given more representation. Moreover, Nehru knew the hazards of forming a Ministry with the League, and as such, he was not prepared to increase the League representation in the Ministry. In the context of coalition governments in 1937, Nehru wrote: 'The non-Congress elements were usually politically and socially conservative; some of them were pure careerists. If such elements entered

Government, they might tone down our whole social programme or at any rate obstruct and delay it. There might even be intrigues with the Governor over the heads of the other Ministers.'[23] Years later (1957) Nehru referred to the criticism that the Congress should have achieved greater agreement with the League in U.P. in 1937, and stated that his fear was that the Muslim League in the U.P. being largely a representative of the big zamindars, might prevent land reform and the abolition of landlordism, that he wished the Ministry to carry out.[24]

It must however be remembered that in the Ministry of six formed by the Congress, two were Muslims. Doesn't this mean that they were adequately represented in the Ministry? What real grievance could Jinnah possibly have? How could one accept the preposterous claim of Jinnah that only the members of the Muslim League could be the true representatives of the Muslim community!

The plain fact is that Jinnah was shocked by the extremely miserable performance of the League in the 1937 elections. He was bent upon making a political capital out of every issue that afforded him some chance to do so. If the Congress had agreed to include two League members in the Ministry, these two would have precipitated a crisis on some issue, big or small and would have come out of the Ministry, thus enabling Jinnah to condemn the Congress organization and to bring further notoriety to it, as an organization opposed to Muslim interests.

In fact, the most appropriate method of studying the U.P. or Bombay happenings is to look at them in the context of the Muslim League strategy and tactics for years together, and not in isolation. The bogus charges that were levelled against Congress ministries in regard to the ill-treatment of the Muslims and injustices done to them, were a part of this strategy. Jinnah, since 1937, became acutely aware of the fact that the only way to strengthen the Muslim League was the one of rousing the religious passions of the Muslims and this he would have done sooner or later, coalition in U.P. or no coalition. It is instructive to remember in this connection that neither the Congress resolution of October 1937, which reiterated its attitude towards Minorities and fundamental rights, nor the efforts of Gandhi, Nehru and others to come to some agreement with Jinnah on the communal issue, bore fruit, as Jinnah had made up his mind to derive maximum advantage through the adoption of negative tactics, and through rousing anti-Hindu sentiment in the Muslim masses and by dubbing the Congress as an organization which represented only the Hindus.

SUBHASH BOSE EPISODE OF 1939

Nehru's role in the Subhash Chandra Bose episode of 1939 also assumed a controversial character, and many people even to this day hold the view that Nehru's role during that grave crisis in the Congress was a dubious one and did not do credit to a person of his reputation and stature.

Before Nehru's role in the controversy is subjected to a close scrutiny, it becomes necessary to trace the events that led to that controversy. The trouble started when Subhash Bose, who was the President of the Congress during the year 1938, sought re-election to that post in 1939. Gandhi and some of the important member of the Congress Party, including Nehru, did not like the idea of Subhash Bose seeking re-election to the post of Congress Presidency. They had Azad in mind as the President of the Congress for the year 1939, and when Azad declined that offer, the Congress leaders decided informally, to lend their support to the candidature of Pattabhi Sitaramayya.

The election for Congress Presidentship took place on January 29, 1939, in which Pattabhi Sitaramayya was defeated by Subhash Bose by 95 votes.

A candidate having the support of Gandhi being opposed was in itself an unprecedented event and as such the defeat of that candidate could not but create sensation. It was in a way an unbelievable event, as by implication it meant the defeat of Gandhi, and Gandhi said so in a statement that he issued after the result of the election became known.

A meeting of the (old) Working Committee was scheduled for 22nd February. Subhash Bose, who was ill then, sent a telegram from Calcutta through which he prohibited the Working Committee from transacting even routine business, even that of a procedural nature. Moreover, through a statement he renewed the charge that some members of the Working Committee were giving up their anti-federation stand. The telegram of Subhash Bose, coupled with his charge against some members of the committee in regard to the federation issue, was taken as a vote of no-confidence, and in consequence twelve out of fifteen committee members resigned. The three who remained as member of the committee were Subhash Bose, his brother Sarat Bose and Nehru. However, Nehru issued a separate statement to the effect that he would not serve on the new working committee to be constituted by Subhash Bose.

The annual session of the Congress began at Tripuri on the 7th of March. On 8th March, Pandit Pant moved a resolution (which had the support of 160 delegates) through which (apart from other matters), a request was made to the President to appoint the Working Committee in accordance with the wishes of Gandhiji. After two days of heated discussion, the resolution was passed in the Subjects Committee.

The crisis deepened in the subsequent days and it finally led to the resignation of Subhash Bose as the Congress President. This is in brief the unfortunate Subhash Bose episode of 1939. Nehru's role during this very grave crisis in the history of the Congress should now be examined in the light of the facts mentioned above and the criticisms to which it was subjected.

The criticism of Nehru's role by people was based on one or more of the following views: (1) Nehru being a democratic socialist like Subhash, should have thrown his lot with Subhash, (2) Nehru did not support Subhash, because he could not go against Gandhi's wishes to who he owed his position (atleast partly) in Indian politics, and (3) Subhash was Nehru's strongest rival and this unspoken rivalry was responsible for Nehru's dubious role in the controversy.

How far was this criticism justified or, whether it was justified at all, could be ascertained, firstly, by carefully examining all relevant facts, and secondly, by finding out as to whether Nehru's role during this controversy was consistent with his approach to issues on which there was a threat of a split in the Congress, in the previous years.

The first thing that should be remembered in this connection is that Subhash Bose had decided to seek re-election inspite of his knowing the fact that Nehru along with most other top leaders of the Congress, was opposed to the idea of his seeking re-election to the Congress Presidentship. How could Subhash or for that matter his supporters expect sympathy and support for Subhash from Nehru and others, after Subhash had taken a decision against their wishes? Even then the role of Nehru during this crisis was far from being antagonistic towards Subhash; in fact, it was helpful, as we shall find out later.

Why did Nehru oppose the idea of Subhash Bose becoming the Congress President again? Nehru's long letter to Subhash Bose dated April 3, 1939, is very important in this respect, as it spells out the reasons for his opposition to the re-election of Subhash as the Congress President. It also throws light on the efforts made by Nehru to prevent a crisis in the Congress.

Briefly, Nehru was opposed to Subhash standing for election, for the following reasons: (1) In those circumstances, it would have meant a break with Gandhi, which Nehru felt, should not take place. (2) It would have meant a set-back for the real Left, as the Left was not strong enough to shoulder the burden by itself and in the event of a real contest in the Congress it would have suffered a defeat and then there would have been a reaction against it. (3) Subhash did not wholly approve of the condemnation by Nehru and others of Nazi Germany and Fascist Italy and may have tried to take the Congress in a direction in which it should not have gone. (4) Subhash did not even stand for definite leftist principles and policies,[25] something which would have made his decision understandable.

The reasons mentioned above need some elaboration. From 1920 onwards, the only person capable of launching an effective movement at the right psychological moment was Gandhi. It would not have been possible for the Leftist group in the Congress to push out Gandhi and others from the Congress, and any such attempt on the part of the Leftists would have very adversely affected the future of this group. Moreover, Subhash hardly had any plan with him that was distinctively leftist in content. In fact Nehru himself was interested in knowing as to where exactly Subhash differed with others. In his letter to Subhash Bose, dated 4th February 1939, Nehru asked Subhash whether his views were at variance from those of his colleagues on the states question or the Hindu-Muslim question or for that matter the question of Kisans and the workers.[26] The implication of this question was clear, it being that Subhash had no distinct policies of his own, and that he could as well have avoided the controversy by not seeking re-election. Probably Nehru had all this in mind when he stated (while giving the reasons for his opposition to the idea of Subhash Bose seeking re-election), 'I felt all along that you were far too keen on re-election....It did distress me for I felt that you had a big enough position to be above this kind of a thing'.[27]

At the time of the Presidential election for the Tripuri Congress, war clouds had started gathering on the horizon. Nehru was very desirous of forming an Anti-Imperialist Front and was more keen than ever about projecting the image of India as a country whose people were wedded to the ideal of democracy. Bose as the Congress President thought Nehru might say and do things which would distort the image of India that Nehru was slowly trying to build up. As such, Nehru was not happy at the idea of Bose becoming the Congress President again.

When twelve out of the fifteen members of the Working Committee decided to resign (the reasons for their precipitate step have already been mentioned), Nehru for two long days tried to persuade the members, to take a far less extreme position than the one taken up by them.[28] However, Nehru's marathon efforts did not bear any fruit.

It is also necessary to know the history behind Pandit Pant's resolution. Nehru was asked to draft a resolution (by Patel, Rajen Babu and others) for the A.I.C.C. expressing confidence in the old Working Committee and in Gandhi's leadership and policy. Nehru drafted a resolution to that effect but he also made it clear to his colleagues that he did not agree with the view-point expressed therein. The resolution drafted by Nehru was not approved and later another resolution was drafted by Rajen Babu and others which was longer and amended one. Nehru tried his level best to make such changes in the resolution as would end an episode and a controversy, but he did not succeed.[29] It is also interesting to know that there was no reference in the resolution drafted by Nehru (on the lines suggested by his colleagues) to the Working Committee being formed as per the wishes of Gandhi.[30]

Nehru, as had been mentioned earlier, did not resign from the Working Committee as twelve of his colleagues did, but nevertheless announced that he would not serve on the new Working Committee. Why did Nehru take such an enigmatic stand? The reason was simple enough, though his act was mistaken for one of deliberate non-cooperation with Subhash. Nehru did not resign with others because he entirely disagreed with the approach of his colleagues. And he announced his decision not to serve on the new Working Committee because during those circumstances (the details have already been given above), it was not possible for Nehru to offer his co-operation to Subhash.[31] While Nehru felt unhappy at the thought that he was not in a position to co-operate with Subhash, he felt unhappier still at the thought that his refusal to resign with his colleagues had resulted in his breaking away from them, thus bringing to an end a chapter of long and continuous association.[32]

In the light of the above facts, it is not necessary to deal with the criticism that Nehru did not support Subhash because thereby he would have lost the sympathy and support of Gandhi, and that would have affected his position very adversely or, for that matter with the criticism that Nehru's dubious role during that period was a result of the alleged rivalry between Subhash and Nehru. It should be very clear, from the facts mentioned above that in those circumstances, on balance, Nehru's stand was correct and logical.

However, to keep the record straight, we may as well deal with those two matters. It should be borne in mind that Nehru had a big enough position in the country in his own right, and that Gandhi valued Nehru's support almost as much as Nehru valued Gandhi's. In the event of basic differences Nehru was capable of taking a stand opposite to that of Gandhi, as was proved at the time of the Dominion Status versus complete Independence controversy. A certain passage in a letter (to Nehru) by Subhash Bose himself serves the purpose of refuting the criticism against Nehru, based on view-point two and three. In a letter to Nehru from Europe dated March 4, 1936, Subhash Bose stated: 'Among the front rank leaders of today you are the only one to whom we can look up to for leading the Congress in a progressive direction. Moreover, your position is unique and I think that even Mahatma Gandhi will be more accommodating towards you than towards anybody else. I earnestly hope that you will fully utilise the strength of your public position in making decisions....Gandhiji will never take a stand which will alienate you.'[33] Again, in the book 'The Indian Struggle', Subhash Bose stated: 'In a certain sense, his (Nehru's) position was stronger than that of Mahatma Gandhi, because he had the support of the entire left which Gandhi had not'.[34] The passages quoted above would prove beyond doubt as to where Subhash stood vis-a-vis Nehru. They also provide an answer to the criticism that Nehru did not support Subhash because he would have lost Gandhi's support and that would have jeopardized his public position.

Nehru's role in the Subhash Bose episode has now, been examined in the context of all relevant facts and the criticism to which it was subjected. Now the only matter which remains to be discussed is about the nature of Nehru's role during this crisis, and whether it was consistent with his role on earlier occasions when there was a threat of split in the Congress.

During this crisis Nehru did his best to straighten out matters in the larger interests of the party and the nation. Repeatedly, he asked Subhash to have a free and frank talk with Gandhi on various matters, so that it may result in rapproachment between the two. Moreover, he wrote letters to Gandhi also, requesting him to follow a conciliatory policy. In one of his letters to Gandhi, dated April 17, 1939, Nehru stated: 'I think now, as I thought in Delhi, that you should accept Subhash as President.'[35]

Even after the Tripuri Congress, Subhash considered Nehru his well wisher and sought advice from him. In his letter to Nehru, dated April 15, 1939, Subhash stated: 'Will it be possible for you to run up here for a few hours? We could then have a talk and I could have your advice as to how to proceed next.'[36]

Nehru's role during this crisis was entirely in line with his role on similar occasions in the past. He always attached great importance to party unity and whenever it was threatened, he tried to bring about a compromise between the rival groups in the Congress, and if the crisis was threatened because of him, he never allowed matters to reach a breaking point.

In 1923, Nehru played a key role in working out the compromise solution, intended to keep the no-changers and the pro-changers in the Congress together. Since that year, on several occasions later, Nehru either played the role of a mediator between two warring factions in the Congress or, took up the work of evolving a formula which would reflect the consensus in the Congress High Command. In fact, even after Independence, Nehru continued to act as a mediator, this time on the international plane, so that quarrels between nations may not affect world peace.

In view of the fact that throughout his political life, Nehru considered unity in the Congress as of paramount importance and strove to perpetuate it, his role during the Subhash Bose episode becomes wholly understandable. If party unity had been threatened because of some person other than Subhash there is no doubt about the fact that Nehru would have acted similarly.

Thus, we can safely conclude that Nehru's actions during the early 1939 crisis in the Congress were motivated by considerations regarding unity in the Congress and advance in the right direction, and not by considerations pertaining to self-aggrandizement.

NOTES

1. *Nehru, the First Sixty Years*, Dorothy Norman, Vol. I, Asia Publishing House, Bombay, 1965 (Text of the Karachi Resolution given on pp. 249-50).
2. Ibid., p. 142.
3. Ibid p. 447.
4. Ibid., p. 130.

5. *The Discovery of India*, Jawaharlal Nehru, Signet Press, Calcutta-20,Fourth Printing, September 1948, p. 28.
6. Ibid., loc. cit.
7. *History of the Freedom Movement in India*, Vol. III, R.C. Majumdar, Firma, K.L. Mukhopadhyay, Calcutta 1963,
8. *An Autobiography*, Jawaharlal Nehru, The Bodley Head, London, 1953, p.532.
9. Ibid., p. 533.
10. Ibid., p. 533, loc. cit.
11. Ibid., p. 532.
12. The reference is to Acharya Kripalani's question to Nehru (in the Indian Parliament), as to whether non-violence was the 'creed' of the nation and Nehru's answer to that question. (Jawaharlal Nehru Speeches, Vol. III, March 1953 - August 1957, p. 382.
13. *An Autobiography*, Jawaharlal Nehru, The Bodley Head, London, 1953, p. 167.
14. Ibid., loc. cit.
15. Ibid., pp, 183-186.
16. Ibid., p. 166.
17. Presidential Address, Punjab provincial Conference, April 11, 1928. (Nehru—The First Sixty Years, Volume I, Dorothy Norman, Asia Publishing House, Bombay, 1965, p. 157).
18. Important Speeches of Jawaharlal Nehru—1922 to 1945, Edited by Jagat S. Bright, The Indian Printing Works, Kacheri Road, Lahore, 1945,pp. 106-107.
19. The Congress success was more impressive than what the figures indicate because out of 1585, only 657 were 'General' or open seats, others were reserved seats.
20. *India's Fight for Freedom*, 1913-1937, Kanji Dwarkadas, Popular Prakashan, Bombay, 1938, pp. 466-467.
21. *India Wins Freedom*, Maulana Abul Kalam Azad, Indian Printing Works, Calcutta 13, Orient Longman Private Ltd, India, 1959, pp. 160-161.
22. Ibid., loc. cit.
23. *The Discovery of India*, Jawaharlal Nehru, Signet Press, Calcutta-20, Fourth Printing, September 1948, p. 320.
24. Indiagram, No. 27 (Feb. 1959), p. 1.
25. A Bunch of Old Letters, Jawaharlal Nehru, Asia Publishing House, Bombay, 1958, pp. 356 357.
26. Ibid., p.319.
27. Ibid., p.357.
28. Ibid., p.353.
29. Ibid., pp. 359-360.
30. Ibid p. 359.
31. Ibid., p. 355.
32. Ibid., loc. cit.
33. Ibid. p. 172.
34. *The Indian Struggle, 1920-1942*, Subhash Chandra Bose, Asia Publishing House, Bombay, 1964, p. 330.
35. *A Bunch of Old Letters*, Jawaharlal Nehru, Asia Publishing House, Bombay, 1958, p. 380.
36. Ibid., p. 378.

8

POLICIES AND DECISIONS IN PERSPECTIVE (II)

[*Note:* This chapter deals with Nehru's views on the changing concept of Democracy, his policy of non-alignment and his decision to continue India's association with the Commonwealth. It also attempts to throw light on his controversial Kashmir and China policy. Nehru's role as an administrator has also been discussed in this chapter.]

THE CHANGING CONCEPT OF DEMOCRACY

As stated in the concluding part of Chapter V, Nehru was accused of leading the country towards totalitarianism after the resolutions on 'Socialistic Pattern of Society' and 'the Co-operative Farming', were passed by the Congress at its Avadi (1955) and Nagpur (1959) sessions respectively.

How far was this criticism justified? It was extremely difficult to believe that Nehru, whose faith and respect for individual freedom was so great, would follow a policy which would result in its total negation. As for the criticism that the sphere of individual liberty was shrinking, due to the corresponding increase in the domain of state activity, we would have to join Nehru first in his survey of 19th century Democracy, in order to understand and appreciate his socialistic policies.

In early 19th century, after the fall of Napoleon, almost everywhere in Europe there took place the repression of the liberty elements. During those years there was little liberty in any European country. In some of those countries there was the king's despotism, whereas in some others, like England, a small aristocratic and rich class was in power. In those circumstances and set of conditions it was but natural that Democracy was considered the remedy for the ills and troubles of the state as well as the people. Thus, in the 19th century, Democracy was a reaction against autocracy and other despotisms. And yet when Democracy finally came, people found out that rights and liberties did not go very far in ensuring happiness; however good and desirable individual freedom might be, it couldn't by itself bring happiness. In other words, the people realized that individual freedom was not an end in itself but a means towards an end, the end being the progress and prosperity of the individual. The right to vote was of little importance to a person who was hungry. Moreover, the extent of his liberty was negligible as, it was possible to purchase his vote or services for the price of a meal. Thus, Democracy in the 19th century, with its excessive emphasis on individual freedom had no solution for the industrial problems that were arising or for those of poverty and class conflict. It laid emphasis on the freedom of each individual to choose a vocation in accordance with his inclination and aptitude so that he might better himself in different ways, and if that happened, society as a whole would obviously progress. But this doctrine of Laissez-Faire failed because the person who was forced to work for a wage was not free in any sense of the word.[1]

Under the system of industrial capitalism, there were no comforts for the factory workers, who were very inadequately paid and remained poor in spite of serving the community. It resulted on the one hand in the labourers becoming very poor and on the other in the coming into existence of a class which lived on industry without working in it. The owners of the industry became very rich and the workers very poor as time passed on and this compelled some earnest people to think of a solution to the problem which was getting worse every day. The solution came in the form of a set of ideas which came to be known as socialism.[2]

Industrialism powerfully affected the people of England and drove them from land to the factories. The factory workers had to live in extremely insanitary conditions; their houses were usually near the coal fields, almost like huts or sometimes even worse. The conditions in factories were appalling and what was worse was that women and small children were made to work for long hours. When attempts were made to improve factory conditions, by legislation the factory owners put up a stout fight against such legislation on the ground, that, it amounted to a 'shameful interference' with the rights of property.[3]

The ideas in regard to individual, freedom which were a reaction against the autocratic rule of kings and governments of the eighteenth century, proved somewhat detrimental to the interests of the society as a whole and led to many complications. The statements in regard to the rights of individuals 'erred somewhat on the other side'. The interest of an individual and that of society might clash and it was not an easy matter in a complex society to give perfect freedom to the individuals by separating them. The democrats in the nineteenth century were full of ideas in regard to liberty, equality and equal right to happiness in case of every person. 'But they realized soon that happiness did not come by merely making it a fundamental right. Apart from other things a certain measure of physical well-being was necessary. A person who was starving was not likely to be happy. This led them to think that happiness depended on a better distribution of wealth among the people.'[4]

So, inevitably people arrived at the conclusion that though individual freedom was very desirable, it could never be an end in itself but only a means towards the end of the development of an individual's personality and happiness. This in its turn meant that if too much of it (individual freedom) affected adversely the end in view, it was better to compromise a little with individual liberty and allow the state to promote social good, which was after all the sum total of individual good. In no country could democracy be real unless the economic standards of the people were satisfactory and that could be ensured by greater governmental functioning.

The peaceful way of progress was in the ultimate analysis a democratic way of progress. In the context of the ultimate aim of democratic thought it was not enough if the right to vote was given to an individual and everything else was left to look after itself. The ultimate aim should not be lost sight of the one of economic democracy, which implied ending the differences between the rich and the poor and between those who had opportunities and those who had either very few or no opportunities at all.[5]

As stated earlier, some important leaders in India were expressing their apprehensions about the future of democracy in the country, in the context of Nehru's socialism. Nehru's reply to those oft repeated apprehensions could as well have been his own words in the *Glimpses of World History*. Referring to persons whose ideal of individual freedom was the 19th century declarations in regard to rights of individuals, Nehru had stated: 'In India today, many of our advanced politicians still talk in terms of the French Revolution and the Rights of Man, not appreciating that much has happened since then.'[6]

In the context of the conditions in India then, the socialistic approach to problems had become imperative and though India had accepted parliamentary type of democracy, it was no longer possible for her to be governed by the 19th century ideas of democracy. India believed in civil liberties and she also desired to progress rapidly so that economic and other disparities could be removed in the shortest possible time. The disparities in India, thought Nehru, would increase if the capitalist approach was followed, and that was the reason as to why the socialist approach had to be accepted.[7] The Socialist approach according to Nehru was not incompatible with democracy in anyway. It was always possible to give the people a large measure of freedom even in the socialist set up. In fact, in a socialistic democracy individual freedom had real content though it might result in the enlargement of governmental sphere to a certain extent. The individuals in the socialist society could have freedom of conscience of enterprise and even that of possessing private property on a restricted scale.[8]

Though the enlargement of the sphere of governmental activity might be desirable and necessary in the context of Indian conditions then, was it not likely that if left unchecked this trend might result in the usurpation of the sphere of individual freedom by the Government. It was very essential to know as to what Nehru's views were on this very vital and all important question. In one of the two lengthy interviews with Nehru that I was privileged to have, I had asked him as to what according to him was the line of demarcation between individual liberty and governmental action. Nehru very promptly replied 'no such line could be drawn'. He elaborated his comment by stating that it depended on the set of circumstances in which any such issue came up before the state. He further pointed out that in the world of today, it was not possible to do away with centrailized authority, which of course resulted in a slight encroachment on individual liberty. And yet, every endeavour should be made to strike a balance between the two, so that the people in a country might enjoy individual freedom inspite of the centralized authority.

When asked about the criticism that was being levelled against him about India going the totalitarian way under his leadership, Nehru deplored the fact that his critics were ignorant of the modern international trend which was neither totalitarian in nature nor of the *laissez-faire* variety of the 19th century. He further pointed out that the world trend today was a via media between the *laissez-faire* of the 19th century and totalitarianism as represented by some countries in the twentieth century; as the evils of both these extremes had been realized by people in different countries. Nehru then gave the examples of the U.S.A. and the U.S.S.R. and pointed out that in the former, which was essentially a democratic country, the sphere of state action was progressively enlarging, whereas in the latter (a totalitarian country) a gradual relaxation of the governmental hold over the people was noticeable.[9]

In a totalitarian set up the individual was sacrificed at the altar of the State; the individual therein was for the State and not the state for the individual. Nehru was very allergic to the idea of a state, wherein the individual lost his identity and became a mere tool in the hands of the state. He believed implicitly in the view that the state was intended primarily to advance the welfare of the individual; at the same time he was also aware of the fact that the individual could not be looked at in isolation and that his obligations to the society should correspond with his rights.[10]

There were no hard and fast rules in regard to the obligations of a state to the individual and vice versa. They must have undergone changes in different periods of history. The earliest state was the one which merely performed the duty of protecting the people of that area from another tribe. Then the world had what was known as a police state. A police state took upon itself the duties of maintaining law and order in the state, protecting the country from foreign aggression and of collecting taxes from the people so as to carry on the administration. In all other matters, the individuals and the groups were left to themselves. The modern state was supposed to do far more. It had to do all those things which were conducive to the growth, progress and happiness of the people living in it. Obviously, when the state did more and more for the individual, the obligations of the individuals to the state also increased. Thus, the rights and the obligations of the individuals living in a state would always go together. If there was a proper integration between the individual and the state, conflicts did not arise but if it was otherwise, it led to many undesirable consequences. Since the modern state considered it to be its duty to work for the overall progress and the happiness of its subjects, its authority was increasingly becoming more and more centralized. Thus, 'the deep problem of, today ... is this: you cannot escape centralized authority, whether it is of the state, whether it is of the big corporation, whether it is of the trade union, or whether it is of any group. They all go on being centralized authorities. Now all centralization is a slight encroachment on the freedom of the individual, and at the same time we cannot escape centralization in modern society. How to balance the two'?[11] Since it was not possible to do away with a large measure of centralization, an effort should be made to limit centralization to the minimum extent and bring about de-centralization in the rest as far as possible.[12]

Since Nehru was fully alive to the dangers of over-centralization of authority, he was very keen on formulating policies in such a way as to strike a balance between centralization and de-centralization. In a country like India, where private resources were not great any project had to be a state project. The river valley schemes in India could not but be state schemes as they could not be taken up by private bodies. A very big project had to be owned either by the state alone or jointly with private enterprise, with some measure of control over it by the former, while leaving a large field for the latter. Thus, there was a public sector of India's economy and a private sector, and also a third one where those two overlapped. So Indian economy had three branches, without any rigid lines of demarcation between them and it was to be seen as to which functioned better. The approach to India's economy was experimental and not dogmatic in any way.[13]

Apart from the efforts that Nehru was making to balance centralization with de-centralization, was there any guarantee of the country not going the totalitarian way? Nehru desired that the answer to the question should be sought in the Constitution of India. So far as the political rights of the individual were concerned, the Indian Constitution had gone as far as any Constitution could go, in order to safeguard them.[14]

Thus, the way that Nehru advocated for India's progress and prosperity was that of democratic socialism and not that of capitalism or communism. In fact, India showed to the world that the issues of production and distribution could be approached not merely through the two methods of capitalist democracy and communism but also through a third one, which took the best from all systems and created something that was in harmony with one's history and philosophy and was suited to the requirements of the country.[15]

It could safely be concluded that Nehru was very eager to function in the framework of democracy and that his policies were far removed from totalitarian policies. His socialistic policies were very firmly rooted in the soil of democracy and drew their sustenance from those firmly established roots. Thus, it could be safely asserted that the apprehensions in regard to the future of democracy in India had no real grounds as they were based on an inadequate understanding of the present day problems of the country and the strategy needed for their solution. Moreover, Nehru's critics seemed to lose sight of the fact that the concept of democracy was a dynamic one and was constantly adapting itself to the needs of changed circumstances. It was not wholly realized that if India did not go the socialist way and solve her basic problems quickly enough, there was every possibility of the Indian people rejecting the democratic pattern and opting for a totalitarian one, because in the eventuality of the people being left with a choice between food and freedom (individual freedom), they might probably choose food rather than starve in freedom.

According to Nehru, democracies failed in the newly independent Asian countries because political democracy preceded economic democracy in Asia. In Europe on the other hand, economic democracy came first and political democracy next. Democratic Governments toppled down in various Asian countries because the challenge of solving the economic problems proved too great for them. Thus, what happened in other countries of Asia served as a warning to India and called for an early solution of its economic problems. And if problems were to be solved quickly enough, before totalitarianism caught up with India, it would have to follow the path of democratic socialism.[16]

Paradoxically enough, while some of Nehru's political opponents criticised him for his so called totalitarian policies, many eminent persons in India and elsewhere paid rich tributes to Nehru for working in the framework of democracy when (with his vast popularity) he could easily have become a dictator Nehru didn't entirely deserve this compliment, firstly, because he couldn't have become a dictator without losing face with the entire world, because he had championed the cause of democracy day in and day out during the pre-Independence period. In fact, the outside world knew Nehru as much as a democrat as a crusader for his country's freedom. Secondly, Nehru did not have within him the makings of a dictator. He was too human and civilized to function as a dictator, and be ruthless as any dictator. As such, his role as a democratic leader was in entire harmony with his past pronouncements and his mental makeup. Hence, let us not give credit to Nehru for not doing something which he couldn't have done.

NEHRU AS AN ADMINISTRATOR

While criticising Nehru's role as a Prime Minister many people have put forward the view that Nehru was not a good administrator. While seeking an answer to the question as to whether Nehru was a good administrator, we must bear in mind the important fact that the common yardstick applied to measure the competence of an administrator cannot be wholly made applicable to a Prime Minister whose work has many more dimensions than that of an administrator at a lower level. Moreover, if a person happens to be the first Prime Minister of a newly independent country, it becomes all the more necessary to consider his role as an administrator in the broader framework of his role as a statesman.

The Prime Minister of a country, more so of a newly independent country, should have before his mind's eye, a very clear picture of the real nature of the problems with which his country is faced and the manner in which those problems have to be solved. Moreover, in the context of the country's past (recent and remote), and its present, he should know exactly the direction in which his country should be taken. He should also have the vision to foresee the possible effects of international trends on the social, political and economic life in his country. All this implies that the Prime Minister should know a great deal about his country's past and present, as also about, international currents and cross-currents, in order to chalk out policies, which are advantageous to his country.

Nehru possessed these pre-requisites in a large measure. As has already been stated in the previous chapter, Nehru started applying, his mind seriously to India's problems, almost from the beginning of his political career. As such, in due course of time, Nehru came to have a very clear idea about the problems of India and the manner in which they should be solved. His profound knowledge of history and the developments that were taking place on the international plane not only enabled him to see India's problems in perspective but also made him eminently suitable for the Prime Ministership of the country.

Nehru thus possessed one very important pre-requisite of a good administrator at his level, the one of thorough acquaintance with the basic problems of his country and the knowledge about the strategy to be adopted for their solution.

A clear perception of what should be done, how and when is an important ingredient of administrative ability, and that comes to a person through a long-standing acquaintance with the problems that he is called upon to solve. Nehru's knowledge of India's problems was so intimate and profound that there was hardly any question of his not understanding them or following wrong methods for their solution. Moreover, he brought to bear upon his work so much of enthusiasm and energy that he rarely failed to inspire those who worked with him or under him.

On basic issues, Nehru had made up his mind even before Independence, and as such there was no question of his wavering or being in two minds over them. In fact, on all basic issues Nehru stood like a rock and did not budge a single inch. It was only on smaller issues that he seemed to waver, primarily because of the intellectual in him, which took note of the good in every point of view.

In so far as day to day administrative work is concerned, it is on record that his notes on the files were always precise and clear and his capacity to dispose of files was something out of the ordinary. His capacity to work very hard in order not to keep any work in pending is too well-known to need any elaborate mention. This is what M.C. Chagla has to say about Nehru as an administrator in his excellent autobiography entitled Roses in December. Chagla states—'I might mention here that Nehru never left his table till about one or two in the morning. Every file which was placed before him was disposed of and every letter that had to be replied to was dictated to his stenographer before lights were switched off. I wrote several letters to him, and I always found that the reply was dictated the day he received the letter. **People do not realize that he was a first-class administrator**. (Emphasis mine)He gave his full mind to the problem in hand, made his decisions, and put it out of his mind, and turned to another which was also dealt with, with the same vigour and precision.'[17a]

As the custodian of India's newly won independence, Nehru could not but be cautious in his decisions, especially those which had a bearing on India's sovereignty and territorial integrity. Obviously, no Prime Minister of a newly independent country can afford to take decisions, which even remotely endanger the hard won freedom.

Nehru's position being pre-eminent in the Indian Government, no important decision could ever be taken against his wishes. This simple fact needs to be stressed in view of the fact that people, while giving credit to Sardar Patel for the Police Action against Hyderabad, talk in such a way as to suggest that Patel was solely and wholly responsible for the Police Action against Hyderabad and that Nehru did not approve of it. A more elaborate mention of this point has been made in one of the subsequent paragraphs.

As stated earlier, Nehru's role as an administrator should be looked at in the larger framework of Nehru's role as the head of a newly independent country's government. He had to perform the delicate and difficult duty of nourishing the tender plant of infant democracy, so that it may grow into a strong and sturdy tree. Nothing can be more unjust to Nehru than an attempt on our part to assess his role as an administrator, by applying the criteria that are normally applied to measure the administrative ability of an executive. A person who takes the country in the right direction, who knows exactly as to what the needs of the country are and how those needs have to be met, and who lays down traditions of immense value is entitled to be considered as a great statesman. Nehru was one such statesman. As such, his work must necessarily be viewed in the context of larger issues and on the back drop of a wider canvass and certainly not in the context of a rigid and narrow definition of a good administrator.

THE RATIONALE BEHIND INDIA'S POLICY OF NON-ALIGNMENT

India's foreign policy, of which Jawaharlal Nehru was the chief architect, revealed a harmonious blending of nationalism with internationalism and pragmatism with idealism. As the first Prime Minister of a free India and as one who had spent the greater part of his life in struggling for the emancipation of his country, Nehru was naturally very anxious to pursue a policy, which would be conducive to the consolidation of the newly won freedom, and to the progress and advancement of the people. And yet, Nehru was not moved to action only on pragmatic considerations. Since Independence, he had striven hard for the preservation of world peace (for India's benefit as also for the good of the entire world) and the liberation of those countries which were still under foreign domination and had consistently raised his voice against all those acts which had resulted in the denial of justice or compromise with liberty.

Ironically enough, inspite of India's efforts to maintain peace and harmony among various nations, its policy of non-alignment had been mistaken by many (in the Western countries) as one of opportunism and 'sitting on the fence'. The people in those countries could not understand Nehru's persistent refusal to line up with the democratic countries of the world in their crusade against world communism. They either mistook India's policy of non-alignment for opportunism or started wondering as to whether Nehru was a 'fellow traveller' or a communist at heart, inspite of his off repeated declaration in favour of a democratic way of life. This confusion in the minds of the western people was a result of an inadequate understanding of the motivating factors that governed the foreign policy of India, a newly independent Asian nation, which symbolised the problems, aspirations, apprehensions and urges of resurgent Asia.

In order to understand India's policy of non-alignment, one must analyse very carefully the motivating factors behind it. It had already been stated in Chapter IV that Nehru was opposed to the communist method, and the communist way of life; it then became a very pertinent question as to why Nehru was opposed to India's joining the Anglo-American bloc and contribute thereby to the efforts of the democracies of the world to check the spread of communism on the international plane. The nations belonging to that bloc desperately believed that communist influence should be countered at home as well as abroad, as any growth in the communist strength on the international plane, would very adversely affect the future of democracy in the world. Nehru's insistence on following a policy of non-alignment, therefore, made the West wonder as to whether he was really wedded to the ideals of democracy and freedom. Those in the West who did not question the *bona-fides* of India's intentions, at least had serious doubts about the wisdom of India pursuing a policy of non-alignment, which (according to them) would adversely affect Indian democracy and Indian interests in the long run.

The dilemma of Nehru's attitude towards Soviet Russia vis-a-vis United States of America, could be resolved if answers were provided to three basic questions that were so often posed by the people of the West. The three questions were, (1) why did India follow a policy of non-alignment when she believed in a democratic way of life? The suggestion implied in that question being that India should line up with the other democratic countries of the world and contribute towards the cause of, making the world safe for Democracy. (2) Why did Nehru actively oppose the steps that were being taken by the West (by way of treaties, pacts, etc.) to arrest the spread of communism in Asia? and (3) Why was India's tone softer towards Soviet Russia as compared to America, when ideologically, India's proximity was greater to the latter?

The urges that prompted Nehru to adhere to a policy of non-alignment inspite of diverse pressures, needed sympathetic understanding and serious consideration as they represented the mind of a nationalist who was striving to reconcile national with international interests and mirrored the hopes and fears of resurgent Asia.

The foreign policy of any country, like its internal policy, was directed primarily to the cause of promoting the interests of its people and India was no exception to it. It was necessarily conditioned by its past, (recent and remote), its geographical situation, considerations of strategy and defence, the values cherished by its people and above all by the contemporary national and international situation. Speaking about India's foreign policy, Nehru said in the Parliament, 'I have often ventured to point out, in this House, that the policy we are pursuing...was a policy which flowed from our historical as well as recent past, from our national movement and from the various ideas that we have proclaimed from time to time.'[17b] The policy to which Nehru made a reference, could be broadly termed as the policy of 'non-alignment', i.e., the policy of keeping away from the power blocs and working for world peace. That policy, according to Nehru, was not only consistent with India's traditions, but was also conducive to the country's immediate needs and interests. 'If the House considers other, different but, nevertheless, comparable countries and situations, it will realize that since India has to guard her newly won independence and solve many problems, that have accumulated in the past, it becomes inevitable that she should follow a policy that will help as best as it can to maintain world peace and also avoid as far as possible entanglements in world conflicts'.[18]

Thus, one very important consideration that prompted India to follow a policy of non-alignment was her intense desire to solve her problems in the shortest possible time. That could be done only when, (1) the freedom of the country was not compromised with, and (2) when world peace was not affected. Thus, Nehru strove for world peace, not only because idealism prompted him to do so but also because only the continuance of world peace could ensure the success of the various steps that were being taken by India, for the advancement and progress of her people. And the one thing that enabled India (and of course Nehru on her behalf) to work for the preservation of world peace was her policy of non-alignment. In a speech delivered in March 1949, Nehru said: 'We do not want war anywhere. We want at least 10-15 years of peace in order to be able to develop our resources'.[19] Thus, it had become absolutely essential for India to work for world peace even on very practical and pragmatic considerations, because in the narrow contracting world of these days, war peace and freedom had become indivisible. Thus, a government in any country in the context of modern conditions, should not rest content with maintaining peace within its borders, but should also make every endeavour to contribute to the maintenance of world peace.[20]

The policy that was being pursued by India since independence might also be termed as a policy of 'enlightened self interest' since it aimed at the promotion of India's welfare, while taking into account the interests of other countries also. For a country like India, which achieved independence a short time earlier and which was full of its own problems that needed immediate attention, a policy of non-alignment in world affairs was a natural policy. The United States of America, which was somewhat critical of India's policy of keeping away from the so called world struggle between communism and democracy, had itself followed a policy of non-entanglement in European affairs after it had attained its independence. That was a period when the western world was breaking up as a consequence of imperialist and revolutionary wars. Those upheavals did affect the United States and still it chose to avoid involvement in that chaotic situation of Europe, as that was a natural thing for a newly independent nation to do. It must be remembered in this connection that the United States remained aloof from what was going on in Europe, inspite of its particular sympathies. The example of U.S.A. should be borne in mind while arriving at any conclusion in regard to India's policy of non-alignment.[21]

If India advocated world peace and worked incessantly for it, she did so, not merely because the continuance of world peace had bearing on India's progress and advancement, but also because the progress and welfare of the humanity as a whole, depended on it. Peace was not only an absolute necessity for people in India in order to progress and develop but it was also of vital importance to the world, and world peace could be preserved not by talking and preparing for war, but by striving for it. The foreign policy of India thus had for its end, not only the good of the Indian people but that of the people all over the world.

The resolution moved by Nehru on the midnight of August 14, 1947 in the Constituent Assembly, requesting its members to dedicate themselves to the service of India and the world, bore an eloquent testimony to Nehru's desire to harmonise India's interests with those of the world. 'At this solemn moment, when the people of India, through suffering and sacrifice, have secured freedom, I...a Member of the Constituent Assembly of India, do dedicate myself in all humility to the service of India and the people to the end that this ancient land attain her rightful place in the world and make her full and willing contribution to the promotion of world peace and the welfare of mankind.'[22] Thus, it would be seen that Nehru was eager to work for world peace and prosperity and was very anxious that the people of India as a whole, should develop a world outlook. Repeatedly he had made it clear that India's policy of non-alignment was not a 'negative' or the 'sitting on the fence', type of policy but one which had for its end the good of the people all over the world. The basic tenets of India's foreign policy were stated clearly and categorically in Resolution V at the Jaipur Session of the Indian National Congress in 1948. An important paragraph therein was as follows: 'The foreign policy of India must necessarily be based on the principles that have guided the Congress in past years. These principles are promotion of world peace, the freedom of all nations, racial equality and the ending of imperialism and colonialism.... It should be the constant aim of the foreign policy of India to maintain friendly and cooperative relations with all nations and to avoid entanglement in military or similar alliances which tend to divide up the world and thus endanger world peace.'[23]

It might be observed that in the long run, peace could be ensured in the world only by supporting every right and just cause. Thus, advocacy of freedom for all nations and opposition to imperialism, colonialism and social discrimination, not only rendered India's foreign policy idealistic and ethically sound but also realistic, because in the ultimate analysis idealism was not something contrary to realism. 'What exactly is idealism? Surely, it is not something so insubstantial as to elude one's grasp. Idealism is the realism of tomorrow. It is the capacity to know what is good for the day after tomorrow or for the next year and to fashion yourself accordingly. The practical person, the realist, looks at the tip of his nose and sees little beyond; the result is that he is stumbling all the time.'[24]

Since independence, India had consistently championed the cause of various dependent countries and had actively worked for their freedom. As India herself was under alien rule for more than a century and a half, she was acutely conscious of the agonies of slavery and the disabilities from which a nation suffered when it was under foreign domination. Moreover,

India believed that the continued subjection of various countries to alien authority would adversely affect world peace and put it in jeopardy.

As long back as in 1946, Nehru had stated that India desired independence not merely for herself. India aspired for freedom in a free world and when she became free she would try her utmost to bring freedom to all subject nations. The world stated Nehru, could not be half free and half slave.[25]

To give only one example out of many, Nehru's role in the liberation of Indonesia from the clutches of Dutch imperialism might be mentioned; it was a notable example of his adherence to the policy of working for the emancipation of countries from foreign yoke. When the Dutch started a police action against Indonesia, a conference was convened by India in January 1949, which was attended by as many as eighteen nations. In his Presidential speech at the conference, Nehru explained the idea behind the convening of that conference. He stated that the freedom of a sister country of theirs was imperilled and once again dying colonialism had raised its head and was challenging the forces which were striving to build up a new structure of the world. The challenge of imperialism had to be met effectively, and any failure on their part to do so would have a very detrimental effect not only on Indonesia or Asia but on the whole world.

The proposals that Nehru put before the conference, were indicative of his mature leadership. He did not issue threats to the Dutch nor did he try to whip up the passions and emotions of the Asian people. On the contrary he urged the conference to follow the peaceful civilized way of solving the Indonesian problem through the medium of the United Nations Organization. That showed, apart from other things, as to how particular Nehru always was not to bypass the authority of the U.N.O. By convening that conference, Nehru revealed himself as a true internationalist, for who the freedom of other countries was a dear as the freedom of his own country.

Nehru had not only followed a policy of helping countries which were under foreign domination but had also done his best to preserve peace in the world by using his good offices and by mediating, in times of international crises. Nehru's role in the Korean affair was a notable one. Though the two Security Council Resolutions declaring North Korea an aggressor and calling for U.N. action to stop it, were supported by India. Nehru criticized the UN action of allowing its troops to cross the 38th parallel as he thought that, that would result in a world war.[26] In fact, Nehru did everything in his power to prevent a world conflagration on the

Korean issue. On July 7, 1950, Nehru sent two urgent messages—one to Stalin and the other to Dean Acheson, Secretary of State of the U.S. Government, endeavouring thereby to seek a peaceful solution to the Korean issue.[27] Again it was Nehru, who agreed to send Indian troops to Korea (in case of a ceasefire agreement) for the purposes of the implementation of the U.N. Resolution, when every other country was reluctant to do so. In his speech in the Lok Sabha on December 24, 1953, Nehru stated that if Indian troops had not gone to Korea, there would neither have been any truce nor any cease-fire and the war, would have continued and would even have expanded. India accepted that job when no other country was willing to do so. Nehru further stated that he had accepted that responsibility on India's behalf and that he would accept it not once but a hundred times again, because I owe a duty not only to my country but to others.[28]

Nehru's role in the Indo-China conflict was also important. For years together, war went on in Indo-China, reaching by 1954 a stage at which it constituted a threat to world peace. The Great Powers of the world, therefore, decided to meet at Geneva in April 1954, in order to discuss the Indo-China issue. Speaking in the Lok Sabha on February 22, 1954, Nehru emphasised the need of ceasefire in Indo-China and made a fervent appeal to the Great Powers, to strive to have a ceasefire in Indo-China. Then they can discuss it in their own way.[29]

In order to settle the Indo-China question, Nehru suggested a six-point plan.[30] The plan, suggested by Nehru, was typical of his endeavours to bring about peaceful solutions to different international problems It also threw light on Nehru's endeavours to eliminate colonialism from Asia and to bring freedom to Asian countries.

Again, in the Suez Canal crisis, Nehru did his very best to avoid a large-scale war by acting as some sort of mediator between England and Egypt. Moreover, he made an earnest appeal to England and the U.S.A. to develop negotiations with Egypt, which would lead to a settlement. Nehru's role in the Suez Canal dispute was a very important one, as could be seen from the speeches delivered by him in the Lok Sabha, from August 1956 to November 1956.[31]

As in the Korean issue and that of Indo-China, India did her best to ease the tension in Congo, and bring about some amicable settlement there. Nehru himself presented a resolution to the General Assembly on behalf of Ghana, the United Arab Republic, Indonesia, Yugoslavia and India.

Explaining the purpose of the Resolution, Nehru said in a speech in the General Assembly three days later, that the main purpose of the resolution was to help in the prevention of a deadlock in the international situation. The world situation had become extremely unsatisfactory and something had to be done in order to avoid a catastrophe. The doors and windows for a discussion of important issues were gradually being closed one after the other and some step had to be taken before all of them were completely closed and bolted.[32]

Not only did India do her utmost at the United Nations Organization, to avoid a world conflagration on the Congo issue, but it also did its best to assist the United Nations in its peaceful operations in Congo. Indian troops were sent to Congo to help maintain peace and order there and on the request of the U.N. Secretary General, Dag Hammersjoeld, India's High Commissioner in Pakistan, Rajeshwar Dayal, was sent to Congo at a very short notice, at a time when India could ill-afford to shift him from Karachi.[33]

The preservation and perpetuation of world peace was becoming increasingly difficult due to the emergence of two power blocs (after the Second World War), representing ideologies, diametrically opposite to each other. The communist countries seemed bent upon liberating the world from the clutches of capitalism; whereas the democratic countries of the world seemed equally determined; to make the world safe for democracy, by combating communist influence everywhere. An incessant 'cold war' was going on between the two power blocs, resulting in mounting tension, and on more than one occasion during those few years, the world was on the very verge of a shooting war. And the one thing which the world could not afford during this Nuclear Age was the breaking out of another world war, which if it unfortunately did, would result inevitably in the complete destruction of the human race and the total annihilation of our civilization.

Inspite of the danger of complete destruction of our civilisation looming large on the horizon, the big powers of the world were unwittingly taking the world towards a world war. They were talking of peace and yet were preparing for war, because they were the victims of 'fear psychosis', as Nehru termed it. 'The very process of marshalling the world into two hostile camps precipitates the conflict which it has sought to avoid. It produces a sense of terrible fear and that fear darkens men's minds and leads them into wrong courses. There is perhaps nothing so bad and so dangerous in life as fear. As a great President of the United States said, there is nothing really to fear except fear itself.'[34]

This 'fear psychosis' prevented the nations of the world from looking at various international problems in perspective. Whenever a problem came before the United Nations Organization (before the General Assembly or the Security Council), the member nations did not take into account the demands of justice and fair play, but always thought in terms of balance of power and how a particular stand on that issue would affect the interests of their own power bloc. The inevitable result of such an attitude on the part of member nations was an increase in world tension. When justice was not done, problems were not solved, and unsolved problems always precipitated international crises and led the world towards a shooting war.

How could that tension be minimised and the drift towards a world war arrested? It certainly could not be done by taking sides blindly and ignoring completely the demands of justice. Nehru had repeatedly stated that India's policy was to judge each issue (that came up before the U.N.) on its own merits and vote on it accordingly[35] so that justice might be done to the aggrieved party. That policy was not only ethically sound but also practically desirable because only the solution of world problems would ensure the continuance of world peace.

It had to be remembered that a country would be in a position to pursue such a policy, when it was not tied up to any of the power blocs, as any such alignment rendered independent and impartial functioning almost impossible. 'By aligning ourselves with anyone power, you surrender your opinion, give up the policy you would normally pursue because somebody else wants you to pursue another policy. I do not think it would be a right policy for us to adopt....Our present policy flows from what we have thought and said in the past, while incidentally it also helps in the maintenance of peace and the avoidance of war in the world today.'[36]

India was in a position to support every just cause, to uphold every right demand and to judge each question on its own merits, because of her adherence to the policy of non-alignment. Any deviation or departure from that policy would not only have been detrimental to India's interest but also to those of the world, as it would have inevitably added to international tension and would have led the world towards a war. The policy of non-alignment therefore was neither a negative policy nor one of opportunism, but one that was ideally suited to the conditions existing in the world at that time. It had for its basis pragmatism as well as idealism, as it sought to harmonise national interests with international interests. It was a positive policy for peace and there was nothing ignoble about it. Explaining some of the considerations that prompted India to follow a policy of non-alignment, Nehru stated that those who refused to join one of the two powerful blocs of nations that confronted each other were accused of sitting on the fence, as if an alternative did not exist. India had pursued a policy of non-alignment and one of cordial relations with other countries not merely because of its national background and the principles which it had made its own. India was convinced that the existing problems could be solved by peaceful methods and that each country could live its own life without imposing itself on others. India's policy, or any step that it took, might not make a big difference to the world issues and yet it might help to turn the scales of peace. Peace was not merely an absence of war but was also a state of mind. It was India's endeavour not to fall a victim to that climate of war and fear and to look at its own problems as well as those of the world very dispassionately. It had to be borne in mind that the continued by-polarisation of the world would inevitably lead to a war, sooner or later.[37]

Nehru, the sensitive nationalist and the keen historian, was extremely allergic to the return of the western Powers to Asia in any form or garb. He knew how the countries of Asia were exploited by these powers for well over one hundred and fifty years and how the people of that continent were subjected to ill-treatment and humiliation by its alien rulers. Apart from geographic and age old ties between various countries, the recent history of common subjection and common suffering had brought the countries of Asia very near to one another, mentally, psychologically and emotionally. Speaking about the domination and exploitation of Asia by European countries and its unhappy consequences, Nehru observed: 'We are today rather overwhelmed with the recent history of 200 years of European domination.'[38]

The people of Asia were treated with contempt and were looked down upon by the alien rulers throughout their rule over Asia. The people of India in particular, with a rich past full of great achievements in various domains, felt greatly insulted and humiliated by the treatment that was meted out to them by the British rulers. As Professor Toynbee very rightly observed: 'India is a whole world herself. She is a society of the same magnitude as our western society; and she is the great non western society that has been, not merely attacked and hit but overrun and conquered by western arms and ruled after that, by western administrators....India's experience of the West has thus been more painful and more humiliating than China's or Turkey's, and much more so than Russia's or Japan's, but just for this reason it has been much more intimate...our western iron has probably entered deeper into India's soul.'[39]

Nehru's mind was full of painful memories in regard to the contemptuous treatment of Indians at the hands of their British rulers, and he knew that the lot of people belonging to other countries of Asia under European rulers was a similar one. As such, Nehru was instinctively drawn towards other Asian countries. Moreover, the problems with which the people of Asia were faced, political, economic and social, were very similar and they required a more or less similar approach. Hence, Nehru considered the conflict between the Soviet bloc and the Anglo-American bloc as 'other men's quarrel' in which Asia need not get interested, as the problems of Asia were peculiarly its own and needed an independent approach for their solution. The underdeveloped countries of Asia would have to devise their own ways and means for rapid development and no traditional methods were likely to help them. Neither the Marxist approach to economic problems, nor the one represented by British Liberalism was likely to help Asia in solving her problems as both of them were somewhat out-of-date and did not have much relevance to the problems of those countries. India was a typical Asian country and when ever Nehru spoke of her problems he always had in mind the Asian background. In February 1955, Nehru stated that either bloc wondered as to how a nation could be so foolish as not to line up with itself. That was indicative of the poor understanding of the people belonging to those blocs, in regard to the mind of Asia. As for India, it had fairly clear ideas in regard to its political and economic structure. The people of India were governed by a Constitution which had rendered the country a parliamentary democracy. Obviously the people desired to function under that Constitution as they themselves had prepared and accepted it. In economic matters also the people of India wanted to go their own way. They neither intended turning communists nor had they any intention of being in the opposite camp. They had chosen a path for themselves and they intended going along it, and would even vary it if they considered it necessary. India wanted to be friendly with other countries and was also eager to build up its strength, but was just not interested in the crusade for or against communism.[40]

India had very strongly opposed treaties and pacts all over the world but more particularly so in Asia. She believed that those so called defensive pacts were very detrimental to the preservation of world peace as they tended to increase 'fear psychosis' and consequently created 'war psychosis'. The NATO, MEDO, SEATO etc, had added to world tension and had very adversely affected the prospects of disarmament and international harmony. Commenting on such pacts and treaties, Nehru said: 'I do not deny the necessity of any country or group of countries protecting themselves or taking steps to protect themselves against possible danger. They may do so by all means. At the same time again and again what a country should decide is whether its policy generally leads towards promoting a peace or war atmosphere. Sometimes I find very little difference—people talk of defence—whether it is defence or something else....One country calls it defence and the other country says that this defence is aimed against it. So they go on mounting armaments.'[41]

While India had raised her voice against defensive treaties (entered into by western powers) in all parts of the world, she had protested more vehemently against the formation of such alliances in Asia. It would be proper to discuss at this stage the reasons behind India's opposition to those defensive pacts, in spite of her opposition to the communist way of life and her efforts on the home front to check the growth and spread of communism.

As had been already stated, Nehru was very sensitive and allergic to the return of western powers on Asian scene and their interference in Asian affairs.

The foremost reason seemed to be India's concern over the preservation of her sovereignty and territorial integrity. Those defensive pacts brought the cold war right at the doors of India and it was but natural that this should worry her.

Apart from other things, Nehru believed that the defensive treaties and pacts sponsored by the western powers in Asia did not serve any useful purpose but merely added to the already existing tension. In this nuclear age, those treaties and pacts made little sense, as only those powers matter which possessed atomic weapons. The countries of Asia were militarily very weak and in terms of atomic warfare they just did not count. Thus, those agreements did not add to the strength of western powers but succeeded only in creating 'war psychosis' and in making the nations of Asia also victims of 'fear psychosis.' There was hardly any justification in spreading that wide network of pacts and treaties when it helped none but was on the other hand detrimental to the preservation of world peace. Speaking during a debate on the President's Address, in the Lok Sabha (February 25, 1955), Nehru made a pointed reference to the futility of such defensive treaties. Nehru stated that he could understand (though he would not approve) military alliances between great powers as they would have some meaning, But he just could not understand military pacts and alliances between a great power and a very small power. In a military sense it had no meaning for him. In the nuclear age of today, in the context of the nuclear war, the countries that count were those which were in a position to use those bombs. When such countries entered into alliances with small countries, their gain was negligible as the small powers had little military value. A war today would mean destruction of humanity; as such military alliances or armaments did not make any sense in the context of thermonuclear bomb.

It was not a matter of much relevance as to how many more bombs one country had than the other. Even the country which had comparatively less bombs could cause great damage to the other country. The fact was that there was hardly any defence against nuclear weapons and it could only mean mutual extermination. Thus, the way out was that of the prevention of wars.

The pacts and alliances made little sense militarily. At best they could serve the purpose of a threat and that was the way in which they were being used by both the blocs. But in the context of nuclear weapons even threatening was of little use, as the big powers that are in possession of those weapons, would not be frightened.[42]

Thus, those pacts and treaties do good neither to the big countries of the West nor to their weak associates in Asia. Apart from other consideration (to which reference had already been made in the previous pages) Nehru considered that very approach to the problem of Communism vis-a-vis Democracy as wrong and highly detrimental to the interests of humanity. Even the so called defensive pacts, succeeded in creating war psychosis and that war psychosis could not but lead to a world war, sooner or later. Hence, Nehru actively opposed those alliances, as he implicitly believed that they were accelerating humanity's drift towards a war.

If the approach of cold war and that of military alliances was persisted with, it could not but lead to a final catastrophe. India was opposed to all pacts and alliances as they added to hatred, fear and apprehension and were therefore very dangerous.[43]

What was the way out then? The way out was of course that of co-existence. The democracies as well as the communist countries of the world should live together, instead of thinking in terms of exterminating each other, because the alternative to co-existence was co-destruction. Though *Panchsheel* assumed international importance only after the Sino-Indian Treaty in regard to Tibet (1954),[44] the importance and necessity of co-existence was emphasised by Nehru, years earlier. Addressing the Indian Council of World Affairs, Constitution Club, New Delhi (March 22, 1949), Nehru had stressed the importance of accepting the fact that each country had the right of having its own political pattern and that no pressure should be brought on a country to accept any other political ideology. In that connection, he commended Indian culture and Indian way of life which stood for the principle of 'live and let live'. Making a direct reference to the need for co-existence on the international plane in the context of existing conditions, Nehru stated that it was high time for each country to realize that it should not interfere with another country's economic policy. Obviously, if a country's policies were right they would deliver the goods and those that did not, would not succeed. Any aggressive interference with the policies of other countries could not but lead to trouble and conflict. It had to be realized that there were different varieties of economic policy in different countries and they were accepted by their people as they had faith in them. If any country made an effort to change forcibly another country's economic policy or for that matter any other internal policy, or brought pressure to bear upon it; that would inevitably lead to counter-pressure, perpetual conflict and trouble of every conceivable nature.[45]

The principle of co-existence, emphasised by Nehru in 1949, needed far greater emphasis in the subsequent years because of the gradual growth in the intensity of cold war. Countries belonging to both the blocs piled up their armaments and feverishly prepared themselves for war because of 'fear psychosis'; the countries in the Anglo-American bloc were afraid of their counter-parts in the Soviet bloc and *vice-versa*. Statesmen of the world talked about peace and yet they prepared their countries for war because of this fear of one another. Nehru realized that the world could ill-afford a war as it would result in nothing short of complete destruction of the human race. The Sino-Indian Treaty on Tibet (1954) which incorporated the principles of co-existence in its preamble was thus the first written pledge on behalf of two nations to live in harmony with each other.

There was always the possibility of nations committing themselves to *Panchsheel* and not adhering to them in practice. Speaking on the concept of *Panchsheel* in Lok Sabha (September 17, 1955), Nehru referred to such a possibility and said: 'This stress on non-interference of any kind-political, economic or ideological is an important factor in the world situation today. The fact that it will not be wholly acted upon here and there is really of little relevance. You make a law, and the law gradually influences the whole structure: of life in a country, even though some people may not obey it. Even those who do not believe in it gradually come within its scope.'[46]

The concept of co-existence was wholly consistent with India's philosophy of life as revealed by India's long and chequered history. The Indians had always stood for a policy of peaceful relations with one's neighbours and for a peaceful approach to problems.

The Chinese invasion of India struck at the very roots of co-existence and it became fairly clear that certain nations would honour the principles of co-existence only so long as they suited their purpose. Of course the principles did not become worthless just because a certain country did not adhere to them, and it was always right to emphasise their importance so that they might go on influencing people everywhere.

The last questions that we had to consider in this connection was about India's comparative softness towards the U.S.S.R. as opposed to the United States, inspite of India's ideological proximity to the latter. It might be remembered that the United States had succeeded in irritating India time and again by her policy of entering into defensive pacts in Asia and thereby stepping on the Asian soil once again. Nehru, with his allergy to the return of western powers to Asia, was naturally critical of the U.S.A. as she was totally insensitive to Asian sentiments and responses. Moreover, the United States annoyed India further by giving military aid to Pakistan and thereby rendering a peaceful solution of the Kashmir problem more difficult. Further, as had been stated earlier, by spreading a large net work of pacts and treaties throughout Asia, the United States had brought the cold war right at the doors of India. The attitude of the United States of America to the question of racial discrimination in S. Africa irritated India considerably. India took to the General Assembly the case of the people of Indian origin in South Africa, who were being subjected to intense ill-treatment by the Government in South Africa which based its policies on racial discrimination. The delegation from S. Africa to the United Nations Organization, maintained that it was a wholly domestic issue and that the General Assembly was not competent to discuss it. India took the case to the General Assembly in June 1946 and it was on the agenda of the General Assembly upto 1948. Throughout that period the United States of America sided with S. Africa and thus disappointed India greatly.[47]

On the other hand the attitude of the Soviet Union towards India was on the whole friendly. The Soviet Union had supported India's stand on the Kashmir issue and on other issues.

Moreover, it should be remembered that Russia was one of India's immediate neighbours and as stated in the previous chapter, Nehru held the view that India's relations with her neighbours should be friendly. Another important matter should also be borne in mind. The first few years after Independence were potentially dangerous from the point of view of the spread of communism in the country as Communism thrives on hunger and poverty and the conditions in India at that time were conducive to the spread of communism in the country. By maintaining friendly relations with Russia, Nehru took the winds out of the sails of the communist party.

These factors coupled with Nehru's admiration for Russia since 1920, explain India's softer attitude towards Soviet Russia.

India's approach to her own problems was consistent with her pronouncements. She had made every endeavour to solve her problems peacefully and through negotiations and discussions. Pakistan's aggression over Kashmir (a part of the Indian territory) was a provocation grave enough to take recourse to arms. And yet India chose to solve that problem peacefully. While India was accused of precipitating matters by taking a police action against Goa and annexing that territory to India (which was India's own territory, hitherto under foreign domination), it was very conveniently forgotten that India made efforts for the peaceful settlement of Goa issue for as many as fourteen years before taking recourse to arms. It must however be remembered that though Nehru had implicit belief in the peaceful approach to international problems, he had made it clear that non-violence was not and could not be a creed with him or the Government of India and that Government was not pledged to it.[48] In a broadcast from B.B.C., London (January 12, 1951), Nehru said: 'I am not a Pacifist. Unhappily, the world of today finds that it cannot do without force. We have to protect ourselves and to prepare ourselves for every contingency. We have to meet aggressions and evils of every other kind. To surrender to evil is always bad. But in resisting evil, we must not allow ourselves to be swept away by our own passions and fears and act in a manner which is itself evil. Even in resisting evil and aggression, we have always to maintain the temper of peace and hold out the hand of friendship to those who, through fear or for other reasons, may be opposed to us. That is the lesson that our great leader, Mahatma Gandhi, taught us and imperfect as we are, we draw inspiration from that great teaching.[49]

INDIA AND THE COMMONWEALTH

It was thought by many in India that India would completely break away from the Commonwealth, after independence. Hence, when Nehru announced in April 1949, India's desire to continue its association with the Commonwealth it came to many as a complete surprise. However, serious students of politics had sensed India's desire to remain in the Commonwealth in 1949 itself. One of the resolutions passed by the Indian National Congress at its Jaipur session (1948) stated: 'In view of the attainment of complete independence and establishment of the Republic of India which will symbolize Independence and give to India the status among the nations of the world that is her rightful due, her present association with the United Kingdom and the Commonwealth of Nations will necessarily have to change.

'India however, desired to maintain all such links with other countries which do not come in the way of her freedom of action and independence and the Congress would welcome her free association with the independent nations of the Commonwealth for their commonweal and promotion of world peace.'[50]

When Nehru agreed on behalf of India to its continued association with the Commonwealth, he was accused by some in India of having gone back on his pledge to the nation (given in the pre-Independence period), to sever India's connection with the Commonwealth, in the post-freedom period. A close study of Nehru's statements of that period would reveal that it was not so.

It was undoubtedly true that during late 'twenties Nehru opposed the idea of Dominion status and favoured the idea of India severing all connections with Britain when it became free. Though he clung to the idea of complete independence for the country throughout the pre-Independence period, he showed his willingness in the 'thirties to co-operate with Britain on a footing of equality and on the condition that Britain gave up her policy of imperialism. In early 'thirties Nehru stated that India would gladly co-operate with Britain in the international field, if the latter did not function as an imperialist power.[51] He could also conceive and welcome 'the idea of a close association between India and England on terms other than those of imperialism.'[52]

When the Second World War broke out and Britain sought India's help and cooperation, Nehru was ready to assure India's active help to Britain inspite of past conflicts, but as a free nation and on terms of equality.[53]

It should also be remembered that the British Commonwealth assumed a different form after India's independence and in the changed context India's continued association with the Commonwealth became necessary as well as desirable. Its continuance in the Commonwealth did not place any restrictions on its freedom to function as it liked. Thus, in the changed set of circumstances the question of going back on the pledge hardly arose.

In a broadcast to the nation on May 10, 1949, Nehru declared that his support to India's continuance in the Commonwealth did not go against his past commitments to the nation as India's freedom was in no way affected by her remaining in the Commonwealth. Elaborating his point in regard to India's status remaining unaffected by its membership of the Commonwealth, Nehru stated that a nation's independence was not lost by its alliance with another country. In fact, India's membership of the Commonwealth was not even wholly in the nature of an alliance, as alliance normally implied mutual commitment, and no such commitments were involved in the Commonwealth, which was a free association of sovereign nations. The strength of the Commonwealth lay in its flexibility and its complete freedom and it was possible for any member nation to go out of it, whenever it chose to do so.[54] One of the reasons for the apprehension that India's freedom would be adversely affected by its continuance in the Commonwealth, was the fact that the British monarch was to continue as the head of the Commonwealth. Explaining the monarch's position, Nehru had pointed out that the Commonwealth was not a super-state in any sense of the term. The British monarch was accepted as the symbolic head of that free association. The monarch had no function attached to that status in the Commonwealth, and he had no place in the Indian Constitution.[55]

In a speech delivered in the Constituent Assembly (May 16, 1949), while moving that the decision to continue in the Commonwealth of

Nations, be ratified, Nehru drew the attention of the members to the first and the second paragraphs of the official statement, issued at the conclusion of the Commonwealth Prime Minister's Conference in London, on April 10, 1949. He stated that whereas in the first paragraph the Commonwealth was referred to as the British Commonwealth of Nations, in the second one it was designated as the Commonwealth of Nations. Moreover, the first paragraph referred to the allegiance to the Crown (existing at that time), that question would hot arise later as India would go outside the Crown area completely, when she became a Republic. While elaborating that point, Nehru made a subtle distinction between the Crown and the King and pointed out that India's subjects would not owe any allegiance to the king and that India would recognise the King merely as the symbol of that free association—the Commonwealth of Nations.[56]

What were India's obligations as the member of the Commonwealth? According to Nehru, there were hardly any. 'Apart from certain friendly approaches to one another, apart from a desire to cooperate, which will always be conditioned by each party deciding on the measure of cooperation and following its own policy, there is no obligation in the nature of commitments.'[57]

Thus, the members of the Commonwealth, according to Nehru, were expected to cooperate and be friendly with one another. To Nehru's critics, it was not very clear as to how it was possible for India to be in the Commonwealth along with a country like South Africa, which persisted with its policy of racial discrimination in spite of India's protest. Nehru admitted that it was a matter which would necessarily give some trouble. Nevertheless he thought that the question did not really arise as entering into an alliance with a nation or a group of nations did not imply committing oneself to something that they might do.[58]

While dealing with the question of India's co-existence with South Africa in the Commonwealth of Nations. Nehru made an important point. He put forward the view that the Commonwealth should not discuss and decide such issues as that of racial discrimination in South Africa. He thought that it was a dangerous thing to bring such matters within the purview of the Commonwealth as they might result in everything taking place, to which India had objected. The Commonwealth might assume the role of a superior body, supervising the activities of its members and functioning sometimes as a Tribunal or Judges. To allow Commonwealth to discuss matters such as those of racial segregation in S. Africa might lead to such a development, and if any such thing happened, it could not but result in the diminution in the independence and sovereignty of member nations. The Commonwealth might discuss such matters in a friendly way, but in no case should disputes be brought before it for their settlement.[59]

What were the factors that prompted Nehru to advocate very strongly, India's continuance in the Commonwealth? It could be said in answer to this question, that defence as well as economic considerations were primarily responsible for Nehru's advocacy of India's continued association with the Commonwealth. A newly independent country could not afford any isolation and the alternative to remaining in the Commonwealth would have been entering into some pact or treaty for India's defence, a much worse proposition: 'If we dissociate ourselves completely from the Commonwealth, then for the moment we are completely isolated. We cannot remain completely isolated, and so inevitably by stress of circumstances, we have to incline in some direction or other. But that inclination in some direction will necessarily be on a basis of give and take. It may be in the nature of alliances; you give something yourself and get something in return. In other words, it may involve commitments far more than at present. There are no commitments today.[60]

Some people in India were of the opinion that India's continuance in the Commonwealth would result in her drifting away from neighbours in Asia, and would also render it difficult for her to cooperate with other great countries of the world. Nehru thought that the contrary was true. India's membership of the Commonwealth actually helped her to come to friendly understandings with other countries and to 'play the part...of a bridge for the mutual understanding of other countries.'[61] Not remaining in the Commonwealth would have necessitated inclining towards this or that bloc, or entering into some treaty or alliance in order to avoid isolation, and this would have prevented India from being friendly with all countries.[62]

Apart from considerations pertaining to the desire to avoid isolation and the desire to cooperate and be friendly with all countries, economic considerations also prompted Nehru to agree to India's continued association with the Commonwealth.

In a speech delivered in the Constituent Assembly on May 17, 1949, Nehru referred to India's economic problems and pointed out that her membership of the Commonwealth would facilitate the task of solving those problems. Even without external help, it would be possible for India to go ahead but that would involve greater time and would obviously be a more difficult task.[63]

From an economic point of view, as stated above, India's association with the Commonwealth was particularly advantageous. India's trade was mostly with the Commonwealth. It was in the Sterling area that India's foreign exchange reserves were tied up. And the armed forces in India got their supplies of arms from Britain.

To conclude, India's continued membership of the Commonwealth was consistent with her sovereign status and was also advantageous from the point of view of her immediate needs and requirements. In it Nehru perceived a good substitute for India's alignment with either of the power blocs, with all the advantage of such an alignment, minus its drawbacks—national and international.

THE KASHMIR DISPUTE

Nehru's role in the Kashmir dispute was subjected to severe criticism in India and to some extent in the outside world, but for different reasons. To begin with, let us try to find out as to what were the grounds on which Nehru's role vis-a-vis Kashmir was criticised in India. Broadly speaking, the criticism was as follows: (1) Nehru's commitment to a plebiscite in Kashmir was wholly unnecessary and wrong, and (2) instead of hastily taking the Kashmir issue to the Security Council, Nehru should have ousted out the raiders from the Kashmir-occupied territory.

The criticism about Nehru agreeing to a plebiscite in Kashmir will necessitate a fairly long answer, as the matter was not half as simple as people imagined it to be. The first thing that should be remembered in this connection is that the Congress Party, very rightly, had not accepted the British view that the paramountcy in a State would revert to the ruler (after the end of the British rule in India), but had claimed such paramountcy to the people. Acceptance of the British view would have resulted in each ruler being given the, right of deciding as to whether his State should accede to India or Pakistan or remain as an independent entity. Thus, there were dangerous possibilities inherent in the acceptance of the British view, and the Congress Party, very wisely rejected that view. Claiming paramountcy for the people implied the right of the people (and not the ruler) in each State, to decide the future status of the State. This naturally meant that, so far as the Indian portion of the sub-continent was concerned, all the States except Kashmir, which had a majority Muslim population, would automatically accede to India, and this is what actually happened, save in the cases of Junagadh, where the Nawab acceded to Pakistan and Hyderabad, where the Nizam declared independence.[64] In so far as the Muslim League was concerned, very understandably, it supported the British view, because only then could it contend that the action of the Nawab of Junagadh as also that of the Nizam of Hyderabad, were technically correct.

Nehru gave expression to his views on the doctrine of paramountcy vis-a-vis the Indian States as early as in May 1939. While dealing with the problem of the Indian States, Nehru stated: 'The only final authority and paramount power that we recognise is the will of the people', and the only thing that counts ultimately is the good of the people.'[65] Incidentally, it may be pointed out, that this statement of Nehru, made eight years before India's independence, showed unmistakably, as to how he always tried to anticipate the problems which the Congress would have to face on behalf of India, pondered over them deeply and sought solutions to them.

Among the Indian States, Kashmir was the only State which had a pre-dominantly Muslim population, though the ruler of the State was a Hindu. As such, the case of Kashmir was different from that of any other state. It was not possible to apply different criteria while dealing with Hyderabad and Junagadh on one hand and Kashmir on the other. Kashmir had acceded to India under very extraordinary circumstances (at a time when the raiders were nearing the capital city of Srinagar) and its accession to India could not but be considered as provisional. India had suggested plebiscite for resolving the Junagadh dispute with Pakistan and as such Nehru's declaration about a plebiscite in Kashmir (in order to ascertain the wishes of the people in regard to the future status of Kashmir), was consistent with India's stand in regard to the paramountcy reverting to the people. Accepting Kashmir's accession to India as final would have made it incumbent of India to accept Nizam's decision to remain independent and Nawab of Junagadh's accession to Pakistan.

As per Nehru's declaration, India accepted the UNCIP[66] (United Nations Commission on India and Pakistan) resolution of August 13, 1948, in regard to a plebiscite in Kashmir, subject to certain assurances by the Commission. These assurances were sought by Nehru in his letter to the Chairman of the Commission dated 20th August 1948.

The Commission gave the assurances sought by the Indian Prime Minister. They were as follows:

(a) The sovereignty of Jammu and Kashmir Government would not be brought into question over the State territory evacuated by Pakistan troops.

(b) No recognition would be accorded to the so-called Azad Kashmir Government.

(c) During the period of truce, the territory evacuated by Pakistan troops would not be consolidated to the disadvantage of the state.

(d) The Commission recognised the paramount need for security, and the time when the withdrawal of Indian troops was to begin, the stages in which it was to be carried out, and the strength of the Indian forces to be retained in the State, were matters of settlement between the Commission and India.

(e) If a plebiscite was held, the resolution would not in any way recognise the right of Pakistan to have any part in it.[67]

As future events, showed, none of these assurances were implemented either by the Commission or for that matter by Pakistan or the Security Council.

A close study of the conditions laid down by Nehru for the acceptance of the Commission's resolution on a plebiscite in Kashmir would reveal that the plebiscite held as per those conditions could have gone in favour of India, especially during that period. So, even from a practical point of view, a plebiscite in Kashmir during 1948-49 was a fairly safe proposition. In fact, more will be said about India's chances of winning the plebiscite during that period, at a later stage of this narration.

Now, let us come to the criticism that Nehru committed a mistake in hastily taking the Kashmir issue to the Security Council. Instead, according to Nehru's critics he should have cleared the Kashmir-occupied area, by ousting out the raiders, which was a simple matter.

This criticism is mostly based on bazaar gossip. People talk about Nehru taking the Kashmir issue to the Security Council at a time when Military Commanders were assuring him that they would be able to oust out the raiders from Kashmir area, within three or four days. Nothing is farther from the truth than the above statement. The facts on the other hand are exactly the opposite.

Firstly, ousting out the raiders from the Kashmir-occupied area was far more difficult than what most people imagined: The raiders were equipped with modern weapons, including mortars, machine guns, Bren and Sten guns, anti-tank rifles etc. They were trained by regular officers of the Pakistan army and to some extent led by them. Moreover, apart from tribal, even regular Pakistan troops were engaged in that fight. As such, it was not easy even to push them back. To oust them out would have necessitated a prolonged war. To make matters worse for India, the winter set in. This meant that it would be impossible for the Indian army to make any progress for several months to come. It was at this stage and during these set of circumstances that the Kashmir issue was referred to the Security Council, and ceasefire agreed to from January 1, 1949. 'Even the Military Commanders in the field, who the Government had consulted, had agreed that the cease-fire was the best solution at that stage'.[68]

Nehru was criticised by some countries for agreeing to a plebiscite in Kashmir and later going back on that commitment. How far was this criticism justified?

A careful study of Pakistan's political tactics convinces us of the fact that at least during the first few years of the Kashmir controversy, Pakistan did not want a plebiscite in Kashmir. During that period Pakistan was by no means confident about winning the plebiscite, as its troops and raiders had perpetrated indescribable atrocities over the people of Kashmir. They had indulged in loot, arson, rape, murder and destruction of property in the State. The circumstances on the whole were favourable to India from the point of view of Kashmir verdict in its favour, in a plebiscite.[69] According to Alastair Lamb, who was by no means pro-India, Jinnah did not look forward to a plebiscite in Kashmir, as he felt convinced that the result would be unfavourable to Pakistan because of Shaikh Abdullah.[70] Moreover, 'when the memory of the horrors of the tribal invasion of October, 1947, was still fresh in Kashmiris' minds, thoughtful Pakistan leaders could not have been convinced that the vote would in fact go in their favour....At this period 1948-1949, a Kashmir plebiscite would have involved a considerable Pakistan gamble.'[71]

During this period, Pakistan tried to evade the issue of a plebiscite in Kashmir by adopting different methods. Years later, Urrutia, who represented Columbia in the Security Council, revealed something very important in his speech in the Security Council on 15th February 1957. He told the Council as to what had happened in the year 1948, when the

United Nations Commission went to India and Kashmir. (Urrutia knew all the details because the Chairman of the Commission was a representative from Columbia, and he had recorded the proceedings of the Commission for the information of his Government. Urrutia had studied those records). Nehru to the surprise of the Commission agreed that subject to certain conditions, the question of Kashmir's future should be submitted to decision by its inhabitants, by means of Plebiscite. The Commission had not expected Nehru's consent to a plebiscite because of the aggression over Kashmir by raiders and Pakistan soldiers. It was thus that India accepted the UNCIP's resolution of August 13, 1948, after Nehru's conditions were accepted by the Commission. The Chairman assured Nehru that India would not be bound by that resolution, if Part I and II of the resolution (withdrawal of Pakistani troops from that area etc) were not complied with.

According to Urrutia the Commission had decided to hold a plebiscite within six weeks to three months at the most. In the light of Urrutia's revelation, is it not surprising that Pakistan went on raising irrelevant issues so that a plebiscite may not take place. Moreover, an extremely just and fair suggestion by India to the effect that the President of the International Red Cross be appointed as the plebiscite Administrator instead of Admiral Nimitz of USA was intentionally rejected. After describing the developments that took place in 1948, Urrutia stated: 'If at that time we had accepted the Plebiscite Administrator proposed by India...plebiscite would already have been held'.[72]

All this was clearly indicative of the fact that Pakistan and its friends were not at all keen about a plebiscite in Kashmir in 1948-1949. Surprisingly enough, during this very period, 'the strongest opposition' to a plebiscite in Kashmir came from Shaikh Abdullah himself. The attitude of Shaikh Abdullah placed the Government of India in an embarrassing position as it had accepted the UNCIP's resolution in regard to a plebiscite in Kashmir. The Shaikh violently opposed plebiscite in Kashmir on the ground that he was the representative spokesman for Kashmir and no poll was necessary.[73] The Shaikh's opposition to a plebiscite is an additional proof of the fact that it was not Nehru who was coming in the way of a plebiscite in Kashmir.

The delaying tactics of the Security Council in finding a just solution to the Kashmir problem, made the Shaikh sceptic about the role of the Security Council and he came to the conclusion that the best way out was for the people of Kashmir to give expression to their wishes through a special convention of the National Conference. Accordingly, a special convention of the National Conference was held in October, 1948, in which a resolution was passed which confirmed the provisional accession of the State to India and pledged its 'fullest support to a final accession to India.'[74] Shaikh Abdullah stated during this convention: 'So far as I am concerned, I feel certain that the political, economic, social and cultural interests of Kashmir demand an immediate and final accession to India and India alone.'[75] It is important to remember that this special convention was held one year after the aggression took place. It is thus safe to infer that the decision was taken after cool and deliberate consideration of the entire issue, and not in a fit of emotion. In the words of B.N. Mullick: 'was any further expression of opinion of the people to settle their future necessary? The whole world would acknowledge that in 1948, the National Conference with its united leadership under Shaikh Abdullah represented 95 per cent of the Muslim population of the Kashmir Valley. Through the Special Convention, the vast majority of the people of the valley had unreservedly decided in favour of permanent accession of Kashmir to India. So far as India was concerned this unanimous decision of the National Conference, which represented practically the entire people of Kashmir, was enough and could be considered as the fulfillment of the pledge that Pandit Nehru had given earlier that...the people of the State would be given an opportunity to decide their future.'[76]

Because of his firm opposition to a plebiscite in Kashmir, and because of his disgust with the dubious role of the Security Council in the Kashmir affair, Shaikh Abdullah decided to convene a Constituent Assembly in order to (apart from other matters) ratify Kashmir's accession to India. The Constituent Assembly which was thus formed in late 1951 ratified the decision taken by the Special convention of the National Conference in regard to Kashmir's accession to India.

A plebiscite in Kashmir became unnecessary after the above mentioned decision of the Kashmir Constituent Assembly, as the people of Kashmir, on their own, took the decision of ratifying the provisional accession of Kashmir to India, thereby making it permanent.

Even otherwise, there was not much chance of a plebiscite in Kashmir because of Pakistan's tactics and approach to the entire problem of plebiscite in Kashmir. As early as on December 21, 1948, Nehru had sought an assurance from the Commission that an appeal to religious fanaticism would not be considered as a legitimate activity, India and the United Nations being secular in their policies. Lozano, on behalf of the Commission gave that assurance to Nehru by stating that any activity that disturbed law and order could not be regarded legitimate. However, Pakistan leaders openly stated time and again that they believed in appeal to religious sentiments at the time of the plebiscite, and Nehru rightly felt that a plebiscite in Kashmir in these circumstances would endanger peace in India and would re-activise communalism greatly. On February 18, 1957, the Foreign Minister of Pakistan stated: 'It would be perfectly legitimate in the case of a plebiscite to draw attention to religious, cultural, linguistic, economic...and other ties, affinities' and other considerations that might sway the choice.'[77] The statement of the Pakistan Foreign Minister referred above was typical of the approach of Pakistan leaders towards the question of plebiscite in Kashmir. Their speeches were not in tune with the assurance given by Lozano to Nehru on December 21, 1948. This assurance, it may be remembered was made public in the Commission's second report.[78]

After taking into account all relevant facts one cannot but come to the conclusion that the criticism against Nehru about his having gone back on his commitment in regard to holding a plebiscite in Kashmir is without any substance.

WAS NEHRU'S CHINA POLICY INDICATIVE OF HIS NAIVETE ?

Over the years, another matter which has come for severe criticism is Nehru's China policy. A very large number of educated Indians still hold the view that Nehru's China policy was a complete failure. It is an undeniable fact that the Indian army suffered a humiliating defeat when the Chinese launched a massive attack over the Indian borders in October 1962. The people of India were not mentally prepared for this defeat, as they had wrong notions about India's military strength. It may be that these wrong notions were a result of India's military successes against Junagadh and Hyderabad immediately after freedom and against Goa a few years later. In so far as Junagadh was concerned, the Indian army merely had to occupy the small portion already brought under control by the peoples' representatives. The opposition encountered by the Indian forces at Hyderabad and Goa was nominal. The military strength of the opponents at both these places was insignificant. India had to fight in the real sense of the word, only in Kashmir and though its success there was noteworthy it became quite clear that defeating the Pakistani forces, who as stated earlier were engaged in that fight, was, not half as easy as defeating the Hyderabad and Goa forces. However, oblivious of these facts the people of India had come to believe that India's military strength was considerable and that Nehru was following a weak kneed policy towards China inspite of it. It was only after the Sino-Indian conflict of October 1962, that we realized that militarily we were very weak and then we went to the other extreme and started wondering as to whether we were good enough even to face Pakistan. The military experts of course knew about our military potential vis-a-vis China. However, the common Indian people never had the opportunity of knowing as to where we stood against China in terms of military strength.

The chief criticism against Nehru vis-a-vis his policy towards China is based on the naive assumption that Nehru was too simple and too gullible a person to comprehend China's evil designs towards India. If Nehru had remained that naive and credulous even after spending more than forty years in politics, he was certainly entitled to get a Nobel Prize (had there been one) for political immaturity. It is true that India was ringing with the slogans of *Hindi-Chini Bhai Bhai* from 1949 to 1956-57. Nehru and the other top persons in the Indian Government repeatedly said during this period that China was India's friend, it was a great peace loving nation and that Sino-Indian friendship was an important factor in the maintenance of world peace. After 1956, progressively, the Sino-Indian relations became more and more strained and ultimately by 1960-61 China and India became openly antagonistic towards each other. And finally when China attacked India in 1962, the Indian leaders accused China of stabbing India into the back. However, in international politics accusations in regard to breach of faith have little or no meaning. In the world of today a nation can afford to remain complacent only at its own peril. The chief criticism against Nehru is that he could not comprehend the devilish designs of a hostile, expansionist and aggressive nation like China and mistakenly took China for a great friend of India and in consequence brought great humiliation to the country in 1962.

While considering this criticism, it is important to bear in mind that what is said publicly on a delicate issue like our relations with China, should not be equated with what we actually feel about that problem. Though Nehru said after the Chinese invasion that the Chinese stabbed us into the back, did not keep faith with us and so on, it does not really mean that we had all along mistaken an enemy for a friend. After speaking for years about the age long friendship between India and China (whatever else he may have had in his mind), Nehru could not have stated publicly that he had never trusted the Chinese. However, all available evidence suggests that Nehru's public pronouncements in regard to the Sino-Indian relationship did not correspond with his private assessment of the situation. B.N. Mullick's book, 'My Years With Nehru: The Chinese Betrayal', gives valuable information about Nehru's policy towards China. The fact is that India just could not have remained complacent about China in the context of the Chinese attitude towards India since the Chinese revolution of 1949. About a year before the Chinese revolution, the Communist uprising in India had begun and at about the time of the Chinese revolution the Government of India was busy in suppressing it. Though India was one of earliest nations to recognise the Peoples' China, China's attitude towards India from the very beginning was one of hostility.

The Chinese Government viewed the Communist uprising in India as the revolt of the progressive forces in India against the reactionary regime of the Congress. China was confident of the fact that the reactionary regime of the Congress would be toppled by the Communist revolutionaries, with the help of the progressive forces and the workers and the peasants. The Indian Government was dubbed as a tool of the Anglo-American capitalists and imperialists, and Nehru was for the Chinese a bourgeoisie with a slavish mentality, heading a Government of Peoples' enemies. The recognition of Peoples' China by India was interpreted as a hypocritical act and as one which was aimed at deceiving the progressive forces in India.[79] Since this was the type of propaganda that was carried on in China, there was no question of India remaining complacent about China. That the strong China would pose a real problem for India was a fact which was realized from the very beginning. Because of this attitude of China, it soon became necessary for the Government of India to send protest notes to China. The first protest note to China was sent on 21st October 1950. From that day onwards, protest notes to China became a regular feature of Sino-Indian relationship. Where was then the question of India living in a dream world of its own vis-a-vis its relationship with China in the context of all these happenings?

The differences between India and China came to the surface in the year 1950, over the question of Tibet. The Chinese stand was that China's sovereignty extended over Tibet also and as such Tibet was politically, an integral part of China. India, felt China, had no right to speak about Tibet and even went to the extent of suggesting that India's wrong policy towards Tibet was a result of U.S.A.'s advice to India in this regard. India on the other hand took the view that India's relationship with Tibet was a result of past agreements, and rights that India had acquired over the years. China according to India had suzerainty over Tibet. Tibet was an autonomous political unit under the Dalai Lama and India had trade and cultural rights in that region; moreover, guarding Tibet's autonomy was partly India's responsibility. The Chinese leaders, instead of negotiating this with India were trying to decide this issue by forceful entry into the region of Tibet. Britain and the U.S.A. were not willing to get entangled in the Tibetan issue by supporting Tibet for different reasons. China had the full support of the U.S.S.R. at that time.[80] The question of sending the Indian forces for the protection of Tibet was also fully considered at that time. However, the then Commander-in-Chief of the Indian Army, General Cariappa, pointed out in no unambiguous terms that it would not be possible for India to spare more than one battalion for Tibet's aid.[81] The position thus was very unenviable. India was not in a position to go to the help of Tibet on its own. Our military weakness left us with no other alternative save that of becoming a silent spectator to whatever China did in Tibet. To add to this was the headache of the McMahon Line. China did not recognise McMahon Line as the correct dividing line between India and China and our military weakness left us with no other alternative except that of protracted negotiations with China on this matter also. The situation as it was developing was thus inherently and potentially dangerous. It is in this context that Sardar Patel's letter to Nehru dated November 7, 1950, has to be considered. Sardar Patel, the Home Minister and the Deputy Prime Minister had drawn the attention of the Prime Minister to the danger to the Indian border from the Chinese side, so that the matter may be fully considered by the Indian Cabinet and suitable measures taken. Had Nehru been oblivious of that danger or if he had considered Patel's fears baseless or imaginary, the Government of India would not have moved into the matter very quickly as it did. Till then there were no security or vigilance on the Sino-Indian border. There were no military posts in this area. All of a sudden the entire border covering thousands of miles was endangered. How to protect that border was the all important question which the Government had now to face. Sardar Patel's letter was thus very timely in the context of the gradual deterioration in the Sino-Indian relationship.

In about a week's time after Nehru received the letter from Sardar Patel the matter was fully considered and the Himmatsinghji Committee was constituted to go into the question of the adoption of suitable measures for the protection of the Sino-Indian border.[82] Thereafter began the process of setting up Intelligence Posts. The first Intelligence Post was set up in the NEFA Region at the end of 1950. From 1954, began the process of setting up Army Check Posts on the Sino-Indian border. A little earlier, that is in March 1952, the Intelligence Service was directed to treat China as India's potential enemy number one and was asked to collect every type of information in that light. To ensure the sympathy of the people on the Sino-Indian border towards India, instructions were issued to give special concession to the Tibetan refugees. Later, by giving refuge to the Dalai Lama in India, China was prevented from creating unrest in the people of that area. The differences between India and China had increased considerably in 1950. They became more accentuated in the subsequent three years with the result that the rights that India possessed in Tibet were abrogated in 1953. After 1954 began the minor attacks on the Indian border.

If this entire historical background is taken into account it would become clear that the Indian Government was aware of the possible danger from China from a very early date. The Indian army and the army experts had gone to Korea with the very competent and shrewd General Thimmayya, in connection with the supervision of the ceasefire in Korea. The General had returned to India, with well-considered ideas in regard to the Chinese military potential. General Thimmayya had always propounded that the Sino-Indian conflict was not one about which the army could do something. It had become evident that India would have to increase its military strength. A little after India became free India's armed forces totalled upto two lakhs and eighty thousand. The Air Force consisted of eight units. Radar arrangements were almost non-existent. Ironically enough, the opposition parties in India during this period were very critical of the Government's considerable expenditure over the armed forces. Inspite of this criticism the Government followed progressively the policy of increasing the strength of India's armed forces. Specially after 1950, when V.K. Krishna Menon was the Defence Minister a big attempt was made to increase the production of arms and ammunition in India. Most of the agreements with the U.S.A. and Britain in regard to the production of arms and ammunition took place during this period. The Indian Intelligence Service was vigilant enough. From June 1962, it became quite evident that there would be a large scale attack on India by the Chinese. After taking into account everything a decision was taken not to use the Air Force during the anticipated conflict. The attack actually began in the middle of October 1962.

It would be evident from what has been stated above that the Government of India was not complacent over the Chinese question. The Government was striving to increase the military strength of the country in view of the danger that it faced from China as well as Pakistan. To say that India failed to increase the military strength adequately so as to cope up with the Chinese attack of 1962 is one thing and to say that India lived in a dream world of its own and naively believed that China would never attack India is yet another. To become militarily strong India needed help from different quarters of the world. It was not possible to get big help from the U.S.S.R., China and U.S.S.R. being friendly at that time. The U.S.S.R. could have indirectly helped India as it actually did during China's attack on India in 1962. The one quarter from which big help was expected-military and otherwise, was from the U.S.A. but unfortunately the U.S.A. was not ready to get itself involved in a war with China extending over the two thousand miles long Sino-Indian border. Not only after the Chinese threat to India had increased but even after the actual Chinese attack on India, the help from the U.S.A. was not much. In fact, the U.S.A. sought excuses to give even the measure of help that it had promised.

In this context a question is asked as to why Nehru asked the Indian Army to oust out the Chinese from the Indian soil, when India was militarily that weak. The question is asked in such a fashion as if Nehru had ordered the Indian troops to attack China. What has to be borne in mind in this connection is that the Chinese forces were right on the Sino-Indian border and almost daily there were incursions in the Indian territory as a result of which India had lost territory to the extent of thousands of square miles. China was not ready to solve this problem through negotiations and it was not possible for India to wage a successful war against China; nor was it possible for India to remain a silent spectator to the progressive usurpation of the Indian territory by the Chinese. Thus, Nehru asked the Indian forces not to give up any post without fighting and to occupy parts of Indian territory hitherto un-occupied and not to leave any such area without fighting. These directives of Nehru were subjected to criticism in such a manner as if Nehru's directives were for a full-fledged war with China inspite of military weaknesses.[83] It is really very sad that instead of facing the fact that India's humiliation in 1962 was a result of India being a military weak country, the army blamed the political leaders and the political leaders the army men and the Indian people on their part blamed both.

This is in brief what happened in 1962 and before it. That Nehru knew about the danger to India from the Chinese quarter[84] need hardly be doubted. In fact his endeavour was to make India strong enough to defend itself against aggression and he knew it too well that the strength to defend one's country comes from the country's overall progress for which the pre-requisite was a period of peace. In order to secure for the country a period of peace Nehru made every endeavour to establish friendly relations with China and in the process put up with many insults and humiliations. He tried every weapon in his armoury to force China to follow peaceful methods. In order to make China answerable for its acts before the bar of world opinion, he advocated People's China's representation in the U.N.O. He concluded with China the *Panchsheel* Agreement and while doing so he tried to break the Sino-Russia axis and make the U.S.S.R. pro-India, an effort in which his success was considerable. He also explored the possibility of getting U.S.A.'s help against China but failed to get much help from that quarter.

There was however one conspicuous failure of Nehru. He could not create in the people of India awareness in regard to the basic validity and correctness of his China policy. While he spoke time and again about the age-long friendship between China and India, he also occasionally dropped a subtle hint about the possible consequences of a two thousand mile military border with China. However, his speeches created an atmosphere which made people believe that China was India's friend. At higher levels, Nehru combined in his speeches an advocacy of peaceful methods and friendly relations with China coupled with important hints about the reality of the situation. Unfortunately, he could not create in India as a whole an atmosphere which would have enabled the people to see his policies in perspective. He failed to create machinery which would have conveyed to the people the real import of his speeches which apparently seemed very idealistic and devoid of realism.

The Chinese scored a point over Nehru by attacking and humiliating India before India was prepared to defend itself adequately. While it was wrong to expect China to keep quiet till India became strong, there was little else that Nehru could do in this regard except following a policy that would result in the avoidance of an armed conflict with China, as long as possible. India's defeat in 1962 not only affected adversely India's international image but it also had a very adverse effect on Nehru's popularity in India. However, it is well to remember that India survived that crisis primarily because of the stability lent by Nehru to the political life in the country ever since India's independence. India's economy and the Indian democracy withstood this shock commendably. In fact India became a stronger nation in more than one sense after the Chinese attack of 1962. Though it is true that we are still not strong enough to defeat China, it is equally true that China realized in 1962 that the Government under Nehru was not so weak as to topple down under the tremendous pressure of the Chinese attack. Though it may not be possible to get back from China the territory usurped by it over the years, China had to stop its policy of the illegal occupation of the Indian territory. During the last few years India has not lost any more territory. It will no longer be possible for China to gain Indian territory in the manner in which it was gained by it from 1956 to 1962. China will have to wage a war against India in order to secure any part of the Indian territory in future.

CRITICISM OF NEHRU'S POLICY OF NON-ALIGNMENT AFTER THE CHINESE INVASION

After the Chinese invasion of 1962, not only the China policy of Nehru but his foreign policy as a whole was subjected to severe criticism. The critics of Nehru lashed at the policy of non-alignment and stated with vehemence that because of this policy India could not gain the friendship of any of the powerful nations and even amongst the other nations India had very few friends. They pointed out that India always found it difficult to rally the support of different nations on any issue which concerned India. Moreover, our foreign policy did not result in the maintenance of cordial relations with our neighbours. And finally, the off-repeated criticism was that the foreign policy of Nehru was a failure as evidenced by the issues of Kashmir and China.

The criticism of the policy of non-alignment on the ground that it has not secured for India the friendship of any powerful nation is based on an inadequate understanding of India's needs as also the currents and cross-currents of international politics. There were only two nations, which could be termed as powerful nations, the U.S.A. being one and the U.S.S.R. the other. Of these two, the friendship of the U.S.S.R. was not possible, for any non-communist country up to 1955. India, a democratic country could have gained a powerful friend like the U.S.A., without losing its separate identify only by joining the American bloc. There was not much evidence to prove that joining the American bloc would have ensured India's protection from external aggression or internal sabotage: nor could it be said on the basis of available evidence that the U.S.A. contributed greatly to the industrialization or for that matter the overall progress of the nations in its bloc. A perpetual condition of war would have prevailed on the Sino-Indian border. It could also have meant a war psychosis developing in India, resulting in preparations for war at the cost of the economic betterment of the people. However, changed circumstances made matters easier for India. India's policy of non-alignment came to be better understood in both the blocs and this resulted in our getting aid from both the quarters. It was because of our policy of non-alignment that we could make the U.S.S.R. a neutral friend and the U.S.A. a helpful one, during our conflict with China. However, the help from the U.S.A. was not much during the Chinese invasion. When the Bangladesh issue cropped up, the U.S.A., China and Pakistan came nearer. In consequence, India had to enter into a defence pact with the U.S.S.R. The fact that the pact had not been approved by some people known politically as the rightists inspite of the U.S.A.'s known animosity towards India clearly indicated that these people would like India to throw its lot with the U.S.A. at all costs, though apparently they might talk about India being in the need of a powerful friend. Since the U.S.A., China and Pakistan had come close enough, it was necessary to do some fresh thinking on the question of the price that India would have to pay for gaining the friendship of the U.S.A. And granting that India was prepared to pay that price, the question would still have remained un-answered as to from who would the U.S.A. protect us. From the day of India's independence onwards, there was no danger to India from the Russian quarter. The threat of aggression came from China and Pakistan.[85] To what extent the U.S.A. would have guaranteed protection to India against China (in the event of India being in the American bloc), was also a question which needed a convincing answer. The subtle point which has to be appreciated in regard to the policy of non-alignment is that it is not so much aimed at gaining the friendship of the powerful nations as to prevent powerful nations from pushing the world into the holocaust of a war as a result of animosity between them. The policy of non-alignment gives a nation a period of continued peace, which it requires for its progress. The test of the success of India's policy of non-alignment lies in the answer to the question as to whether India has succeeded as a result of this policy, in getting a period of peace to become militarily strong, at least to the minimum possible extent.

The criticism that India could not gain friends even among nations other than powerful, is also untenable. The question relating to India which was constantly before the United Nations was the question of Kashmir; the other question which occasionally came up for discussion at the United Nations was in regard to Indo-Pak conflicts in general. On both these there was little likelihood of the members of the American bloc being favourable to India. Pakistan being in the American bloc and India being consistently opposed to imperialism, the western countries were not in India's favour. The Muslim countries also are usually against India in any matter involving Pakistan. In such circumstances, it is not easy for a non-aligned country like India to gain many friends in different parts of the world. The question as to how many nations voted in favour of India on any particular issue is not very important in international politics. What is important to understand is whether different nations are generally friendly to one's country or not. The number of the countries which are consistently hostile to India is indeed very small. In fact, barring views on one or two questions, the relations of India with other countries are quite friendly. The criticism that India could not establish friendly relations with the neighbouring countries is only partly true. Countries like Sri Lanka and Nepal have to make attempts to emphasise their separate identity in order to boost up national pride and it is in the light of this policy that public utterances of their leaders have to be considered. Barring, what is publicly stated by important people belonging to these two places, India's relations with them are very friendly. To think that no occasion of differences should develop between India and the neighbouring countries is to expect what is well nigh impossible. Differences are bound to arise. However, what is important to remember is whether these differences have assumed the form of mutual antagonism. Not only no such feeling of antagonism has developed, but what is more important still, these small neighbouring nations have become more and more convinced about the fact that they need not entertain any apprehensions in regard to a possible attack from India or in the case of Nepal, India doing something inconsistent with its Protectorate obligations. Barring China and Pakistan, India's relations with other neighbouring countries are quite friendly. Of course it is possible to argue that it does not speak well of India's foreign policy that two of its more powerful neighbours should be consistently hostile to her. It is important to remember in this connection that the hostility of these two countries towards India has immediate political as well as historical reasons and no person endowed with any measure of objectivity would ever deny the fact that during the last few decades India tried every possible method to straighten out her relations with them, and it is difficult to imagine as to what more could have been done.

Sometimes in a naive way we expect India's foreign policy to yield two fruitful results. Firstly, we expect that our foreign policy should result in the solution of the Kashmir problem, and secondly we expect the Soviet Union and the U.S.A. to stand by our side in order to defeat China. Both these expectations are indicative of a rather immature approach to international problems. Every nation formulates its foreign policy in such a way as to benefit it to the utmost. It is wrong to expect any other country to help India to solve its problems on humanitarian grounds or on considerations of justice and fair play. The only criterion of judging the success of India's foreign policy is the one of finding out as to how far that policy has helped India to step up its industrial progress and increase its military strength, without compromising with its freedom in any way. Judging from this point of view, it could safely be said that India's foreign policy has helped it to further the objectives mentioned above.

NEHRU, PATEL AND THE POLICE ACTION AGAINST HYDERABAD

Since very often a comparison is drawn between Nehru and Sardar Patel, invariably to the disadvantage of the former, it would be worthwhile to find out as to what was Sardar Patel's exact position in Nehru's Ministry as also in the Congress Organization. It is an undeniable fact that this senior leader of the Congress was endowed with great organizational capacity and was also a great administrator. His influence in the Congress organization was tremendous and if we think in terms of the Congress organization only, his position was on par with Nehru. However, it was not possible for Sardar Patel to take a decision bypassing Nehru, and as a rule Sardar Patel did not try to do that. Whenever Patel differed with Nehru, he tried to convince Nehru about the correctness of his stand and obtained thereby Nehru's support for that policy. Whenever Sardar Patel failed to get Nehru's approval for any action proposed by him, he gave in to Nehru. The Sardar was old and in none too good health when he became the Deputy Prime Minister in Nehru's Ministry. In March 1948, he suffered from a severe heart attack and from that time onwards the great Sardar was constantly conscious of the fact that he was moving in the shadow of death and that not much time was left for him. From March 1948, there was no question of Sardar either attempting or even desiring anything higher than what he had already achieved. Nehru on his part knew the great worth of Patel and treated him with utmost respect. In later years, Nehru treated Pandit Pant with almost equal measure of respect. However, neither Patel nor Pant could go against Nehru's wishes. There were many occasions when the relations between Sardar Patel and Nehru became strained. Whenever the strained relations reached a point of crisis, the Sardar expressed his desire to resign from the Ministry. However, people in Sardar's circle always dissuaded him from doing do so. Nehru never asked for Sardar's resignation nor tried to part company with him at any time. However, there does not seem to have arisen any occasion when Sardar Patel submitted his resignation and insisted on its acceptance and Nehru on his part entreated him not to press for its acceptance. Sardar Patel's position, though very important in Nehru's cabinet, thus had its own limitations. Sardar passed away in 1950. When people talk in such a way as if nothing worth the name was done by the Indian Government under Nehru in the subsequent fourteen years (because of the so called ineptness of Nehru as an administrator), it becomes unhappily necessary to examine Sardar Patel's position in the Indian Cabinet, as has been done above.

A very commonly held belief in India is that Nehru was opposed to the Police Action against Hyderabad and but for Sardar Patel it would not have taken place. Nobody seems to be bothered with the question as to whether such a decision of historic importance could have been taken by Sardar Patel without the concurrence of Nehru—a Prime Minister with an overwhelming influence over vital decisions. The fact of the matter is that the decision about the proposed Police Action (though euphemistically called the police action, it was actually a regular military operation) was taken as early as in March 1947 in view of the fast deteriorating conditions in Hyderabad State and the growing belligerence of the Razakars— the semi-military outfit in Hyderabad. It had become very clear by the beginning of 1948 that the Nizam of Hyderabad was in no mood for the accession of his state to the Indian Union and was only playing for time, through long and wasteful negotiations. Both Nehru and Patel had referred to the continued existence of the state of Hyderabad as a separate entity, as a 'cancer in the belly of India' which was dangerous to the unity and territorial integrity of the Indian Union. All available evidence goes to show that the decision to start military operations if nothing else succeeded, was taken in early 1948 and instructions were sent to the army to get ready for that eventuality. Nehru's letters to the chief ministers throw abundant hints about the governments intended action. The only difference, if any, was in regard to the timing of the proposed action. Nehru was actually aware of the fact that if this issue of international ramifications got complicated, what with Pakistan's intervention and the possible support of the Muslim countries (the daughter-in-laws of the Nizam belonged to the family of the last caliph of Turkey), the infant country's future would be in jeopardy. As such, he desperately sought a peaceful solution to the problem till the end. An additional reason for Nehru's desire to postpone the military operations scheduled for September 13, 1948, was the passing away of Mohd. Ali Jinnah—the Governor General of Pakistan just 2 days before the operations were to start. Nehru thought that it would not be in fitness of things for the operations to begin just at the time when the neighbouring state was in mourning because of the passing away of its Governor General. Nehru, it may be borne in mind had come to the conclusion as Patel did that a Police Action against Hyderabad was the ultimate solution, if nothing else helped. That Nehru had made up his mind in regard to Police Action against Hyderabad is confirmed by what he wrote in his letter to the Chief Ministers dated 1 July 1948. The letter carries a very significant sentence which is as follows: 'The present position in regard to Hyderabad is this, we are ready at a short notice to invade Hyderabad.'[86]

Having said that Nehru himself had made up his mind about the Police Action against Hyderabad, it must be said to the credit of Sardar. Patel that he adhered to the governments decision, taken earlier, to start the military operations on the scheduled date. In retrospect, one does feel that any delay in this matter would have resulted in great complications for India. But saying this is very different from saying that it was because of Sardar Patel that the Police Action against Hyderabad took place. As has already been stated above it was the governments decision, headed by Nehru, to resort to Police Action against Hyderabad if nothing else succeded. Evidently, the Police Action against Hyderabad would never have been taken, had Nehru been opposed to it.

GANDHI'S ADVICE ABOUT THE DISSOLUTION OF THE CONGRESS PARTY

Nehru and other Congress stalwarts are far too often criticized for going against Gandhi's advice to dissolve the Congress Party in the form in which it existed till freedom and convert it in a 'Lok Seva Sangh'. Had that idea been implemented, it would have created all sorts of problems to the newly independent country. In the interests of a strong and stable government at the Centre as well as in the States, a strong well organized and highly popular party was the pre-requisite and the Congress party fulfilled all these requirements. During the period of India's struggle for freedom the roots of the Congress party had extended even to the rural areas of the country and its name had become synonymous with India's aspiration for independence. It had become a household name during that period. It dissolution or it assuming a different form would have resulted in utter confusion for the people of India and it would have adversely affected our plans to give a concrete shape to our ideals and objectives.

NEHRU—THE ARCHITECT OF MODERN INDIA

It was Jawaharlal Nehru who played the most decisive role in the first seventeen years of our freedom, as the first prime minister of the country. Among the top leaders of the Congress, his influence over the provisions of the Indian Constitution was the greatest. In fact, many provisions of the Constitution were based on the resolutions moved by him from time to time in the pre-Independence Congress sessions. Thus, the Constitution as a whole bears the stamp of Nehru's ideas on political, social and economic matters. Again, it was Nehru who tried to create in the country by words and deeds an atmosphere in tune with the letter and spirit of the Constitution. To ensure the proper implementation of his ideas he chose as his associates persons of undoubted talent and ability such as Benegal Narsing Rao, Benegal Rama Rao, Girijashanker Bajpai, Sardar Panikkar, K.P.S. Menon and others. C.D. Deshmukh and V.K. Krishna Menon were two diametrically opposite persons by temperament and training and yet Nehru valued both of them and took them into confidence because of their conspicuous ability and undoubted brilliance. There was a time when people said that Nehru's economic policies were far too much influenced by C.D. Deshmukh and later the same thing was said about the influence of Krishna Menon over Nehru's political decisions. However a close student of Nehru's politics cannot but conclude that Nehru did not allow his policies to be governed by others, beyond a certain point, however eminent they may have been. Nehru's relationship with C.D. Deshmukh and V.K. Krishna Menon bears testimony to this fact.

Nehru, during the period of India's struggle of freedom did not part company with Gandhi, not only because he was profoundly influenced by

Gandhi's personality and some of his ideas but also because of the fact that he realized that in the context of the objective set of circumstances, it was only Gandhi who had the capacity to lead the movement and any break up with him on ideological or other grounds would adversely affect India's movement for freedom. However, while following the Mahatma in many important ways, he prepared the minds of his compatriots for the acceptance of many non-Gandhian ideas, specially in the economic domain, by moving appropriate resolutions in the various sessions of the Congress. In the post-Independence period it was primarily because of Nehru's leadership that India became a stable democracy based on the firm foundations of secularism. If one wants to understand what Gandhi and Nehru meant to the country, one should imagine India without Gandhi or for that matter an India without Nehru—so immense was the impact of these two stalwarts on India, after 1920.

Critics of Nehru could not be blamed for finding fault with some of his policies and decisions and even if we concede that they were right in their judgement, the fact remains that Nehru was a towering personality and that on balance his achievements were far greater than his failures.

However, in all fairness to Nehru it must be pointed out that his critics have been less than fair to him in recent years. His policy of non-alignment in general and the China and Kashmir policy in particular, have been subjected to a great deal of criticism. That this criticism, stems from a very inadequate understanding of the motivating considerations behind the pursuit of those policies would be obvious to any one who cares to examine the relevant facts carefully. Moreover, the image of Nehru as the Hamlet of Indian politics or one who was not practical or realistic, is a very distorted one. Nehru never wavered on basic issues. If at all he was an idealist it was only in the sense that he could take a long range view of matters, by projecting his mind into the future and by sensing the requirements of today as well as tomorrow.

The River Valley Projects, Steel Plants, Scientific Laboratories, Technical Institutes, Cultural Centres and many such important schemes of far reaching importance were launched by Nehru. On the side of social justice he took the initiative in taking up the Hindu Code Bill inspite of stiff opposition within the Congress party itself. Nehru himself felt that this was his most notable achievement in the post-freedom period.

I have gone into considerable details in this book to show as to how Nehru's role was a multi-dimensional one during India's struggle for freedom and how in the post Independence period he strove tirelessly to bring into reality the India of his dreams, through his statesmanlike approach to different problems. When one takes into account all these facts one cannot but agree with the view that Nehru was indeed 'the architect of Modern India'!

NOTES

1. *Glimpses of World History*, Jawaharlal Nehru, Lindsay Drummond Ltd., London W.C. 1., Fourth Edition, January 1949,pp. 404-405.
2. Ibid., loc. cit.
3. Ibid., p. 533.
4. Ibid., p, 529.
5. *Jawaharlal Nehru's Speeches* (1949-1953). The Publication Division, Ministry of Information and Broadcasting, Govt. of India, Calcutta, 1954, pp. 93-96.
6. *Glimpses of World History*, Jawaharlal Nehru, Lindsay Drummond Ltd., London W.C. 1., Fourth Edition, January 1949, p. 530.
7. Conversations with Mr. Nehru, Tibor Mende, Secker and Warburg, London, 1956, pp. 76-77.
8. *The Unity of India*, Jawaharlal Nehru, Lindsay Drummond London, W.C 1, 1948, p.118.
9. During the course of the author's second interview with Nehru, New Delhi, October 26, 1960.
10. *Talks with Nehru*, Norman Cousins, London, Victor Gollanez, 1951, p. 22.
11. Ibid., loc. cit.
12. Ibid., p. 14.
13. Ibid., pp. 24-25.
14. Ibid., p.25.
15. The Mind of Mr. Nehru, Interviews by R.K. Karanjia, George Allen and Unwin, London, 1961, pp. 100-101.
16. To the author in New Delhi, 26th October 1960.

17a. Roses in December, M.C. Chagla, Ninth Edition, January 1990, Bharatiya Vidya Bhavan, Bombay, pp. 442-443.

17b. *Jawaharlal Nehru's Speeches* (1949-53), The Publication Division, Ministry of Information and Broadcasting, Govt. of India, Calcutta, 1954, p. 144.

18. Ibid., loc. cit.
19. Independence and After: A Collection of the more important speeches of Jawaharlal Nehru from Sept. 1946 to May 1949, The Publication Division, Ministry of Information and Broadcasting, Govt. of India, Calcutta,1950, p. 258.
20. *Jawaharlal Nehru's Speeches* (1949-1953),The Publication Division, Ministry of Information and Broadcasting, Govt. of India, Calcutta, 1954, p. 129.
21. Ibid, p. 145.
22. *Speeches of Jawaharlal Nehru*, Vol. II, edited by Jagat S. Bright, M.A., Indian Printing Works, New Delhi, 1958, p. 534.
23. *Background of India's Foreign Policy*, N.V. Rajkumar, A.I.C.C., New Delhi, 1953, p. 96.
24. *Jawaharlal Nehru's Speeches* (1949-1953), The Publication Division, Ministry of Information and Broadcasting, Govt. of India, Calcutta, 1954, p. 183.

25. *Speeches of Jawaharlal Nehru*, Vol. II, edited by J.S. Bright, M.A, Indian Printing Works, New Delhi, 1958, p. 480.
26. Jawaharlal Nehru's Press Conferences 1953, Information Service of India, New Delhi, p. 26,
27. *The Time of India*, Bombay, 8th July 1950, p. 1.
28. *Jawaharlal Nehru's Speeches* (1953-1957), The Publication Division, Ministry of Information and Broadcasting, Govt. of India, Calcutta, Delhi, 1959, p. 244-245
29. Ibid., p. 246,
30. The six-point plan was quoted by Nehru, in his speech in the Lok Sabha on April 24, 1954, (India's Foreign Policy, Selected Speeches of Jawaharlal Nehru, from September 1946 to April 1961), The Publication Division, Ministry of Information and Broadcasting, Govt. of India, Delhi, 1962, p. 399-400.
31. Ibid., pp 527-38.
32. Ibid., pp. 225-26.
33. Ibid., pp. 513.
34. Ibid., p. 398.
35. Ibid., p. 192.
36. Ibid., pp. 192-93
37. *India News*, January 30, 1954, p. 452.
38. Independence and After: A collection of the more important Speeches of Jawaharlal Nehru from September 1946 to May 1949, The Publication Division, Ministry of Information and Broadcasting, Govt. of India, Calcutta, 1949, p. 250.
39. *The World and the West*, A.J. Toynbee, Oxford, London, 1953, p. 34.
40. *Jawaharlal Nehru's Speeches* (1953-1957), The Publication Division, Ministry of Information and Broadcasting, Govt. of India, Culcutta, 1958, pp. 284-85.
41. At the Press Conference, on July 27, 1953 (Jawaharlal Nehru's Press Conferences1950-53, Information Services of India, New Delhi. p. 7).
42. *Jawaharlal Nehru's Speeches* (1953-1957),The Publication Division, Ministry of Information and Broadcasting, Govt. of India, 1958,pp. 281-82.
43. Ibid., pp. 362-63.
44. The concept of co-existence or *Panchsheel* owed its birth to the agreement between India and China in regard to Tibet (1954). The Preamble to the agreement stated: 'The principles and considerations which govern our mutual relations and the approach of the countries to each other are as follows: (i) Mutual respect for each other's territorial integrity and sovereignty; (ii) Mutual non-aggression; (iii) Mutual non interference in each other's internal affairs; (iv) equality and mutual benefit; and (v) Peaceful Co-existence.' (Ibid., p. 262)
45. Independence and After: A Collection of the more important Speeches of Jawaharlal Nehru from September 1946 to May 1949, The Publication Division, Ministry of Information and Broadcasting, Govt of India, Calcutta, 1949, pp. 259-60.
46. *Jawaharlal Nehru's Speeches* (1953-1957), The Publication Division, Ministry of Information and Broadcasting, Govt, of India, Calcutta, 1958, p. 307.
47. *India in World Affairs* (1947-1950), K.P. Karunakaran, Oxford University press, 1955, pp. 159-60.
48. *Supra*, pp. 56-57.
49. *Jawaharlal Nehru's Speeches* (1949-1953), The Publication Division, Ministry of Information and Broadcasting, Govt of India, 1954, pp. 134-135.

50. *Background of Indian Foreign Policy*, N.V. Rajkumar, A.I.C.C., New Delhi, 1953, p. 6.
51. *Recent Essays and Writings*, Jawaharlal Nehru, Kitabistan Allahabad, 1934, p. 22.
52. *India and the World*, Jawaharlal Nehru, George Allen and Unwin Ltd, London, 1936, p. 228.
53. *China, Spain and the War*, Jawaharlal Nehru, Kitabistan, Allahabad and London, 1940, pp. 180-181.
54. Independence and After: A Collection of the more important Speeches of Jawaharlal Nehru from September 1946 to May 1949, The Publication Division, Ministry of Information and Broadcasting, Govt. of India, 1949, pp. 266-68.
55. *India's Foreign Policy*, Selected Speeches, September 1946 to April 1961, Jawaharlal Nehru, The Publications Division, Ministry of Information & Broadcasting, Govt. ofIndia, 1961, p. 133.
56. Ibid., p. 135.
57. Ibid loc. cit.
58. Ibid., p. 139.
59. Ibid., pp. 139-140.
60. Ibid., p. 144.
61. Ibid., loc. cit.
62. Ibid., loc. cit.
63. Ibid., p. 146.
64. *My Years with Nehru: Kashmir*. B.N. Mullick, Allied Publishers Pvt. Ltd, p. 4.
65. *Nehru—The First Sixty Years*, Vol. I, Dorothy Norman, Asia Publishing House, Bombay, 1965, p. 610.
66. Earlier, on January 1,1948, India had taken the Kashmir issue to the Security Council. The appointment of a Commission was a subsequent development.
67. *The Kashmir Story*, B.L. Sharma, Asia Publishing House, 1967, Bombay, p. 57.
68. My Years with Nehru, B.N. Mullick, Allied Publisher Pvt. Ltd, pp. 6-7.
69. 'If a plebiscite had been held in Jammu and Kashmir sometime in 1949, there was a good chance that the majority of the people would have voted for India, because the wounds inflicted by the Pakistani raiders on the peaceful people of Kashmir were still fresh in their minds and India was held in much respect as their saviour. The National Conference was also a united body and had complete control in the valley. Pandit Nehru's prestige amongst the Kashmiris was very high. They remembered that he was the one leader who had gone to Kashmir in support of the people' liberation struggle and had courted arrest by Maharaja. Even the assessment of the British at that time was that there was an even chance for India to pull off the plebiscite'. (Ibid., p. 7).
70. *Crisis in Kashmir*, Alastair Lamb 1947-1966, Routledge and Kegan Paul, London, 1966, p. 50.
71. Ibid, p. 57.
72. *The Kashmir Story*, B.L. Sharma, Asia Publishing House, Bombay, 1967, pp. 132-135.
73. *My Years with Nehru-Kashmir*, B.N, Mullik, Allied Publishers Pvt. Ltd, Delhi, p. 11.
74. Ibid., p. 182.
75. Ibid., p. 183.
76. Ibid., p. 154.
77. *The Kashmir Story*, B.L. Sharma, Asia Publishing House, Bombay, 1967, p. 140.
78. Ibid., loc. cit.
79. *My Years with Nehru: The Chinese Betrayal*, B.N. Mullik, Allied Publishers Pvt. Ltd, Delhi, pp. 61-62,

80. Ibid., p. 72.
81. Ibid., p. 80.
82. Ibid., p. 122.
83. Ibid., pp. 365-366.
84. 'When in 1952...we had asked his (Nehru's) advice about the targets, he had clearly visualised that the two enemies whom India would have to confront would be Pakistan, which would utilise Pan-Islamism in its support and China which would utilise international communism for its...own ends... .'
85. Ibid., p. 84.
86. Jawaharlal Nehru Letters to Chief Ministers (1947-1964), Vol. I, 1947-49, Govt. of India, 1985, New Delhi, p. 147.

APPENDIX I

JAWAHARLAL NEHRU'S ROLE IN INDIAN POLITICS: BEFORE INDEPENDENCE

[*Note:* This lecture and the one that follows (Appendix (ii)) were delivered by the author at the Centre of Nehru Studies, Shivaji University, Kolhapur, on 17th of September, 2008.]

Vice-chancellor of Shivaji University and the Chairman of the first lecture, Dr. Salunkhe. Dr. Chousalkar, Mrs. Rajurkar, members of the Faculty, distinguished guests and dear students.

At the very outset I deem it my pleasant duty to thank those who are associated with the Department of Political Science and the Centre of Nehru Studies. Shivaji University, for the opportunity that has been given to me to speak on Jawaharlal Nehru this morning. I had the privilege of delivering three lectures at this very place four years back and I still carry in my mind very happy memories of those lectures.

The calendar years and dates are proverbial for their similarity but the 27th of May 1964 was different. It recorded not only the death of a very extraordinary person, but also the end of an era. On that day, a human dynamo ceased to function. Never in the recent history of India did a person mean so much to so many in so many different ways. I have Mr. Chairman, witnessed national mourning in the very real sense of the term, only on two occasions. Firstly, when Mahatma Gandhi was assassinated and secondly on the passing away of Jawaharlal Nehru.

Those who are fifty-five years old today or around that age have only a vague memory of having seen Nehru and for those who are younger still, Nehru is just a part of history. As ill-luck would have it, the younger people have a much distorted image of Nehru before their mind's eye. I do not want to deal with the question as to how and why these distortions have taken place and whether they are a result of an inadequate understanding of Nehru's ideas and policies or a consequence of deliberate and calculated efforts of those who were opposed to all that he had stood for. This question warrants a detailed and elaborate answer, but constraints of time prevent me from taking up this matter.

I belong to a generation which was profoundly influenced by the rare qualities of Jawaharlal Nehru's heart and mind, as also by his books, speeches and the quality of his leadership. It was always a matter of great aesthetic joy to see this incredibly handsome person, standing erect in an open car, in order to acknowledge the greetings of thousands of people who used to gather on both sides of the street in order to have a glimpse of him. Nehru was known for his great courage-physical and moral. He used to rush into crowds of mad rioters, their minds full of communal frenzy and snatch away daggers from the hands of such people, in total disregard to his personal safety. On the moral plane, he had the courage to criticise openly some of the ideas of Mahatma Gandhi in spite of the fact that Gandhiji had declared on more than one occasion that Jawaharlal was his political successor. Wherever and whenever liberty was compromised with, his used to be the first voice of protest. Even in the pre-Independence period he was known for his uncompromising support for democracy and his opposition to Nazism and Fascism. He could not sleep for days together when the Republicans suffered a set-back during the Spanish civil war of 1936.

Nehru's books drew worldwide attention. His autobiography, first published from London in 1936, underwent eighteen reprints in the very first year. The entire world realized the significance of India's struggle for independence under the leadership of Mahatma Gandhi, through Nehru's autobiography. After going through Nehru's autobiography, people in the West started referring to Nehru as 'Gandhi's Western face'. As early as in 1940, John Gunther, the author of 'Inside Asia',' Inside Europe' and other internationally acclaimed books, referred to Nehru as 'one of the six best writers of English prose'.

What I have stated so far, would give you some idea in regard to the great influence that Nehru wielded on my generation. There are several other matters to which I could refer in the context of his influence over us, but the constraints of time do not allow me to do so.

It is commonly believed that the correct evaluation of the role of a political leader is not possible during his own time and that some time should be allowed to pass before any such evaluation or assessment is attempted. Such a belief implies that the people belonging to the period to which the great man belongs are too near to him and too emotionally involved in contemporary events to take a detached and fairly objective view of the policies pursued by that leader or for that matter, the decisions taken by him. This view, though broadly speaking fairly correct, suffers from one inherent limitation. The attitude of admiration bordering sometimes on the verge of worship by contemporary people, towards a political figure, is a result in a considerable measure of their acute awareness in regard to the difficulties and peculiarities of circumstances in which that political leader had to function. As the time passes on the contours of those difficulties and peculiarities of the situation become increasingly less and less distinct and in consequence a proper assessment of the leader's work is rendered difficult. In this respect, the people of the contemporary generation have the distinct advantage of being a part of the entire set up in which that political leader operated. In so far as I am concerned, Mr. Chairman, I had the good fortune of belonging to the period in which Nehru had to meet different challenges under most trying circumstances and now I have the advantage of seeing Nehru from a distance, in terms of years. I can say very honestly that today, Nehru appears to me a bigger man still, than what he did earlier.

People belonging to a subsequent period have to contend with two challenges when they, attempt to evaluate the role of a political leader, belonging to an earlier period. The first of course is the one of becoming mentally a part of the earlier period and the second being the one of getting the facts correctly. Getting the facts correctly is always a difficult proposition but it becomes all the more difficult over a period of time as facts get twisted or are replaced by information which has no basis in facts. Moreover, it is also important to bear in mind that in the objective set of circumstances the choice before a leader is not always between good and better but it is sometimes between bad and worse. We have to take into account all these factors, while evaluating the role of a great leader. In so far as Nehru is concerned, as I had the opportunity of stating earlier, the distortions vis-a-vis his policies and ideas are so numerous that it requires a special effort on our part to reach the truth.

When a person's political career spans over a period of more than four decades, as was the case with Jawaharlal Nehru, some of the policies pursued by him or for that matter some of his decisions are bound to become controversial. A controversial decision by its very definition means that while some agree with that decision a few others do not. Nehru, who was one of the top most leaders of India for decades together, could not have escaped some controversies. Due to exigencies of time, I will not be able to deal with all of them. All that I can hope to do is to deal with only some of them and that too very briefly. However, I may state at this stage that if one takes into consideration all relevant facts pertaining to most of these controversies and examine them without pre-conceived notions, one would come to the conclusion that Nehru had strong reasons to pursue the policies that he did. My principal concern today will be to place before you a broad picture of the significant role that Nehru played in the pre-Independence period as also in the period that followed Independence, so that the younger members in the audience may know as to what Nehru meant for India. This has become all the more necessary, in view of that fact that Nehru's image today, as ill-luck would have it, is a much distorted one.

As is well known, Nehru was born with the proverbial silver spoon in his mouth. How was it that a person who was born in an aristocratic family and who had spent as many as seven years of his formative life in England and who was influenced by his stay in that country in different ways, become anti-British? The answer to this question lies in the experiences and influences on Nehru, during his childhood. It was during this period that seeds of nationalism were sown in his mind. As a child, he used to listen to the talk of his cousins which was invariably related to the overbearing character and insulting manners of the English people and the Eurasians towards Indians. He came to know from such talks as to how the people of India suffered at the hands of their alien rulers. An Englishman who killed an Indian was almost always acquitted by jury of his countrymen. Compartments were reserved for Europeans in railway trains, which the Indians were not permitted to occupy even when they were empty and when the train otherwise was terribly crowded. There was also reservation of benches and chairs for Europeans in parks and other places. This policy of discrimination and one that resulted in the humiliation of the Indian people at the hands of their British rulers filled Nehru's mind with anger and resentment against the British authority in India. To add to this were the stories that he heard from his father's Munshi-Mubarak Ali, about the excesses committed by English troops during the revolt of

1857, made Nehru anti-British authority in India, though he did not entertain feelings of anger against individual Englishmen.

It was in the month of May, 1905, that Nehru sailed for England to pursue education. A few months later Bengal was partitioned by the British, resulting in great unrest all over India. The great movement that was started to annul the partition of Bengal was led by Bal Gangadhar Tilak, Lala Lajpat Rai, Aurobindo and Bipin Chandra Pal. Nehru and other Indians at Cambridge University were greatly influenced by this movement and almost all of them became Tilakites or the followers of Tilak. It was roughly during this period that Nehru was vaguely attracted to Fabianism and other socialistic ideas.

The single greatest influence on Nehru in terms of personalities, was that of Gandhi, who he met for the first time at the fag-end of 1916, a little before the historic Lucknow Session of the Congress. Gandhi had returned to India in January, 1915, after a sojourn of about twenty years in South Africa. The impact of Gandhi's personality on young Nehru's sensitive and impressionable mind was tremendous and yet as far as approach to political problems was concerned Gandhi seemed to Nehru 'very distant, different and un-political', though he had admired Gandhi's heroic fight in South Africa. The opinion that Nehru formed when he met Gandhi for the first time however underwent a complete change soon afterwards. Nehru worked as some kind of secretary to Gandhi, when Gandhi visited Punjab soon after the Jallianwala Bagh tragedy. It was during this period that Nehru's faith grew in the wisdom and political insight of Gandhi. In addition to sound judgement Gandhi had a unique capacity of winning over sceptics and those who were opposed to his policies and programme. Josh Mallihabadi, the great Urdu poet tells us in his extremely readable autobiography in Urdu entitled 'Yaadon Ki Barat' as to how he felt greatly disappointed when he saw Gandhi for the first time during the Congress Session of 1918 and how he wondered as to how such an ordinary looking person could lead India's movement for freedom. He however, changed his opinion completely after spending a half hour with Gandhi a little later. He tells the readers of his autobiography that he felt convinced after that short meeting that India just couldn't have a better leader than Gandhi. Mr. Chairman, another anecdote comes to my mind when I think of Gandhi's capacity to convince others about the soundness of his judgement. C.R. Das, the great leader from Bengal, attended the Nagpur Session of the Congress held in 1920, with the avowed purpose of 'crushing'

Gandhi. He had decided to oppose Gandhi's resolution the next morning. Gandhi sent a small note to C.R. Das around 10 p.m. and requested Das to see him for a few minutes. The brilliant leader from Bengal with a razor sharp intellect entered Gandhi's tent, metaphorically speaking, roaring like a lion, only to come out of it like a meek lamb after 10 minutes. At the end of the meeting C.R. Das was so convinced about the correctness of Gandhi's stand that he thumped the table in front of him and said, 'Damn it Gandhi, you are always right and we are always wrong'. A little later, C.R. Das went to the tent of the delegates from Bengal and asked them to support the resolution that Gandhi was to move the next morning. I thought Mr. Chairman, that I should narrate these anecdotes in order to drive home the fact that Gandhi's political insight and sense of judgement influenced not only Nehru but almost everyone else who came in contact with him.

The Gandhi-Nehru relationship provides a key to the understanding of the developments that took place in the political domain, in the pre-Independence period. But to deal with them in details would necessitate a separate speech. I shall therefore try to be as brief as possible and highlight only such matters wherein Nehru was influenced by the Gandhian ideas and Gandhi's approach to different problems, as also those where he was openly critical of them. Nehru points out in his autobiography as to how Gandhi made the Congress a dynamic organization and discouraged all empty and fruitless talk. Before Gandhi's advent, the Congress by and large had indulged merely in talking and passing resolutions which were not taken seriously by anybody. To the earnest Nehru, full of patriotic zeal, Gandhi's insistence on action appealed all the more as he was tired of the empty talk, pious platitudes and noisy politics of the day.

Gandhi's insistence on fearlessness had an immense effect on Nehru, as the dominant impulse under the British rule was fear. Gandhi used to say that there was nothing to fear in this world except fear itself. It was Gandhi, who made the people of India so fearless as to enable them to come out openly against the oppressive rule of the British. To Gandhi, courage was the one sure foundation of character and without it there was no morality, no religion, no love. Cowardice, according to Gandhi was a contagious crime. Being a fearless man himself, Gandhi's appeal to the people to shed fear, made a deep impact on Nehru's mind.

Though Nehru approved Gandhi's emphasis on village industry, he did not agree with Gandhi's views on the use of big machines. Gandhi was opposed to the use of big machines for a variety of reasons but I will not deal with that question because of the paucity of time. Nehru was all in favour of tractors and big machinery as he felt that the only way of solving many of India's urgent problems was through rapid industrializations of the country.

As on big machines, Nehru also did not agree with Gandhi's concept of Trusteeship which appeared to Nehru wholly impracticable and unrealistic. To give power and wealth to an individual and expect him to use it entirely for public good was according to Nehru, entirely unreasonable, as even the best of us could not be trusted that way.

Gandhi's insistence on the adoption of good means for the achievement of good ends met with Nehru's approval. Gandhi thought that the Machiavellian dictum that 'ends justify means' was wrong ethically and harmful even from a practical point of view. To him means and ends were convertible terms and as such should be equally pure. Gandhi likened the means to a seed and the end to a tree, and thought that there was the same inviolable connection between the means and the end as there was between the seed and the tree. Nehru spoke almost Gandhi's language, when he addressed the Columbia University in October 1949. He said that there was always a close and intimate relationship between the end that was aimed at and the means that were adopted for its attainment. It was just not possible to separate the means from the ends, as they were connected very intimately and inextricably. In his book, *The Discovery of India*, Nehru has expressed the opinion that he considered Gandhi's stress on right means as one of his greatest contributions to Indian public life.

Though Nehru was greatly influenced by Gandhi's insistence on the purity of means even in political life, he accepted Gandhi's programme of non-violent struggle for the achievement of India's freedom, primarily on pragmatic considerations. He of course, admired and approved the moral and ethical side of non-co-operation and Satyagraha, though he did not give absolute allegiance to non-violence or accept it forever. He was attracted to it more and more because the belief grew on him that in the context of India's background and traditions and also that of existing conditions that was a right policy for them to pursue.

Nehru was convinced of the futility of violent means for the achievement of freedom and thought that acts of terrorism and the killing of individual officers by bomb or pistol was a bankrupt's creed. It was simply absurd and ridiculous, thought Nehru, to imagine that such acts could shake a powerfully organized government, however much they might terrify and frighten individuals. In his presidential address at the Lucknow Congress, delivered on April 12, 1936, Nehru described terrorism as a sign of 'political immaturity in people'. It was therefore very understandable that he should have welcomed Gandhi's technique of non-violence. Gandhi had placed it before the country not only because it was a right method but also because of the fact that it was, very effective. To Nehru however non-violent method of resistance was not an unchallengable creed or dogma. It was for him essentially a policy and a method which promised certain results and in the ultimate analysis it was to be judged by those results only.

Nehru's autobiography and his other writings, as also his speeches, make it fairly clear that but for his faith in the effectiveness of the non-violent movement he would not have supported it. The pragmatist Nehru realized more quickly than others that Gandhi's method was the only feasible and effective method in those circumstances. In his presidential speech at the Lahore Congress of 1929, Nehru pointed out that the people of India had neither the material nor training for organized violence and that in the absence of those pre-requisites it was a folly to adopt violent methods. Any effective movement for the liberation of a country should necessarily be one which had mass support and such mass movements had to be peaceful except when there was an organized revolt. In the '*Glimpses of World History*', Nehru gave expression to similar views. He pointed out as to how, for the disarmed people of India, armed rebellion was out of the question. Even if the people of India did make such an attempt, it could be very easily put down by the British authority in India.

After the Russian revolution of 1917 a large number of young Indians with leftist ideas started entertaining dreams of a similar revolt in India, without realising the utter impracticability of such a dream coming true in the totally dissimilar conditions of India. Such young men were not drawn to the ethical side of Gandhi's non-violent movement for freedom. It was primarily because of Nehru that they became conscious of the fact that there was no real alternative to the technique of non-violence in the peculiar conditions that existed in India. When the pragmatic implications of the non-violent movement became evident to them, they turned from violence to non-violence.

As I had stated at the beginning of my speech, Nehru was drawn to socialistic ideas when he was studying at Cambridge University. However, after his return to India even that academic interest in socialism receded into the background of his mind when he took a plunge in to the freedom movement. Though he read a few books on socialism during the First World War period, the socialistic ideal did not take deep roots in his mind till his visit to Soviet Russia. It was roughly during the late 'twenties that he did considerable reading of Marxist-Leninist literature and this coupled with his visit to Russia, resulted in his becoming a confirmed believer in the socialistic ideal, though he did not approve of the communist method of reaching it. A study of Marx and Lenin however produced a powerful effect on his mind and which in turn enabled him to see history and current affairs in a new light. He gained a new perspective on history and thence forward considered India's struggle for freedom as one of the world problems in which people elsewhere ought to be equally interested. India was a typical example of imperialist domination and the success of Britain in retaining its hold over India had tempted other countries to undertake imperialist adventures. The global view that Nehru took of India's movement for freedom, was reflected in two of his statements of that period, one being that India's movement for freedom was not an isolated phenomenon but was on the other hand a part of a wider movement against colonialism and imperialism and the other being that it was not Britain that was India's enemy but it was imperialism and wherever imperialism was, there India could not willingly remain.

The study of Marxist-Leninist literature resulted in Nehru taking the view in the 'thirties that democracy was incompatible with capitalism as democracy symbolised power of the many and capitalism gives power only to the few. Even in a democracy the government under a capitalist setup could only be that of the possessing classes for the advancement of their interest. It would be possible thought Nehru to have a government by the people and for the people only when power went in to the hands of the masses and that happened only under socialism.

At this stage, it would be relevant and appropriate to discuss Nehru's socialism in relation to democracy. Nehru's public utterances for more than three decades make it abundantly clear that he had always desired to raise the superstructure of socialism in India, on the firm foundations of democratic principles. Nehru's faith in a democratic way of life primarily resulted from the influence of the Indian way of life and that of the 19th century liberalism, on his mind. Probably it was also the result of the impact on Nehru's mind, of the evils of the suppression of individual liberty and the denial of basic rights—a normal feature of the British rule in India. Moreover, the Indian National Movement of which Nehru was an integral part was itself based on the democratic urges of the Indian people for self-rule.

Nehru's first major pronouncement in favour of socialism came through his Presidential address to the Lahore Congress of 1929. In this address, Nehru stated that he was a socialist and a republican and that he did not believe either in kingship or in the capitalist order, which produced kings of industry. He further stated that India too would have to go the socialistic way if she sought to end her poverty and inequality.

Throughout his political career Nehru lent his support to the ideology of socialism with a surprising degree of consistency and constantly stressed the fact that it was most essential to bear in mind the needs of the country, while accepting it. In other words, his approach was never very rigid and doctrinaire. The socialistic measures that Nehru advocated in the pre-Independence period included the abolition of the Princely States, which were the remnants of the old feudal order, the abolition of Zamindari and similar systems, which resulted in poverty and inequality, progressive taxation, nationalisation of key industries and similar such measures.

Even in the pre-Independence period, Nehru believed in the concept of Planning, so as to ensure a balanced progress of the country. Since Subhash Chandra Bose was aware of Nehru's interest in planning, he made Nehru the Chairman of the Planning Committee when he (Bose) became the president of the Congress in 1938. The Committee did commendable work in spite of the obvious limitation on its functioning. It can thus be said that it was Nehru who made India 'Planning conscious' in the pre-Independence period itself.

Nehru not only strived ceaselessly for the liberation of India from foreign yolk, but also constantly applied his mind to the socio-economic and political problems that Independent India would have to face and sought solutions to them. Through his books and speeches in the pre-Independence period as also through the large number of resolutions that he moved in the different sessions of the India National Congress, he more or less placed before his countrymen the blue print of Independent India's policies and programme. Thus, when we became free on the 15th of August, 1947, we were fairly clear in our minds about the direction in which we should move and the path that we should follow. I may be permitted Mr. Chairman, to make a mention in this connection of some of the resolutions that Nehru moved in the Congress sessions during that period—resolutions which are indicative of his vision and capacity to project his mind into the future and sense the needs and requirements of the days to come. As early as in 1927, twenty years before India became free, Nehru moved a resolution on India's foreign policy, at the Madras session of the Congress, through which the broad approach of India to various international problems was highlighted. Yet another resolution of great significance was drafted by Nehru but was moved by Gandhi at the Karachi session of the Congress of 1931, a historic resolution which has come to be known as Resolution on Fundamental Rights and Economic Programme. This resolution was in the nature of a pledge by the Congress in regard to the rights that the people would enjoy in Independent India. Some of the clauses of the resolution suggest very clearly that India's future political setup would be secular in nature and content. Nehru's resolution on the abolition of Zamindari, passed at the Lucknow session of the Congress in 1936, was indicative of Nehru's earnestness to give an economic content to freedom.

The Indian National Congress followed a policy of non-interference in the affairs of the Princely States for a considerably long time, before freedom. This, in spite of the fact that the Princely states, to use the words of Nehru, represented 'probably the extreme type of autocracy in the world'. Even Gandhi, upto the year 1938, stuck to the policy of non-interference in the affairs of the Princely States, which were almost 600 in number and barring few exceptions, civil liberties were non-existent in them. Gandhi, evidently, wanted to win over the Princes and make them see reason. Nehru on the other hand was very keen on extending the national movement to the Princely States too and bring the people there in the main stream of the national movement. In fact, he wanted those remnants of feudalism to vanish from the map of India, in the interest of democracy and the political unity of the country. His was the most important role in shaping the Congress attitude towards the Princes and he played the most active role in the All-India States' Peoples Conference, as its president for years together.

It is hardly necessary for me to stress the fact that but for the incessant and intense efforts of Nehru, there would not have been the necessary measure of political awakening in the people of the Princely States. While the role of Sardar Patel in the consolidation of the newly won freedom. has been acclaimed on all sides and rightly so, the efforts made by Nehru towards political awakening in such States in the pre-Independence period, seem to go unnoticed. With all respect for Sardar Patel, I may venture to state that his work towards the integration of the Princely States with the Indian union, would have become all the more difficult, if the people of these states had not stood solidly for the accession of these states to the Indian union—this being the direct result of the efforts made by the All India States' Peoples Conference—the moving spirit of this organization being Jawaharlal Nehru, for more than 15 years before Independence.

I had stated Mr. Chairman, in the earlier part of my speech as to how under the influence of the Marxist-Leninist literature, Nehru considered India's movement for freedom as a part of a wider movement against colonialism and imperialism. To that, I may add here that he was opposed to Nazism and Fascism too, which were opposed to the ideology of democracy and which stood for authoritarian rule at home and imperialism abroad. Nehru was so intensely opposed to Fascist Italy and Nazi Germany that he refused to meet Mussolini in 1936 and turned down an invitation from Hitler to visit Germany in 1938. He projected India's image on the international plane as a country that was not opportunistic but as one which stood for democracy and human equality. It was because of this that President Roosevelt brought pressure on the British government during the course of the Second World War, to transfer power into Indian hands. Roosevelt assured Churchill, the then Prime Minister of England that India would support the cause of democracy on the international plane—the guarantee being Jawaharlal Nehru.

Mr. Chairman Sir, during the last one hour or more, I made an endeavour to deal with Nehru's role in India's movement for freedom. I hope that the members of this distinguished audience would agree with me when I say that Nehru played a most vital part in the freedom movement through his multi-dimensional approach to it. I thank you ladies and gentlemen for being so attentive and for giving me a patient hearing.

Courtesy: Centre of Nehru Studies, Shivaji University, Kolhapur and Paramount Publishing House, Hyderabad – New Delhi.

APPENDIX II

JAWAHARLAL NEHRU'S ROLE IN INDIAN POLITICS: AFTER INDEPENDENCE

Chairman of the meeting Shri Kishor Bedkihal, Dr. Chousalkar, ladies and gentlemen.

As I stand before you to speak about Nehru's role in Indian politics, as independent India's first Prime Minister, my mind goes back to a cartoon by R.K. Laxman that had appeared in the Shankar's weekly, during the early years of our independence. The cartoon revealed the immense burden that Nehru was carrying on his shoulders and the superhuman effort that he was making in order to render his dreams about India's future, into realities. The title of the cartoon was 'The show must go on'. The cartoon showed Nehru playing different musical instruments at the same time in a musical concert. The different instruments carried on them the names of different portfolios that Nehru was holding at that time. He was playing a couple of instruments with his mouth, a couple of instruments with his left hand, a couple of instruments with his right hand, an instrument with his toes and then the cartoon shows a tabla to his right, which was yet to be played. Nehru turns towards the audience and asks: 'is there a tabla player in the audience?' and after getting an answer in the negative starts playing the tabla too, with his right hand. That cartoon showed in unmistakable terms as to how Nehru was shouldering numerous responsibilities of bewildering variety almost single-handedly in order to put India on the right track.

Nothing would be more erroroneous than an attempt to evaluate Nehru's achievements in arithmetical terms. To judge Nehru on the basis of the problems that he had solved and those which he couldn't, would indeed be very misleading as Nehru's legacy was the one of hundreds of problems that had accumulated during 150 years of British misrule. The statistical approach to Nehru's achievements would be as misleading as the assertion by an expert in Statistics who declared that if a person had one of his hands in a refrigerator and the other on a burning stove, on an average, he would be comfortable!

India's population was around forty crores when it became free. During that period Nehru once said that there were as many problems in India as the people living in it. On yet another occasion Nehru stated that every age was represented in India, from the Cow dung age to the Nuclear age. To carry such a complex society forward and that too through the process of democracy was indeed a very difficult task. Moreover, the party that he led was not really suited to independent India's requirements, as it was far from homogenous. The Congress was essentially a heterogeneous organization, having within its fold people holding all shades of opinion. It was however quite understandable that it should be so, as it was primarily intended to serve the purpose of winning freedom for the country. It was because of this that all those who broadly agreed with the Congress strategy to win freedom, became its members. Their views on other political matters being not of immediate relevance, diversity in them did not very much matter during that period. To take the country quickly in the direction of progress through the instrumentality of such a party was not easy; as groups within the Congress pulled in different directions.

It has to be borne in mind that the task of the first Prime Minister of a newly independent country is far more difficult than that of his successors. He has to do the pioneering work in every sphere and lay down traditions and practices which his successors could follow with advantage. Nehru had to face the added difficulty of bringing about changes in a static and tradition bound society. As if all this was not enough, immediately after assuming office, he had to face the tremendous refugee problem, which shook the economy of the newly independent country to its very foundations.

In spite of the overwhelming difficulties that he faced, Nehru proceeded ahead with the task of laying down firm foundations of democracy in India. While democratic structures toppled down in various parts of Asia like structures made of playing cards, democracy took strong roots in India primarily because of Nehru's mature and democracy-oriented leadership. He made every effort to establish the finest traditions of democratic behaviour. In order to facilitate his presence in the Parliament as often as possible, during the periods when parliament was in session, he established yet another office in the Parliament House itself. I am Mr. Chairman, reminded here of and incident which revealed Nehru's keen desire to adhere to the norms of proper parliamentary behaviour. On a certain day, Nehru asked Shri G.V. Mavalankar—the Speaker of the Lok Sabha, to make it convenient to see him at his office in the parliament premises. The upright Speaker sent a note to Nehru stating that since he (the Speaker) was the highest authority in so far as the parliament house was concerned, it would be in fitness of things if the Prime Minister came over to his chamber. Nehru, without taking the slightest offence, immediately went to the Speaker's chamber and offered his apologies to him.

When Nehru was in one of the two Houses of the Parliament, he more often than not assumed the role of a school teacher, telling the members as to how they should maintain dignity and decorum in the House. Nehru himself was an ideal parliamentarian. His behaviour in the Parliament was always consistent with the highest traditions of parliamentary behaviour. He made it a point to congratulate even the members of the opposition when their contribution to a debate was significant. In so far as Nehru's speeches in the Parliament are concerned they compel our attention as much for their content as for the dignified manner in which they were delivered.

In spite of his firm belief in socialism, Nehru as the Prime Minister, taking into account the objective realities of the situation, followed a policy of 'mixed economy'. He had come to grips with practical problems and it was no longer possible for him to talk merely in theoretical terms.

Nehru realized that higher living standards for the people of India could be ensured only through a progressive increase in production and since India was essentially an under developed country with inadequate capital and shortage of technical personnel, it was necessary to allow public as well as private capital to come into play. In the conditions in which India found herself, immediately after freedom, it was wise and prudent to support mixed economy rather than go headlong in socialist direction.

In one of his speeches during that period, Nehru told his listeners as to how, in day to day administration, 'isms' do not very much come into the picture. In that connection, he gave an interesting example. He said that the government had invited plans for the construction of a dam over a river from two engineers, one belonging to U.S.A.—a capitalist country and the other to the Soviet Union—a communist country, but the plans that these two submitted were identical for the simple reason that there was no such thing as a capitalist dam or for that matter a communist dam. From an engineering point of view a dam was simply a dam. He further stated in that speech that he was not enamoured of the 'isms' and his approach was and that of his country should be a phlegmatic approach in considering any problem. Whatever be the method, stated Nehru, so long as it brought about necessary changes and gave satisfaction to the masses would justify itself and give hope.

Though Nehru followed a policy of gradualism and moderation to begin with, he was nevertheless leading the county slowly towards socialism, in spite of the opposition from many of his countrymen. In December 1954, Nehru initiated a proposal in the parliament in regard to the amendment of a certain part of the constitution, so that the courts may no longer have the right of determining the amount of compensation for the property confiscated by the state. In the same session proposals in regard to the nationalisation of the Imperial Bank of India were made known to the parliament by the then Finance Minister, C.D. Deshmukh. In this very session of the Parliament, the Lok Sabha passed a resolution which was as follows: 'This House, having considered the economic situation in India and the policy of the government in relation thereto, is of the opinion that (1) the policy of the government is in harmony with the statement of 6th April 1948, (2) the objective of our economic policy should be a socialist pattern of society, and (3) towards this end the tempo of economic activity in general and industrial development in particular should be stepped up to the maximum possible extent'.

The Congress following Nehru's line of thinking passed at its Avadi Session (January 1955), an important resolution, which took India a step further, in the direction of a socialistic state. This resolution (known as the 'socialist pattern' resolution), which was passed unanimously, envisaged the establishment of a socialistic pattern of a society in India. It stated in part, I quote, 'planning should take place with a view to the establishment of a socialistic pattern, in which the principal means of production are under social ownership or control, production is progressively speeded up and there is equitable distribution of the national wealth...the public sector must playa progressively greater part, more particularly in the establishment of basic industries.' This resolution was followed by the resolution on 'The Co-operative Farming', which was adopted at the Nagpur Session (1959) of the Congress. The resolution on 'Co-operative Farming' could not make much headway in practical terms because of opposition to it by a sizable section of Congressmen.

Sometimes it is asked as to whether Nehru would have approved of the policy of liberalisation, which the Congress adopted in later years. This is essentially a hypothetical question and such questions have no definite answers. All that could be said by way of answer to this question is that Nehru's approach to problems was never rigid and doctrinaire and that his approach to this question would have depended on his understanding of national and international currents and cross-currents. Incidentally, I may mention that I had the privilege of holding lengthy interviews with Nehru and I found that while answering my questions he always took into account not only the situation in the country but also the international trends, because he was aware of the fact that in the world of today, no country was an island by itself. I hope that it would not be out of place if I were to mention here that during the course of those interviews, Nehru treated me with extreme courtesy and kindness, in spite of the fact that he was at that time a world figure and I was just a young man around thirty years old. When the veteran leader C. Rajagopalachari, the first Governor-General of independent India, referred to Nehru after Nehru's death as, 'the most civilised among us all, when many of us are not even civilised,' I was most forcefully reminded of the gracious treatment that was meted out to me by Jawaharlal Nehru.

Very rightly and appropriately Nehru is described as the architect and builder of Modern India. I had stated in my earlier lecture Mr. Chairman, as to how Nehru gave a deep thought to the problems that independent India would have to face and sought solutions to them through the resolutions that he moved in Congress sessions. Even if one goes through his books, such as his autobiography, *The Discovery of India* and the Unity of India, one gets an idea of his insight into India's problems and the clear perception that he had in regard to the manner in which they could be solved. He was convinced that the pre-requisite for India's social and economic progress, as also for its political stability, was its industrial, technological and scientific advancement. Even in the pre-Independence period, he used to remind his countrymen that India's independence would be a nominal one unless it makes rapid progress and gains strength, as weak nations always fall a victim to economic imperialism. Thus, Nehru, as the first Prime Minister of independent India ensured the all round progress of India through taking up River Valley Projects, by setting up of

Steel Plants, establishing technological institutes and scientific laboratories. People in the United States refer to India as one of the emerging super powers, for which the credit should go in a large measure to Nehru's vision.

The essential factor in the proper growth of a nation according to Nehru was the capacity of its people to look at problems in perspective. They should imbibe from the past whatever was really good and at the same time they should keep pace with the present by keeping the windows of their mind open. Nehru once likened the past of a country to the roots of a plant and the present to the air and sunshine above terra firma. If the roots are neglected the plant would not survive. At the same time the plant would not grow and there would not be branching out and flowering of the plant, unless it is provided with sunshine and free air. So what is required is a deep respect for the accumulated wisdom of the past combined with the ability to accept everything that is good about the present.

India's foreign policy of which Jawaharlal Nehru was the chief architect, revealed a harmonious blending of nationalism with internationalism and pragmatism with idealism. As the first Prime Minister of independent India and as one who had spent the greater part in struggling for the emancipation of his country, Nehru was naturally very anxious to pursue a policy, which would be conducive to the consolidation of the newly won freedom and to the progress and advancement of the people. And yet, Nehru was not moved to action on pragmatic consideration only. Since independence, Nehru had striven hard for the preservation of world peace, for India's benefit as also for the good of the entire world and the liberation of those countries which were still under foreign domination. Moreover, he consistently raised his voice against all those acts which resulted in the denial of justice or compromise with liberty.

Nehru used to point out repeatedly that while other goals were important, the foreign policy of India, like its internal policy, was directly intended to promote the interests of its people. He preferred the term external policy to the term foreign policy on the grounds that there was nothing foreign about the country's foreign policy and that it primarily aimed at the country's good. It was necessarily conditioned by its past, recent as well as remote, its geographical situation, considerations of strategy and defence, the values cherished by its people and above all by the contemporary national and international situation.

The policy that Nehru followed in the context of international situation, came to be known as a policy of 'non-alignment'. In the post-Second World War period, two power blocs emerged on the global scene, representing ideologies, diametrically opposite to each other. The communist countries seemed bent upon liberating the world from the clutches of capitalism whereas the democratic countries seemed equally determined to make the world safe for democracy, by combating communist influence everywhere. The result was an incessant 'cold war' between the two power blocs. During that period, the world came very near to a shooting war on more than one occasion. And the one thing the world could not afford during this Nuclear age was the breaking out of another world war, which if it unfortunately did, would inevitably result in the complete destruction of the human race and the total annihilation of our civilisation. Nehru decided that India should not align itself either with the Anglo-American bloc or the Russian bloc, in the interests of world peace, as also for the good of India. He strongly put forward the idea that the nations of the world should learn to co-exist in spite of their ideological differences as the alternative to co-existence in this Nuclear age was co-destruction. In so far as India was concerned, it could not entertain the idea of joining the Anglo-American bloc, in spite of its ideological affinity to the nations belonging to that bloc because two powerful communist countries—China and the Soviet Union were its immediate neighbours and friendly relations with your neighbours is a matter of prime importance in international politics. India could not consider the option of joining the Soviet bloc either as the nations in this bloc had authoritarian type of governments. Moreover, Nehru considered the conflict between the Anglo-American bloc and the Soviet Union bloc as 'Other Men's Quarrel' in which India was not interested. He put forward the view that the newly independent countries of Asia and Africa had problems peculiar to themselves and that neither the approach of the developed democratic countries nor the one represented by the nations in the Soviet bloc would help them to solve their problems. Nehru's point of view was accepted by a large number of nations belonging to Asia and Africa and in a very short span of time the concept of non-alignment gained strength and momentum.

India's adherence to the policy of non-alignment was in harmony with the basic tenets of India's foreign policy (apart from other considerations) which were clearly and categorically stated in resolution V at the Jaipur Session of the Indian National Congress in 1948. That the resolution represented in totality the views of Nehru, hardly needs a separate mention.

I may be permitted to quote an important paragraph from this resolution. 'The foreign policy of India must necessarily be based on the principles that have guided the Congress in past years. These principles are promotion of world peace, the freedom of all nations, racial equality and the ending of imperialism and colonialism....It should be the constant aim of the foreign policy of India to maintain friendly and co-operative relations with all nations and to avoid entanglement in military and similar alliances which tend to divide up the world and thus endanger peace'. The part of the Jaipur resolution that I quoted just now would prove in no uncertain terms that only through the policy of non-alignment could India realize the ideals for which it stood from the pre-Independence period. In this connection, I may venture to state that in the long run peace could be ensured in the world only by supporting every right and just cause and this would be possible only when you are not tied up to any particular bloc and are in a position to judge every issue on its merits, independent of other considerations. Thus, it could be said that India's policy of non-alignment was a logical corollary to the ideals it had cherished since the pre-Independence period. Advocacy of freedom for all nations and opposition to imperialism, colonialism and social discrimination, not only render India's foreign policy idealistic and ethically sound but also realistic, because in the ultimate analysis idealism was not something that was contrary to realism. As Nehru once said, 'what exactly is idealism? Surely, it is not something as insubstantial as to elude one's grasp. Idealism is in fact the realism of tomorrow. It is the capacity to know what is good for the day after tomorrow or for the next year and to fashion yourself accordingly. The practical person, the realist, looks at the tip of his nose and sees little beyond; the result is that he is stumbling all the time'. In the context of the nuclear weapons and the explosive international situation, Nehru realized to a greater extent still the importance of Gandhi's insistence on the peaceful approach to problems. On the international plane Nehru functioned as a true disciple of Gandhi, seeking peaceful solutions to complex problems. However, it needs to be emphasised that Nehru as a statesman was conscious of the limitations of non-violence in state matters. In the pre-Independence period, as I had opportunity of stating during the course of my first lecture, Nehru had accepted the technique of non-violence for gaining freedom, primarily on pragmatic considerations. Similarly in the post-Independence period too the practical utility of a non-violent and peaceful approach to problems carried conviction with Nehru. However, his post-Independence speeches too give ample evidence of the fact that Nehru was profoundly influenced by Gandhi's theory of ends and means. It must however, be borne in mind that Nehru never accepted non-violence as a creed and this became evident when Nehru participated in a debate on Goa in Lok Sabha. Nehru, in his reply to the debate spoke about the Government's anxiety to bring about the union of Goa with India and turned to the question of the methods that were to be employed for that purpose. Nehru stated that Acharya Kripalani had asked him a straight question as to whether the Government was pledged to non-violence and his reply was that it was not. He further stated that he could not conceive any Government pledged to non-violence in the circumstances that existed. If a Government was pledged to non-violence, it would neither maintain army, navy or air force nor perhaps even a police force. One might have an ideal and yet the circumstances might not be conducive enough to give a concrete shape to that ideal. He reminded the members of the parliament that Gandhiji, the very symbol of non-violence, gave his blessings to the idea of Indian Army going to Kashmir, so that Kashmir could be saved from the raiders. Nehru said later that the right of the state to resort to violence was conceded even by Gandhiji and the Government would not give up that right in the context of contemporary conditions.

Mr. Chairman, Nehru was in favour of a state with a strong Centre and he saw to it that the Constitution rendered it as such, both in the context of India's past and the present. He however faithfully followed the principle of the decentralisation of powers at lower levels, indicating thereby the validity and relevance of some of the Gandhian ideas. By way of conclusion, I may state that while Nehru criticised some of the Gandhian ideas, he accepted a few others which were germane to present day conditions at the national and international level.

Nehru was a man of rare courage and in no other period of his life did his courage manifest itself to the extent to which it did, immediately after India became free. Being secular to the very core and acutely aware of his responsibilities as the Prime minister, he made super-human effort, in very adverse circumstances, to crush the fierce communal riots that had broken out in Northern India and particularly in the city of Delhi. Almost single handedly he fought the forces of communalism that threatened to shake the very foundations of secularism in India. His was the one voice of sanity at a time when men had lost their reason. He personally took the lead in going to the help of the minority community at grave personal risk. On one occasion, he saved two Muslim children, who were about to be murdered by a mob. On yet another occasion, he rushed into a furious mob which was looting Muslim shops in Delhi's Connaught Circus area and brought the situation under control through the force of his personality.

D.F. Karaka, editor of a Bombay weekly, known as Current, was a chronic critic of Nehru. Even he accepted the fact that secularism was almost an instinct with Nehru. I doubt as to whether anyone else in India, with the possible exception of Gandhi, did more to strengthen the forces of secularism in India, through words and deeds, than Nehru.

Nehru was keenly aware of the fact that in the context of India, democracy necessarily implied secularism. If the constitution of India stands for secularism in spirit and content, it is in no small measure due to the efforts of Nehru. His resolution on Fundamental Rights and Economic Programme, passed at the Karachi Session of the Congress in 1931, to which I made a reference in my first lecture, bears testimony to his faith in the secular ideal.

The great scientist, Albert Einstein, once asked Nehru as to what was the most difficult task that he was facing as India's Prime minister. Nehru's prompt reply was that it was the one of making a highly religious society secular in its outlook.

The problem of rendering the Indian society secular is a very complex one and I think that we have yet to go very far to achieve our objective. Nehru is believed to have said a few months before his death that he was endeavouring to fit the ideal of secularism within the framework of Indian culture. I feel that the concept of secularism will increasingly become more and more clear through judicial decisions. I hope that in none to distant a future, secularism in India will assume a more acceptable form without losing anything on the conceptual side. Be it, as it may, the fact remains that India's partition was the biggest challenge to secularism in India and but for Nehru's efforts the cause of secularism would have had an immense setback.

Since the beginning, Nehru followed a policy of including in his Ministry men of outstanding ability, who were not the members of the Congress party. It was an act of great statesmanship on his part for which Nehru has not received the praise that he deserved. It could not have been easy for Nehru to include such persons, as the pressure on him to include his party men in the Ministry must have been considerable. The composition of his Ministry from time to time reminded one more of a National government than a Party government. Nehru realized that what the country needed at that juncture was the services of persons of great administrative experience and expertise and he showed not only wisdom but also courage in looking beyond his party to choose such persons. The inclusion of persons like B.R. Ambedkar, John Mathai, Shanmukham Chetty, T.T. Krishnamachari, C.D. Deshmukh, M.C. Chagla, V.K.R.V. Rao, Gopalaswamy Iyengar and others in the Ministry, proved highly beneficial to India at that point of time. This policy of Nehru, indicative of his mature leadership often goes unnoticed and therefore I thought that I should draw the attention of the listeners to this act of far sightedness.

I may be permitted Mr. Chairman to revert back to Nehru's role in the pre-Independence period and make a mention of a couple of things to which I should have referred in my first lecture. At a time when the Congress leadership was not prepared to look beyond the goal of Dominion status for the country, Nehru, along with Subhash Chandra Bose stood for the goal of Complete Independence for the country and forced the Congress leadership to accept that goal. It was thus that India's political objective changed from Dominion Status to that of Complete Independence at the Lahore Session of the Congress held at the fag-end of December, 1929, under the presidentship of Jawaharlal Nehru. At that time, the British Commonwealth of Nations stood for imperialism and since Nehru stood for the liberation of all countries under foreign rule, it was but understandable that he should have opposed the objective of Dominion Status. However, India after Independence decided to remain a member of the Commonwealth of Nations, as it came to be known later. It was a wise move on Nehru's part, as the Commonwealth of Nations was a loose association of totally independent states, radically different from the British Commonwealth of nations. India stood to gain in economic terms by its membership of this body. Moreover, Nehru perceived in it a good substitute for India's alignment with either of the power blocs, with all the advantages of such an alignment, minus its drawbacks-national and international.

There is one more matter to which I would like to refer here, primarily related to the pre-Independence period. The heterogeneous nature of the Congress party was not conducive to the pursuit of the socialistic ideal and yet Nehru did not allow a split to take place in the party on that score, as he was acutely aware of the fact that the primary objective of the country at that time was the achievement of independence for the country and that India could ill-afford a split in the Congress party on an issue, which was of secondary importance at that time. Similarly, Nehru had realized that Gandhi was indispensable as the leader of India's movement for freedom and that differences with him on economic and other matters should not be allowed to jeopardize his position as the supreme leader of the country. Any split in the Congress party or for that matter repudiation of Gandhi's leadership, could have resulted in disastrous consequences in terms of the ultimate objective of freedom for the country. Nehru as such, very wisely avoided any course of action which would have weakened the national movement at that crucial stage in the country's history.

Mr. Chairman, people who come to me in order to discuss Nehru's role in Indian politics often ask me to spell out the details in regard to the mistakes that Nehru committed during his political career. I tell them half jocularly and half seriously that their generation knows a great deal about Nehru's failures and that I cannot possibly add to their knowledge on that score and when I say that I have in mind the distortions that have taken place about Nehru's ideas and policies during the last few decades. I must confess Mr. Chairman that because of my habit of transplanting myself mentally to the period to which the person in question belongs and the options available to him, as also because of my desire to get the facts correctly, I do not find it easy to pin point in a categorical fashion the failures of a historical figure, be it Nehru, Tilak, Gokhale or Gandhi. My experience tells me that a person goes up in the esteem of the listeners or the readers as the case may be when he spells out the failures of a given person and is complimented for his so called acute sense of judgement. The members of the distinguished gathering here, I feel sure, do not belong to this category.

Any attempt to discuss the controversies surrounding some of the decisions of Nehru would inevitably necessitate a detailed discussion about the controversies and that would require one or more separate lectures. I shall therefore deal with those controversies in the briefest possible manner Probably the first controversial decision of Nehru was his refusal to accommodate one more Muslim League minister in the Congress cum League Ministry of 7 members, which was to assume office in U.P. after the General Elections, 1937. Out of 7 members, 3 were to be Muslims, 2 representing the Congress and 1 representing the League. Nehru considered the League representation in the ministry adequate. At this stage the Muslim League demanded that there should be 2 League members in the ministry—a demand that was very understandably rejected by Nehru and Gandhi is believed to have supported Nehru's decision. The Congress had fared very well in the 1937 elections, whereas the Muslim League had fared badly. In view of this Nehru desired that the League should abide by the Congress Manifesto and Jinnah in search of a pretext to blame the Congress, in order to boost up the image of the League which had not done well in the elections, refused to cooperate with the Congress and accused the Congress for the failure of the talks. The crux of the matter-is that, Jinnah as usual, wanted to rouse the Muslims against the Congress. The next controversy relates to Nehru's interpretation of the Cabinet Mission plan in the press conference of July 10, 1946.The interpretation had possibly the support of Gandhi. Nehru's interpretation made Jinnah furious. He withdrew Leagues support to the Cabinet Mission plan and gave a call for Direct Action. The Cabinet Mission Plan was full of complexities. It sought to make the centre very weak and the proposed Constituent Assembly suffered from inherent limitations. Nehru's view has to be understood in the context of the above two deficiencies in the plan. In so far as the story of India's partition is concerned it begins at the fag-end of the 19th century, when Sir Syed Ahmed Khan talked about Hindus and Muslims being two nations. Even Gopal Krishna Gokhale and Bal Gangadhar Tilak are held responsible for the eventual Partition of the country, though to my mind, quite wrongly. The emergence of Pakistan was a result of several factors, the principal factors to my mind being the British policy of 'Divide and Rule' and the shrewd manner in which Jinnah exploited the Muslim sentiments. 'The last straw that broke the camel's back' as the hackneyed expression goes, was the British Prime Minister Clement Attlee's announcement in the House of Commons an 20th Feb, 1947. Atlee gave expression through that speech to the British Government's firm decision to leave India by June, 1948, at the latest regardless of the fact as to whether there was any settlement among Indian political parties or not The Congress was left with only two alternatives-either to accept partition of the country or to face a civil war. It was in such circumstances that Gandhi, Nehru and Patel, eventually accepted the idea of India's partition. A ridiculous story takes round to the effect that Nehru accepted the idea of India's partition, under the influence of Lady Mountbatten. That the Congress was getting ready for the acceptance of the idea of India's partition became abundantly clear when it passed a resolution for the division of Punjab in two parts, on the 8th of March, 1947, thirteen days before Lady Mountbatten stepped on the Indian soil.

As the time is running out, I shall deal in as brief a manner as possible, with three other controversies surrounding Nehru, they being about Tibet, Kashmir and China. India could do nothing in regard to Tibet as Britain and U.S.A. were not willing to get entangled in the Tibetan issue by supporting Tibet for different reasons. China had the full support of U.S.S.R. at that time. India did not have enough military strength to defend Tibet single handedly. Nehru thus had no alternative but to remain passive when Chinese took hold of Tibet. The story of Kashmir has for its basis the two nation theory of Mohammed Ali Jinnah. Kashmir was the only princely State in India with a Muslim majority. Jinnah, apprehensive of Kashmir's accession to India because of a Hindu ruler conspired with the tribals to take possession of Kashmir by force, the tribals being supported by regular Pakistani forces. A considerable part of Kashmir was already under the occupation of Pakistan by the time the Maharaja acceded to the Indian Union. Whether Nehru should have taken the Kashmir dispute to the Security Council is a debatable issue. However, experience tells us that Big Powers always manage to fish in troubled waters regardless of the fact as to whether a certain issue is before the Security Council or not. In so far as the question of plebiscite in Kashmir is concerned it is a known fact that Pakistan backed out of it as Nehru' conditions for a free and impartial plebiscite under U.N. supervision were not to its advantage. In so far as Nehru's readiness for plebiscite is concerned there was nothing new about it. Sardar Patel in a similar situation had put forward a proposal for a referendum in Hyderabad over the question of its accession to India on October 24, 1947. The Kashmir problem has its origin in the two-nation theory though it assumes different forms from time to time.

The popularly held belief that Nehru had no idea about the real intentions of China and was gullible enough to treat China as India's friend has absolutely no basis in facts. B.N. Mullick's book 'My years with Nehru: The Chinese Betrayal' gives valuable information about Nehru's China policy. As early as in March 1952, the Intelligence Service was directed to treat China as India's potential enemy number one and was asked to collect every type of information in that light. The opinion of the Commander-in-Chief was sought in regard to India's preparedness to face a possible Chinese attack and his advice to Nehru was to continue the *Hindi-Chini Bhai Bhai* refrain since India would not be militarily equipped to defend its very long border with China for 25 years more. The verdict of knowledgeable people is that Nehru's policy in the context of the objective set of circumstances was basically right but China attacked India before we got ready for that eventuality.

Mr. Chairman Sir, since I am at the fag-end of my second speech on Jawaharlal Nehru, this is what I would like to say by way of conclusion. Nehru may have gone wrong on certain occasions, as every statesman does, but on balance, his achievements outweigh by far, his perceived failures. In normal course of things one comes across intellectuals and thinkers who have very little or nothing to do with politics on the operational side or, we have politicians who are far from thinkers. In Nehru, we had the rare combination of a politician and a thinker. His study of history and contemporary conditions enabled him to comprehend the problems with which India was faced and the maladies from which it suffered. He not only understood India's problems but also made every possible effort to seek remedies to them through the resolutions that he moved in Congress sessions. Some years later, as the Prime Minister of the country, he took concrete steps to solve the socio-economic and political problems that he had perceived in the pre-Independence period with a vigour and sense of commitment which few could equal. His vision of India was one of a country that was socially and economically advanced and politically mature. He wanted the people of India to preserve all that was worthwhile about the past without losing sight of what was essential for the present. He realized that a country like India could not but be democratic and secular and when he talked about socialism he always had the peculiar problems of India in mind. If India is on the way to become a super power, it is primarily because of his vision and untiring efforts. Mr. Chairman Sir, if my speeches today contribute to a better understanding of the significant role that Nehru played on the national and international plane, I will feel more than rewarded.

Ladies and gentleman, I can assure you that I will cherish the memory of my two speeches at the Centre of Nehru Studies, for a long time to come.

Courtesy: Centre of Nehru Studies, Shivaji University, Kolhapur and Paramount Publishing House, Hyderabad – New Delhi.

BIBLIOGRAPHY

Azad, Maulana Abul Kalam, *India Wins Freedom*, Printed at Inland Printing Works, Calcutta 13, Orient Longmans Private Ltd., India, 1959.

A Student (Ed.), *Nehru Flings a Challenge*, Hamara Hindustan Publications, 1943.

Bright, Jagat S., *Important Speeches of Jawaharlal Nehru* (From, 1922-1945), The Indian Printing Works, Kacheri Road, Lahore, 1945.

Bose, Subhash Chandra, *The Indian Struggle 1920-1942*, Asia Publishing House, 1964.

Brecher, Michael, *Nehru: A Political Biography*, Western Printing Series Ltd., Briston, Oxford University Press, 1959.

Bright, J.S., Important Speeches and Writings of Subhash Bose: Being a collection of most significant speeches, writings and letters of Subhash Bose from 1927 to 1945, Second Revised and Enlarged Edition, Indiau Printing Press, Kacheri Road, Lahore, January 1947.

Bright, J.S., *Jawaharlal Nehru: A Biographical Study*, The Indian Printing Works, Lahore, 1945.

Bahadurlal, *The Muslim League: It's History, Activities and Achievements*, Agra Book Store, 1954.

Besant, Annie, *India: A Nation, The People's Book*, printed by Ballantune Hanzen and Co., Edinburgh and London.

Bowles, Chester, *Ambassador's Report*, Collins Paper Ltd 14 St. James Palace, London 5. 101.

Bowles, Chester, *The New Dimensions of Peace*, A Pennant Book, Published by arrangement with Harper and Brothers, in U.S.A.

Bowles, Chester, *Ideas, People and Peace*, The Bodley Head, London.

Cousins, Norman, *Talks with Nehru*, Gollanez, 1951.

Campbell-Johnson, Allan, *Mission with Mountbatten*, Robert Hale Ltd., London, 1951.

Carr, Edward Hallett, *The New Society*, Macmillan and Co. Ltd., London, 196.

Das, M.N., *The Political Philosophy of Jawaharlal Nehru*, George Allen and Unwin Ltd., 1961.

Dehlvi Md. Rahim, *Jawaharlal Ki Kahani* (Urdu), Naya, Kitab Ghar, Urdu Bazar: Delhi I, Second Edition, 1947.

Desai, A.R., *Social Background of Indian Nationalism*, Popular Book Depot, Lamington Road, Bombay-7, Second Revised Edition, 1954.

Dhawan, Gopinath, *The Political Philosophy of Mahatma Gandhi*, Navajivan Publishing House, Ahmedabad, 1951.

Dutt, R. Palme, *India Today and Tomorrow*, Revised Abridged. Edition of 'India Today', Printed at New Age Printing Press, Delhi. Published by him for People's Publishing House Ltd., New Delhi.

Emerson, Rupert, *From Empire to Nation the Rise of Self Assertion of Asian and African Peoples*, Harward University Press, Cambridge, Massachusetts, 1960.

Fisher, Louis, *The Life of Mahatma Gandhi*, Vol. I & II, Bharatiya Vidya Bhavan, Bombay, 1953.

Gokhale, B.G., *The Making of the Indian Nation*, Asian Publishing House, Madras, Bombay, Calcutta, New Delhi, June 1958.

Gunther John, *Inside Asia*, Harper and Brothers, New York: and London, 1942.

Husain S. Abid, *The Way of Gandhi and Nehru*, Asian Publishing House, Bombay, 1959.

Hartog, Mabel (Lady Hartog), *India New Pattern*, George Allen & Unwin Ltd., Ruskin House, Museum Street, London.

Hayes Carlton, J.H., *A Political and Cultural History of Modern Europe*, Vol. II, The Macmillan Company, New York.

Hayes, C.H.J., *Contemporary Europe Since 1870*, The Macmillan Co., New York, Revised Edition, 1958.

Hayes, Carlton, I.H. Baldwin, M.W. Cole, C.W., *History—Europe*, Revised Edition, Fourth Printing, U.S.A., 1959.

Harbert, S., *Nationality and its Problems*, Methuen and Co Ltd., 36 Essex Street, W.C. London.

Hutheesing, Krishna, *With No Regrets*, Oxford University 31 Press, Bombay, 1944.

Kanji Dwarkadas, *India's Fight for Freedom*, 1913-1937.

Karaka, D.F., *Nehru: The Lotus Eater from Kashmir*, Richard Clay and Co. Ltd., London, 1953.

Krishnamurti, Y.G., *Jawaharlal Nehru: The Man, his Ideas*, The Popular Book Depot, Bombay, 1942.

Kabir, Humayun, *The Indian Heritage*, Asian Publishing House, Bombay, Calcutta, Third Edition (Revised and Enlarged), Nov. 14, 1955.

Karunakaran, K.P., *India in World Affairs* (August 1947 January 1950), Geoffrey Cumberlege, Oxford University First Edition, 1952.

Kedourie Elic, *Nationalism*, The Anchur Press Ltd., London, 1960.

Kripalani, J.B., *Gandhi, the Statesman*, Ranjit Printers and publishers Delhi, Madras, 1951.

Kohn Hans, *The Idea of Nationalism—A Study in its origin and background*, The Macmillan Company, New York, 1948.

Kundra, J.C., *Indian Foreign Policy (1947-1954): A Study of relations with the Western Bloc*, Vara & Co. Publishers Ltd., Bombay-2.

Lamb, Alastair, *Crisis in Kashmir*, Routledg and Keganpaun, London 1966.

Levi, Werner, *Free India in Asia*, University of Minnesota Press, Minnepolis, U.S.A.

Low, Francis, *Struggle for Asia*, Fredecick Mulle, Ltd., London.

Lumby, E.W.R., *The Transfer of Power in India*, George Allen & Unwin Ltd., 1954.

Mullick, B.N., *My Years with Nehru: The Chinese Betrayal*, Allied Publishers private Ltd.

Mullick, B.N., *My Years with Nehru: Kashmir*, Allied Publishers Private Ltd.

Mende, Tibor, *South-East Asia between two Worlds*, Turntile Press, London, 1955.

Mende Tibor, *Conversations with Nehru*, Seeker and War-burg, London, 1956.

Moon Parker Thomas, *Imperialism, and World Politics*, The Macmillan Company, New York.

Moraes, Frank, *Jawaharlal Nehru: A Biography*, Macmillan Co., New York, 1956.

Moraes, Frank, *Yonder one world: A Study of Asia and the World*, The Macmillan Company, New York. 1958.

Moraes, Frank, *The Revolt in Tibet*, The Macmillan Co., New York, USA.

Nehru, Jawaharlal, *An Autobiography*, The Bodley Head, London, 1953.

Nehru, Jawaharlal, *Soviet Russia—Some Random Sketches and Impressions*, Chetana Ltd., Bombay, 1929.

Nehru, Jawaharlal, *Glimpses of World History*, Lindsay Drummond Ltd., 2, Guilford Place, London W.C. 1., Fourth Edition, January 1949.

Nehru, Jawaharlal, *The Discovery of India*, Signet Press, Calcutta-20, Fourth .Printing, September 1948.

Nehru, Jawaharlal, *The Unity of India*, Lindsay Drummond, 2 Guilford Place, London, W.C. 1, 1948.

Nehru, Jawaharlal, Letters from a Father to his Daughter-Being a brief account of the early days of the world, written for children, Oxford University Press, Bombay, 1959.

Nehru, Jawaharlal, *Recent Essays and Writings*, Kitabistan, Allahabad, 1934.

Nehru, Jawaharlal, *India and the World*, George Allen and Unwin Ltd, London, 1936.

Nehru, Jawaharlal, *China, Spain and the War*, Kitabistan, Allahabad and London, 1940.

Nehru, Jawaharlal, *A Bunch of Old Letters written mostly to Jawaharlal Nehru and some written by him*, Asia Publishing House, Bombay, 1958.

Nehru, Jawaharlal, *India's Foreign Policy*, The Publication Division, Ministry of Information and Broadcasting, Government of India, 1961.

Nehru, Jawaharlal, *India Today and Tomorrow*, Azad Memorial Lectures, 1959, Orient Longmans, 1960.

Nehru, Jawaharlal, *Mahatma Gandhi*, Signet Press, Calcutta, 1949.

Nehru, Jawaharlal, *Independence and After—A Collection of Speeches (1946-1949)*, The publication Division, Ministry of Information and Broadcasting, Government of India, Calcutta.

Nehru, Jawaharlal, *Jawaharlal Nehru's Speeches (1949-1953)*, The Publication Division, Ministry of Information and Broadcasting, Government of India, Calcutta, 1954.

Nehru, Jawaharlal, *Jawaharlal Nehru's Speeches (1953-1957)*, The Publication Division, Ministry of Information and Broadcasting, Government of India, Calcutta, Delhi, 1959.

Nehru, Jawaharlal, *Letters to Chief Ministers (1947-1964)*, Vol. 1, Oxford University Press, London, 1989.

Nanda, B.R., *The Nehrus: Motilal and Jawaharlal*, George Allen and Unwin Ltd., 1962.

Narsimha Char, L.T., *The Quintessence of Nehru*, East Midland Printing Company Ltd., London, 1961.

Nehru Abhinandan Granth Committee, *Nehru Abhinandan Granth—A Birthday Book presented to Jawaharlal Nehru*, Prime Minister of India on completion of his Sixtieth Year, November 14, 1949, published for the Nehru Abhinandan Granth by Vishwanath More of the Aryavarta Prakashan Griha.

Nene, M.G. and Barde, S.M., *India in Transition*, Shivaji Printing Press, Bombay-14, 1947.

Nuseibeh Nazem Zaki, *The Idea of Arab Nationalism*, Vail-Ballon Press, I.N.C., Binghampton, New York, USA. Cornell University Press, Uthaco, New York.

Padelford and Lincoln, *International Politics*, The Macmillan Company, New York.

Patel, Satyavrata Ramdas, *Foreign Policy of India: An Inquiry and Criticism*, N.M. Tripathi, Private Ltd., Princess Street, Bombay, 1960.

Pyarelal, *Mahatma Gandhi—The Last Phase*, Vol. I (1956) and II (1958), Navjivan Publishing House, Allahabad.

Russell, Bertrand, *Roads to Freedom Socialism, Anarchism and Syndicalism*, J.K. Sharma at the Allahabad, Law Journal Press, Allahabad, published by Kitabistan, Allahabad, 1946.

Sen, N.B. (Ed.), *Wit and Wisdom of Nehru*, New Book Society of India, New Delhi.

Sharma, B.L., *The Kashmir Story*, Asia Publishing House, Bombay, 1967.

Smith, D.E., *Nehru, and Democracy*, Orient Longman, Bombay, Calcutta, Madras, First Edition, February 1958.

Spencer Cornelia, *Nehru of India*, The P.T. Book Depot, Educational Publishers, Bombay, Bangalore 4, Lucknow, Madras, Revised Edition, 1952.

Srivatsa, *Pandit Jawaharlal Nehru—A Study at close quarter*, Dikshit Publishing House, Madras.

Sampurnanand, *Memories and Reflections*, Asia Publishing House, Bombay, Calcutta, New Delhi, Madras, London, New York, 1962.

Seligman, E.R.A. (Editor-in-Chief), *Encyclopedia of Social Sciences*, Vol. 11, The Macmillan Co., New York.

Srinivasan, N., *Democratic Government in India*, The World Press Ltd., Calcutta, 1954.

Sturzo Don Luigi, *Nationalism and Internationalism*, Printed by J.J. Little and Ives Company, New York, U.S.A., 1946.

Tandon, P.D., *Nehru Your Neighbour*, Signet Press, Calcutta, 1947.

Tagore, Rabindranath, *Nationalism*, Macmillan Company, New York, 1917.

Tendulkar, D.G., *Mahatma: Life of Mohandas Karamchand Gandhi*, in Eight Volumes, Bombay, 1951-54.

Thayer W. Philip (Ed) Philips Williams. T (Assistant), *Nationalism and Progress in Free Asia*, The John Hopkins Press Baltimore, 1956.

Thomson Ian, *The Rise of Modern Asia*, Printed by Butler and Tanner Ltd., Published by John Murry Ltd., London.

Venkata Raman, T.S., *A Treatise on Secular State*, Madras 1950.

Wanlass Lawrence, C., *Gettle's History of Political Thought*, Allen and Unwin Ltd., London, W. 1., Second Edition, Seventh, Impression.

INDEX

1951 General Elections, 89

A

a Hinduised look, 80
Abdullah, Shaikh, 162-64
Abyssinia, 33, 35
Acharya Kripalani, 21, 204
Admiral Nimitz, USA, 163
Advisory Council, 87
Afghanistan, 115
Africa, 10, 38, 114, 119, 202
Air Force, 169, 170
Ali, Sayid Fazal, 85
All India Congress Committee (AICC), 55, 126
All Parties Conference, 83
Allahabad Session, 73
All-India Language, 95, 96
All-India Muslim League, 72
All-India States' Peoples Conference, 115, 194-19
All-India Teachers' Conference, 2
All-India Trade Union Congress, 55
All-Parties Conference, 117, 119
All-Parties Report, 118
Ambedkar, B.R., 206
America, 48, 118
American bloc, 173
Andhra, 84
Anglo-American bloc, 140, 152, 202
Anglo-American capitalists, 167
Anglo-American imperialists, 167
Army Check Posts, 169
Ashoka's period, 74
Asia, 38, 114, 148, 202
Avadi Session, 69, 130, 199
Avadi, 69
Azad, Abul Kalam, 78

B

B.B.C., 154
B.G. Kher, 120
Bajpai, Girijashanker, 178
Balkan wars, 79, 80
Baluchistan, 73
Bengal, 83
Bhagwad Gita, 17, 12, 21
Bhavnagar session, 98
Big Business, 59
Bihar High Court, 65
Boer War, 11
Bombay, 122
Bose, Subhash Chandra, 123-25, 127-28, 206
Britain, 32, 34, 35, 97, 119, 156, 169, 209
British mis-rule over India, 108
British policy of 'Divide and Rule', 208
British, 38, 77
  Government, 9, 33, 77, 80
  imperialism, 112
  India, 115
  liberalism, 149
  rule in India, 11, 58, 193
  rulers, 148
Brooks, Ferdinand T., Irish Tutor, 12
Buddhism, 57

C

Calcutta session, 84, 118
Cambridge University, 13, 31, 53, 54, 188, 191
Capitalism, 34, 38, 43
Capitalist system, 34, 36
Caste, 58
Central Europe, 35
Ceylon, 115
Chagla, M.C., 138, 206
Champaran (Bihar), 22

Chauri Chaura incident, 19
China, 30, 33, 35, 47, 57, 107, 149, 166, 167, 170, 172, 173, 174, 179, 202, 209
aggression over India, 104
Chinese
attack, 170
invasion of 1962, 172
quarter, 171
Churchill, 195
Civil Disobedience Movement, 19
Civil war, 82
Class struggle, 46
Cold war, 146, 152, 202
Columbia University, 17, 190
Columbia, 162-63
Commonwealth, 155-59, 206
Communalism, 81
Communism, 54
problem of, 151
Communist Party, 44, 45
Communists, 47, 49
Congo, 145, 146
Congress Election Manifesto, 89
Congress High Command, 128
Congress Organization, 175
Congress Party in Parliament, 95
Congress Party, 159, 207
Congress resolution on Independence, 118, 122
Congress Session, 188
Congress victories, 106
Congress Working Committee, 55, 56
Congress, 106, 108-9, 111, 113, 118, 120, 124, 160, 179, 193, 197, 207-8
Congress-League Coalition ministry, 119
Connaught Circus, 3
Constituent Assembly, 77, 142, 143, 156, 158
Constitution Club, 152
Constitution of India, 91
Co-operative Farming, 199
Count Cavour, 9
Cultural Centres, 179

D

Dalai Lama, 168-69
Dar Commission, 84, 85
Das, C.R., 188, 189
Dayal, Rajeshwar, India's High Commissioner in Pakistan, 146
Dean Acheson, 145
Dehra Dun Jail, 3
Democracy, 33, 35, 36131,, 133, 135, 136, 151, 179, 192, 197
definition of, 33
Deshmukh, C.D., the then Finance Minister, , 69, 178, 199, 206
Direct Action, 208
Directive Principles of State Policy, 92, 110
Doctrine of 'revolutionary violence', 42
Dominion Status versus complete Independence, 117
Dominion Status, 118, 119, 127, 155, 206
Draft Constitution, 62, 63
Dravida Munnetra Kazhgam, 96
Dutch imperialism, 144

E

East and West Punjab, 4
Economic Policy, 109
Economic Programme, 90, 205
Egypt, 82, 145
Einstein, Albert, 205
England, 12-13, 109, 131, 145, 187
Enlightened self interest, 142
Europe, 30-32, 38, 54, 97, 118, 119

F

Faizpur, 112
Fascism, 34-35
Fascist Italy, 32, 125
Fear psychosis, 147, 150
First Five Year Plan, 97
First World War, 29, 54, 192
France, 34
French, 97
Fundamental Rights, 90-91, 109-10, 122, 205

G

Gandhi and Nehru
differences between, 26
Gandhi, Indira, 98
Gandhi, Mahatma Gandhi, 11-13, 15-26, 47-48, 56-57, 104-6, 115-7, 121-28, 155, 177-79, 184, 185, 188-91, 194, 203, 207
Gandhi's agrarian movement, 22
Gandhi's movement, 13
Gandhi's Western face, 185

Gandhian ideas, 13, 22
Gandhi-Nehru relationship, 15, 26, 189
Garibaldi, 9
General Cariappa, 168
General Elections, 1937, 207
General Thimmayya, 169
Geneva, 145
Germany, 75, 97, 114, 195
Ghana, 145
Ghose, Aurobindo, 9, 188
Glimpses of World History, 20, 38, 132, 191
Goa issue, 154
Goa, 204
Gokhale, 15, 207
Gokhale, Gopal Krishna, 208
Good administrator, 137
Great Britain, 34
Gunther, John, 12, 40, 185

H

Hammersjoeld, Dag, U.N. Secretary General, 146
Haripura, 112
Harrow Public School, 9
Himmatsinghji Committee, 168
Hindi-Chini Bhai Bhai, 166, 209
Hindu Code Bill, 179
Hindu community, 93
Hindu Law, 92
Hindu Society, 93
Hinduism, 73
Hindu-Muslims problems, 78
Hindus, 74
Hussain, Dr. Zakir, 3
Hussain, Zakir, 4
Hyderabad
    Police Action against, 138, 176, 177
Hyderabad, 160

I

Idealism, 143, 203
Imperial Bank of India, 69
Imperialism, 35, 38, 114, 119, 192
Imperialist war, 111
Imprisonment, 46
India National Congress, 193
India, 10, 35, 54, 93, 119, 132, 135, 137, 145, 157, 159, 163-64, 166-68, 174
    blue-print of free, 109, 112-13
    Independent, 116, 193, 194
    past or present, 78
    rural, 23
    Unity of, 58, 200
India's ancient literature, 13
India's economy, 172
India's Five Year Plans, 87
India's foreign policy, 111, 139, 175, 201
India's partition
    idea of, 73
Indian Army, 162, 170, 204
Indian Constitution, 111, 178
Indian Council of World Affairs, 152
Indian democracy, 172
Indian Economics, 23
Indian Intelligence Service, 169
Indian National Congress, 9, 78, 143, 194, 202
Indian National Movement, 193
Indian Parliament, 20
Indian States Peoples' Conference, 116
Indian States, 160
Indian Union, 176
Indian unity, 75
Indo-Aryan languages, 75
Indo-China conflict, 145
Indonesia, 145
Indus Valley Civilization, 74
Industrial capitalism, 131
Industrial Revolution, 42
Industrialism, 131
Industrialized Capitalist state, 38
Intelligence Posts, 169
International Red Cross, 163
Iraq, 82
Islam, 73
Italy, 78
Iyengar, 4
Iyengar, Gopalaswamy, 206
Iyengar, H.V.R., 4

J

J.V.P. Committee, 85
Jaipur Session, 143, 155, 202
Jallianwala Bagh tragedy, 17, 188
Jamiat-ul-Ulema-i-Hind, 120
Japan, 149
Jinnah, Mohammed Ali, 72-74, 82-83, 120, 122, 177, 208-9

Junagadh, 160, 165
Justice Mahadev Govind Ranade, 43

K

Kaira (Gujarat), 22
Kanji Dwarkadas, 120
Karachi Congress, 58, 90, 109
Karachi Resolution, 56, 91
Karachi Session, 205
Karaka, D.F., 205
Karnataka, 84
Kashmir Constituent Assembly, 164
Kashmir, 160, 163, 172, 174, 179, 204, 209
    dispute, 159, 161
    Indian Army going to, 21
Kashmiri Brahmin community, 12
Kashmir-occupied area, 162
Kelkar, N.C., 115
Kerala, 84
Kerensky and Bolshevik Revolution, 29
Khan, Aga, 78
Khan, Liaquat Ali, the then Prime Minister of Pakistan, 4
Korea, 169
Korean issue, 145
Krishnamachari, T.T., 206
Kunzru, H.N., 85
Kuttaghar, 2

L

Lady Mountbatten, 208, 209
Lahore Congress, 19, 53, 55, 191, 193
Lahore Session, 106, 118, 206
Land reforms, 62
Language policy, 75, 86, 94
Laxman, R.K., 196
Leninist ideas, 37
Liberalism, 58, 59
live and let live, 152
Lok Sabha, 151, 153, 204
    debate on Goa in, 20
Lok Seva Sangh, 177
London, 185
Lord Ismay, Chief of Lord Mountbatten's staff, 82
Lozano, 165
Lucknow Congress, 18, 37, 59, 61, 111, 191
Lucknow Session, 188

M

Machiavellian dictum, 17, 190
Madras session, 73, 117
Mahabharata, 12, 21
Maharashtra, 84
Mallihabadi, Josh, 188
Manchuria, 33
Marx, 42, 43, 49
    times of, 41
Marxian philosophy, 49
Marxism, 40, 48, 49
Marxist philosophy, 30
Marxist-Leninist ideas, 31, 32, 39, 50
Marxist-Leninist literature, 11, 13, 29, 33, 37, 54, 192
Mathai, John, 206
Maulana, 121
Mavalankar, 6
Mavalankar, Shri G.V., 198
Mazzini, Joseph, 9
McMahon Line, 168
MEDO, 150
Menon, K.P.S., 178
Menon, Krishna, 29
Menon, V.K. Krishna, 169, 178
Minorities, 122
Mullick, B.N., 164, 167, 209
Munshi Mubarak Ali, 9, 187
Music Party, 6
Muslim Law, 92
Muslim League, 73, 120, 121, 122, 160
    Subjects Committee of, 82
Muslims, 74

N

Nagpur Session, 69, 83, 130, 188, 199
Naini prison, 2
Narain, Jaya Prakash, 104
Narayan, Daridri, 57
Narrowly national, 38
National Conference, 164
National Congress, 155
National Integration Committee, 98
National movement, 113
National Planning Committee, 59
NATO, 150
Nazi Germany, 32, 125
Nazi regime, 114

NEFA Region, 169
Nehru anti-British authority in India, 188
Nehru Committee, 83, 118
Nehru joined Trinity College, 10
Nehru, Jawaharlal, 1-4, 8, 12, 15, 19, 43, 74, 75, 85, 106, 123, 126, 128, 133, 137, 175-76, 178, 185, 187, 190, 195, 197, 200, 207
  Architect of Modern India, 178-80
  as the Prime Minister, 107
  Autobiography, 19
  China policy, 165
  ideas, 178
  legacy, 196
  literary style, 2
  popularity, 104
  resolution, 117
  role in Indian politics, 108
  wrote English, 2
Nehru, Motilal, 10, 12, 117
Nepal, 174
New York, 5
Newspaper Editors, 93
Nizam of Hyderabad, 176
Nobel Prize, 166
Non-alignment, 45, 140, 141, 148, 172, 173, 179, 203
Non-co-operation, 190
Non-Gandhian ideas, 179
non-violence, 21, 191, 204
North India, 12
North Korea, 144
North West Frontier Province, 73
Northern India, 204
North-West areas, 73
Now or Never, 73

O

Other Men's Quarrel, 202

P

Pakistan, 107, 159-62, 166, 170, 174
  Army, 162-63
  aggression over Kashmir, 154
Pal, Bipin Chandra, 9, 188
Panchsheel Agreement, 171
Panchsheel, 152-53
Pandit Pant, 124, 176
Pannikar, K.M., 85
Parliament, 92
Patel, Sardar Vallabhbhai, 85, 112, 114, 116, 120, 126, 138, 168, 175, 176, 177, 194, 209
Pattabhi Sitaramayya, 85, 123
Persia, 30, 82
Planning Committee, 193
Political democracy, 43
Political immaturity in people, 191
Post-election period, 120
Post-freedom period, 89, 179
Post-Independence period, 60, 67, 104, 106, 109, 111, 116
Post-Independence role, 108
Post-Revolution Russia, 39
Post-Second World War, 202
Prasad, Rajendra, 112
Pratapgarh episode, 23
Pre-Independence Congress sessions, 178
Pre-Independence period, 98, 105, 112, 114, 117, 136, 155, 187, 189, 193, 203
Pre-Independence role, 108
President Roosevelt, 195
Princely States, 194, 195
Professor Toynbee, 148
Provincial Assembly, 120
Punjab, 73

R

Radar arrangements, 169
Rai, Lala Lajpat, 9, 188
Rajagopalachari, C., 200
Rajaji, 112
Rajen Babu, 126
Ram Rajya, 57
Ramayana, 12, 21
Ramdhari Singh 'Dinkar', 48
Ranade, 43
Ranjit Pandit, 5
Rao, Benegal Narsing, 178
Rao, Benegal Rama, 178
Rao, V.K.R.V., 206
Republic of India, 5
Revolt of 1857, 9-10
Ricardo, 43
River Valley Projects, 135, 179, 200
Rowlatt Act, 16
Rowlatt Bills, 16
Russia, 29, 30, 31, 39, 44, 47, 149

Russia-Bolshevik revolution, 18
Russian revolution, 36, 191
Russian, 97
Russo-Japanese Pact, 39
Russo-Japanese war, 11

S

S.R.C. Report, 86, 87, 88
Sardar Panikkar, 178
Satyagraha Sabha, 16
Satyagraha, 190
Schedule Caste, 91
Scheduled Areas Conference, 95
Scheduled Tribes, 95
Scientific Laboratories, 179
SEATO, 150
Second Asian Conference, 5
Second World War, 29, 36, 39, 44, 146, 156, 195
Secularism, 90, 92
Security Council, 161, 162, 164
shameful interference, 132
Shanmukham Chetty, 206
Shudrak's Mricchakatika, 5
Sind, 73
Singh, Sardar Ajit, 9
Sino-Indian border, 168, 169
Sino-Indian conflict, 166, 169
Sir Mohamed Iqbal, 73, 80
Sir Syed Ahmed Khan, 78, 208
Smith, Adam, 43
Social change, 42
Social justice, 42
Socialism, 38, 53, 54, 57, 131, 192
Socialist, 54, 113, 133
Socialistic Pattern of Society, 69, 118, 130
South Africa, 15, 153, 157, 188
South India, 95
Sovereign Legislature, 63
Soviet Russia, *See* Soviet Union
Soviet Union bloc, 152, 202
Soviet Union, 39, 45, 54, 59, 112, 118, 134, 140, 153, 168, 170, 172-73, 175, 192, 198, 202, 209
Soviet's invasion of Finland, 39
Spain, 33, 35
Spanish civil war, 35, 185
Special Convention, 164
Sri Lanka, 174
Stalin, 145
State Assemblies, 88
State Governments, 88
States Reorganization Commission, 86, 89
States Subjects Conference, 115
Steel Plants, 179, 201
Subjects Committee, 124
Suez Canal crisis, 145
Swaraj Party, 117
Syria, 82

T

Technical Institutes, 179
Technological progress, 43
Tensing Norgay, 3
The Co-operative Farming, 69, 130, 199
The Discovery of India, 31, 47, 190, 200
The Indian Struggle, 127
Tibet, 167, 168, 209
    Sino-Indian Treaty on, 152
Tibetan refugees, 169
Tilak, Bal Gangadhar, 10, 188, 207-8
    emergence of, 9
Totalitarian policies, 136
Tripuri Congress, 128
Tripuri, 112, 124
Trusteeship
    Concept of, 25, 26
Turkey, 30, 78, 79, 82, 149, 177

U

U.P. Conference, 32, 60
U.P. Provincial Congress Committee, 55
U.P., 120-22, 208
U.S.S.R. *See* Soviet Union
UNCIP, 160
    resolution, 163
United Arab Republic, 145
United Nations (UN), 164, 174
United Nations Commission, 163
United Nations Organization (UNO), 144, 146, 147, 154, 171
United States of America (USA), 29, 43, 75, 134, 140, 142, 145, 153-54, 168, 169, 170, 172, 173, 175, 198, 209
Upanishads, 12, 21
Urrutia, 162, 163

V

Vedanta
  philosophical teachings of, 48
Village industry, 24

W

War Danger, 111
War psychosis, 150
Western civilisation, 32
Western countries, 139, 149
Working Committee, 123, 126
World war, 144

Y

Yugoslavia, 95, 145

Z

Zamindari, 61, 65, 66, 193
  abolition of, 194
  old system of, 60
Zonal Councils, 87